VISIONS OF HAPPINESS

JUDITH ASHLEY

Copyright © 2018 by Judith Ashley

All rights reserved. No part of this publication may be reproduced, distributed or transmitted in any form or by any means, including photocopying, recording, or other electronic or mechanical methods, without the prior written permission of the publisher, except in the case of brief quotations embodied in critical reviews and certain other noncommercial uses permitted by copyright law. For permission requests, write to the publisher, via the contact page below.

Windtree Press
http://windtreepress.com

Publisher's Note: This is a work of fiction. Names, characters, places, and incidents are a product of the author's imagination. Locales and public names are sometimes used for atmospheric purposes. Any resemblance to actual people, living or dead, or to businesses, companies, events, institutions, or locales is completely coincidental.

Book Cover by Christy Keerins, Covered by CLKeerins
Visions of Happiness/Judith Ashley – 1st Edition

Print ISBN 978-1947983342
Ebook ISBN 978-1947983335

❦ Created with Vellum

This book is dedicated to every woman and child who has lived in fear for their very lives, who've made difficult choices in order to survive and who, I hope, find the courage to make their Vision of Happiness their reality.

ACKNOWLEDGMENTS

I am blessed to have people who whole-heartedly support me on my writing journey. For *Visions of Happiness* the list includes Sarah McDermed and Lois Regn as editors, Christy Keerins as cover designer, Lt. Col. Boyd C. Yaden, USAF Retired for helping me figure out how to kill the bad guy while staying within the story I wanted to tell.

And as always the #ftb forum at Rose City Romance Writers, my fellow authors at Windtree Press and Goal-Reporters. A special Thank You to Maggie Lynch, whose faith in me and the stories I write, has supported me through times of doubt.

CHAPTER 1

Saturday - September 13, 2003
Fremont Park
Fremont, Oregon

His son's tug on his hand along with the childish voice pulled Mark Parker toward the swing set.

"Papa, papa, come see! Look! Look, Papa, it's Lily!"

Not for the first time Mark wondered how this five-year old bundle of energy could tire him out. Of course it didn't help that he'd been On Call last night. He'd been paged and as a result of a serious auto accident spent a couple of hours in surgery. He stifled a yawn and let Ethan pull him across the park to a woman he knew well.

He and Lily Hughes Montgomery were longtime friends and recently he'd become friends with her new husband, Jackson. He didn't recognize the other woman standing by a little girl on a non-moving swing.

As he and Ethan closed the distance he saw the other woman was close in height to Lily's five foot three. Instead of being blond like his friend, she had rather non-descript brown hair. The dark-haired little girl in the swing? Must be her daughter.

"Lily, Lily!" Ethan's high-pitched shout carried across the span of grass as he pelted toward her.

Mark lengthened his stride and reached the swing set just as Lily bent down to scoop Ethan into her arms. She paused on the uptake. "My goodness, Ethan, you've grown so much I don't think I'm strong enough to pick you all the way up."

Ethan giggled, gave Lily a smacking kiss on one cheek and patted the other with a grubby hand.

"Sorry about that, Lily." Mark reached into his pocket for the ever-present tissue.

After setting the wiggling boy down, Lily patted Mark's arm. "No need for tissue or apology. I don't want him to see me wipe my face after such an exuberant greeting."

"Hi, I'm Ethan." He stood just to the side of the barely moving swing.

Mark watched with a soupcon of pride as Ethan introduced himself to the little girl and held out his hand. Ethan's manners were improving thanks to his grandmama. A few seconds tick by before the little girl spoke.

"I'm Emma." A small frown wrinkled between her eyebrows. She didn't shake Ethan's hand, didn't reach toward him at all.

"Papa, I want to swing, too." Ethan tugged on his papa's hand.

Mark picked his son up and after putting him in a swing, made sure the safety belt was latched. Holding the chains, he pushed the swing hard enough that Ethan squealed with delight.

Emma's swing barely shifted. The thought crossed his mind to push it but something held him back. He wasn't a child welfare expert but seeing how thin and pale Emma was, he'd bet a good amount that she was not being well cared for. Was that why Lily was here?

As he moved back to Lily's side, visions from that December night when Ethan was brought into the Emergency Department a battered and bewildered four year old with straw-textured hair and a haunted look in his eyes were etched forever in his memory. His stomach churned, his jaw tightened and his hands fisted. He would do whatever it took to keep this bundle of joy in his life. Ethan's brown hair was now thick and his blue eyes clear and bright. Yes, there were still nightmares but not as frequent as in the beginning.

"Mark?" Lily tapped his arm.

Her touch jolted him out of the memories. "Hmm?"

"I want to introduce you to my friend, Jocelyn Edwards." Lily's blue eyes held a hint of worry in their depths as they searched his.

"Sorry, got called out last night so I'm a bit short on sleep."

Lily smiled. "And a promise is a promise so here you are."

"Something like that." He focused his attention on Jocelyn and extended his hand. "To finish the introductions, I'm Mark Parker."

The cool, slim hand that slipped into his had a firm grip. "I'm pleased to meet you," she said her voice tinged with a bit of an accent that telegraphed she wasn't local. Her baggy jeans had seen better days but then so did the pair he had on. Her worn lightweight top looked two sizes too big and was no match for the brisk breeze blowing today.

"Jocelyn is one of the women hosting the Women of the 14th Moon Gathering next year." Lily turned a beaming smile in her friend's direction. "We're always grateful when people step forward because it's a special time of year for many of us."

"I thought that happened over Labor Day Weekend?" Hearing Ethan's raised voice, Mark's attention snapped to the swings. He leaned as if to stride in that direction but Jocelyn was already there.

With her hand on his arm, Lily continued. "It does but planning always begins the year before. Jocelyn and three other women stepped forward this year. I'm in a supportive role."

He couldn't hear what Jocelyn was saying but she had both children's attention as she held the two swings steady. Ethan's eyes filled with tears and his lower lip trembled.

"What the hell!"

Lily's hold firmed. "Let her handle it".

He glared his exasperation at her. "Let her handle what?"

Shifting he stared back at the scene unfolding on the swings. His son was saying something to the little girl. What was her name?

Emma – yeah, that was it. He more clearly saw the child. Her eyes were huge, her body rigid with fear. What the hell had happened?

Lily shifted, her arm now wrapped around his.

"What?"

"Let Jocelyn take care of it. Emma frightens easily. Remember Ethan when you first met him? That's where Emma is now."

He stared Lily down wanting her to say more.

She shook her head "It's not my story to tell. In fact I may have said more than I should."

"Papa?" Ethan called to him.

Mark strode to the swing quelling the urge to push the petite woman aside. "What's up?"

"Can Emma come to get ice cream with us?"

His son's voice was riddled with concern but his upturned face held such hope.

"That's up to her mom."

"Can she?" Ethan zeroed in on Jocelyn.

For a moment Mark felt a twinge of sympathy. His son's pleas were hard to refuse.

Jocelyn straightened but he noticed her hand remained on Emma's shoulder. Her mousy brown hair blew in wisps around her face having come undone from the pony tail. Her hazel eyes had flecks of green and gold. Would they change colors with her mood or the lighting or maybe the color of clothes she wore?

"We don't want to intrude on your time with your son." Her tone was polite, her gaze straight on. No flirtation in sight.

"It won't be an intrusion." Mark relaxed another notch. She wasn't coming on to him, she wasn't gushing about his being a single father, and she hadn't hurt his son. She was just doing her best by her daughter. He could accept and even admire that.

Ethan watched the two adults as if it were a tennis match. Emma? Her big blue eyes were glued on her mom.

Lily piped up. "I think we should all go get ice cream. My treat because I'll be scoping out the flavors and I'll want to know your opinion of your ice cream to report back to Jackson." She turned to

Jocelyn. "I don't know if I've mentioned that my husband considers himself a master at homemade ice cream. He and Grant, you know Hunter's husband, have a competition."

"I thought wives couldn't interfere." Mark grinned and tossed that comment into the conversation.

Hand on her hips, Lily blew a lock of blond hair out of her eyes. "We can't interfere. However, we can say that the ice cream at such-and-such an ice cream parlor has a new flavor or their whatever flavor is really good. We just have to give the same information to both of them."

"Jackson won't try to persuade you to keep your findings a secret?" Jocelyn asked.

A smile tipped Mark's lips. He could see the wheels turning as Jocelyn tried to figure out what was going on.

Lily grinned. "That's half the fun. What my husband won't do to try to persuade me." She crooked her fingers around the last two words.

"Okay, you two," Mark said, turning to the swings. "If you want ice cream, we need to go now."

Mindful of Emma, he approached Ethan from as far away from her as he could and helped his son unbuckle the safety belt. "I've got you now," he said and lowered Ethan to the ground.

Ethan ran over to Emma. "My papa can help you get down. He's really nice." Ethan turned to Mark, "You're really nice, aren't you Papa?"

Mark squatted down so he was eye-level with Emma. "May I help you out of the swing, Miss Emma?"

Wide blue eyes darted a glance over his shoulder.

"I'll hold the swing steady for you." Jocelyn appeared behind the swing. Her white knuckled hands gripped the chains.

Mark unbuckled the safety belt and slid his hands under Emma's arms. With as much care as he could muster he lifted her until her legs were free. She weighed maybe thirty pounds and she was four years old? True her bone structure was small but she was barely more than skin and bones. He shifted her to his hip and held her for a second, breathing in her perfume-free clean scent. His brow wrinkled as he breathed again. Ethan loved his strawberry-scented shampoo.

He slid her to the ground but kept her hand in his for another second before literally handing her to her mom. Throughout this process Jocelyn had stood alert and immobile, obviously ready to step in if he did something wrong. *As if.*

Ethan, who'd been a few feet away with Lily, dashed over. "Let's go, Emma." He grabbed her hand and tugged in the direction from which they'd come.

"Whoa there." Mark called. "Let's decide where we're going for ice cream first. And," he turned to Jocelyn, "whether Emma and her mom want to ride with us."

"Do you have a second car seat?"

"Wouldn't suggest it if I didn't." He heard the irritation in his tone before catching Lily's arched brow.

"The closest ice cream parlor is two blocks away. We could just walk there," Lily proffered.

"I'm not sure Emma can go that far and back." Jocelyn's hand rested in a protective manner on her daughter's shoulder.

"Let's see. If she can't walk all the way back after resting and eating ice cream—I'll carry her," Mark offered.

"But—," Jocelyn started to protest.

Lily spoke up. "With you right beside me as well as Ethan nearby, she'll be fine. Let's give it a try. And, if that doesn't work, I'll go get your car and bring it to you."

Hand-in-hand, Ethan and Emma headed across the park.

Lily and Jocelyn followed close behind. Their chatter about next year's 14th Moon drifted past Mark leaving him to his own thoughts. Thoughts that wondered what had happened to this fearful little girl who walked with a severe limp.

CHAPTER 2

Jocelyn Edwards' head began to ache because of her red-flagged-awareness of the intense male presence prowling along on the other side of Lily. The idea that the invitation to spend an hour in the park was intended to introduce her to Dr. Parker was dismissed. Her friend had seemed surprised, pleased, but surprised when Dr. Parker and his son showed up.

Tears threatened and her throat closed with emotions she would not name as she watched Ethan holding Emma's hand. He chattered on and on about all kinds of things. A few words drifted back "Grandmama" "Grandpapa" "Papa." Yes, "Papa" was in virtually every sentence out of the little boy's mouth.

And Papa? He stalked along, lost in his thoughts—at least that was her guess. The frown on his face communicated that whatever he was thinking wasn't a happy thought. Jocelyn's worry meter ratcheted up a notch at the intensity in his stare as he watched Emma alongside Ethan.

Focusing on Ethan, Jocelyn wondered if Emma would ever be that happy. He was a handsome little boy. So full of life and vitality.

"Jocelyn?" Lily's quiet voice jerked Jocelyn back to the present.

"Sorry." She stumbled but caught herself before falling. "Mind wandering a bit. Nightmares last night so neither Emma nor I got much sleep."

Lily turned her head in her direction. "You could have called and cancelled."

Jocelyn shook her head and swallowed tears. "Emma was so excited to come to the park and see you. She likes you and I didn't have the heart to disappoint her over an outing like this."

When the ice cream parlor came into view, Ethan pulled on Emma's hand. Jocelyn's pulse sped up and she started forward. Then Ethan said something to Emma and she shook her head. He put his arm around her daughter, his head bent. He must have said something because Emma nodded. Then, with his arm slung around her daughter's shoulder, they walked on.

How could a five-year-old have such a connection to her daughter? Adults were put off by Emma. Well, not Lily or Audrey Smith, who watched Emma while Jocelyn worked. Emma felt safe in Audrey's warm and welcoming home. As the oldest she could hold babies and help out by picking up toys tossed from high chairs and out of playpens.

Even though it added an extra hour to her day to keep her at Audrey's, it was worth it. The drive home was full of Emma's chatter about what had happened during the day. For now, Audrey's was a sanctuary for Emma.

In a year? She had no idea what their life would be like in a year. Since getting away from Tony, they'd never stayed anywhere longer than a few months. She shivered at the memory of the comment the social worker made when she applied for medical insurance for Emma. "Your daughter may never heal from her father's abuse." Two months later that thought still chilled her to the bone.

What was wrong with her today? Her thoughts were flitting all over the place. Keeping track of the conversation with Lily was impossible. What had she missed?

Lily's hand on her arm helped her focus. "I just commented that Emma is slowing down, seems tired but she did much better than I thought she might."

Jocelyn internally rallied and said. "Ice cream is a big motivator and I think having Ethan holding her hand helps."

Once inside the old-fashioned ice cream parlor with bright pictures of sundaes, ice cream cakes, milk shakes and cones of various sizes, Lily steered the children to the restroom to wash their hands. Jocelyn perused the prices, mentally calculated the change in her purse. If she did without, Emma could have a one-scoop cone.

Her solemn-faced daughter appeared, Lily next to her. Emma looked longingly at the case of ice cream but didn't move from Jocelyn's side. Ethan was already up on the ledge, just the right width for kids so they could look and choose what they wanted.

"Emma," Mark held his hand out. "May I help you up here?"

"Come on, Emma." Ethan waved from his perch. "They got everything."

A wistful look on her face, Emma glanced at Jocelyn but didn't move.

"Did I fail to mention this is our treat?" Mark laid a hand on Ethan's shoulder. "We were the ones who suggested it."

"Actually, I was the one who suggested it," Lily said and laughed. "However, I won't battle you for the check." She turned to Jocelyn and Emma. "The big decisions are which flavor and one scoop or two?"

Ice cream decisions made, they settled down at the inside tables. She and Lily sat at the grown-up table and Mark sat with the children. She'd acquiesced to his request to call him Mark and she reciprocated by asking him to call her by her given name also.

Jocelyn pinched the inside of her elbow trying to keep herself focused on the conversations. Once she'd almost missed Mark asking her how she liked her ice cream because he'd spoken in a normal tone. Where she worked the men often raised their voices and her boss was a yeller.

And Tony? Tony had shouted and cursed at her. His threats were often followed by action. External bruises might be gone but inside? Inside the damage was there. She was hypervigilant, had nightmares, startled easily and was always aware of where Emma was. If she, a grown-up, had been terrified, defenseless and helpless.... . Her gaze quickly checked Emma.

She shivered as memories faded, her focus once again on the children. The reason she hadn't left the very first time Tony's temper soared was sitting across from her very daintily and primly eating ice cream from a bowl. She'd have rejoiced if Emma had ordered a cone and ice cream melted and dripped down her hands, maybe even down to her elbows. Just a little mess would be a good sign.

Instead, her four-year-old daughter's manners were perfect. Little bites, spoon down until she'd swallowed. Her head tilted slightly from Ethan to Mark. The "never look at another person when you are eating" rule was just one of many Tony had instituted to control them. What was also crazy making is that he'd often change the rule and slap you because you weren't looking at him. Meal time with Tony had been fraught with peril.

"He's really very good with children," Lily was saying.

Jocelyn tuned back in. "Mark?"

Lily nodded. "And he isn't even a pediatrician. He's an orthopod. But children seem to warm up to him even if at first they're a bit standoffish."

Doctor Mark Parker. That name was familiar from her searches for a doctor who could help Emma. Jocelyn shifted toward Lily. "Why do you think that is?"

Lily's response was immediate. "Because they know instinctively he'll do them no harm."

"But if they are in pain—?" Jocelyn's eyes widened in disbelief.

Lily waved away her words. "He always tells them the truth. What will hurt, what won't. He talks to them about what they can do to help him help them. Brings them in as members of the team. They know he listens to them, really hears what they are trying to say, helps them put words to what they feel physically and emotionally."

Jocelyn smiled. "In other words he has a good bedside manner?"

Lily leaned closer and caught her gaze. "In other words he is a kind, caring, compassionate, gentle man who is very good at his job. I trust him implicitly. Even when I don't like what he is saying."

Leaning back, a slight smile on her face, her gaze unfocused she continued. "I was in a serious accident less than a year ago. I was so frustrated because I couldn't use my arms for what seemed like a lifetime or two but was actually more like six weeks.

"Mark was always calm, rational when I was neither. He said 'no' to my getting out of the immobilizers and back to work and that was it. No debate, not even a discussion although he always told me I was more than welcome to get a second opinion. So very frustrating! But so what I needed."

"So an ortho-orthopod," Jocelyn stumbled on the word, "is an orthopedic surgeon, right?"

"Correct. Mark works out of St. Agatha's. His office is in the adjoining medical building."

Jocelyn sighed. She was positive the insurance she had for Emma through child welfare would not list his name. No, Dr. Parker was out of her reach. They would make do with Emma's referral to the medical school for an assessment.

And that referral was what prompted her to ask Lily a couple of questions when they were sitting down to dinner at 14th Moon. Someone had mentioned Lily's background in child welfare although she now worked with vulnerable adults. Jocelyn knew, to become a doctor you had to practice on someone. Lily had assured her there was always an attending physician. She sighed. *I just wish Emma didn't have to be someone's practice project.*

"Uh huh," Ethan's voice carried through her murky thoughts.

Emma's vehement denial, "No, he can't," startled her.

Lily's hand on her arm stayed her for the second it took to assess what was going on. "Mark's there. He can handle it." Her friend's words and the soft pat on her arm eased Jocelyn's tension.

Mark looked cool, calm and collected except for the fingers tapping on his knee. He leaned over and spoke directly to Ethan whose mulish look did not abate. Mark then turned to Emma and said something. She shook her head, her eyes averted and downcast.

Jocelyn's hands fisted and she struggled to breathe. Lily's hand on her arm was the only thing keeping her in her seat.

Elbows on the tiny table, Mark looked comfortable rather than ridiculous as his conversation with Emma and Ethan continued. Ethan kept shaking his head but the mulish look was gone.

Jocelyn shivered when the realization struck that Emma was safe with Mark. Tony wasn't here now. Tony didn't know where they were. And if she had anything to say about it, Tony never would.

When she glanced over at Lily, her friend's face sported a large grin. "Did you see how upset Ethan was?"

Jocelyn quirked an eyebrow, confusion evident. "He was angry at his dad."

"I know. How wonderful is that! When he was first living with Mark, he was terrified to express anything. He did his best to not be noticed at all."

She'd had a suspicion Mark was not Ethan's biological father. Looking again, she noted their differences—more than the difference in hair and eye color. Ethan's light brown hair and sky blue eyes were framed by an oval face. Mark's hair was a darker brown. He had high, defined cheek bones and milk chocolate colored eyes.

Not that biology was a guarantee. Emma didn't look like Tony, whose Italian heritage shown in his coloring and features. Emma's hair was a lighter brown and her eyes were a dark blue.

The conversation at the children's table ended, Emma came over and leaned against her side. Automatically she sheltered her daughter with her own body. The ice cream she'd eaten threatened to make a reappearance as memories of the times when sheltering Emma from Tony's abuse hadn't always worked.

Fighting the rising tide of food back, Jocelyn focused on the inward and outward flow of air through her nose. This, the third move they'd made since escaping from Tony, felt different. They'd been here in Fremont for four months. Her hope was she and Emma could stay here a year. The idea, the dream of being here a year was what prompted her to volunteer to be the Intercessor at the next 14th Moon.

In this moment staying in trust was challenging especially when her mantra was move forward or get caught. But staying in trust felt right to her. She was where she needed to be until another door opened and another path beckoned her forward.

Her first long term plan included Emma having the surgery and healing from it before next Labor Day. Then they'd move the week after Emma's last follow-up appointment. They'd have been in Fremont a record breaking fourteen months. There was something about this city on the river with the snow-capped mountains in the background that felt like home. Tears threatened as the thought of leaving this all behind surged forward. She pushed the tears and thoughts aside. Keeping Emma safe was her priority.

The future weighed heavily as her head began to throb. Rubbing her temple with her free hand, she rolled her neck in an effort to release the taut tendons and muscles. Emma's hand gripped her jeans.

"May I?" Mark's breath whispered across her cheek.

She jerked. "What?"

"May I help with your headache?" Mark's voice was low-pitched and calm.

She saw his silhouette in the window. Mark was not Tony. She relaxed a fraction, looked over her shoulder and caught his gaze. "How?"

"There are a couple of pressure points, like in acupuncture, that usually help when the headache is new."

Jocelyn hesitated before reminding herself Mark wasn't Tony, they were at an ice cream parlor and Lily was sitting next to her. Then she nodded.

A brush of fingers swept her hair away from her neck. A gentle touched kneaded the tendons at the base of her head and worked its way down to her shoulders. His warm fingers knew where she was the tightest. As the taut muscles eased, she took a deep breath. His clean scent filled her lungs. Her headache lessened as the tension ebbed. One part of her body eased but another part of her body stirred to life. A part she'd purposefully ignored. A part she'd willed dead.

CHAPTER 3

Dr. Mark Parker glanced down his patient schedule for the day. Since Ethan had come into his life, he did more and more pediatric work. He was one of three partners in Fremont Specialty Orthopedics. One of his partners specialized in hip surgery, the other in sports injuries. He was more of the generalist, although when he looked at today's appointments, he was seeing two children and four elderly patients who had fallen. Between them, he'd be checking two broken arms (pediatrics) and broken wrists, legs and a collar bone between his other patients.

Emma Edwards perched in the back of his mind. Her gait was off as if one leg was shorter than the other or a broken bone had healed at an angle. Tempted to call and ask Lily for information, he rubbed a hand down his face. *What the hell am I doing?*

He sighed. A question he didn't have a pat answer to.

By the end of the day, the little girl still on his mind, he gave up. Sitting in his office, feet up on his desk, he faced the picture of Ethan on the credenza under the window. Using his cell phone, he called his friend.

"Hi Lily, do you have a few minutes?" He kept his voice upbeat.

"For you? Of course I do. What's going on?" Lily's voice shifted from one of friendly welcome to a more professional tone.

Mark smiled knowing Lily was most likely reaching for paper and pen thinking he was calling about an elderly patient who had an attentive family lost in the maze of senior services.

"I noticed that Emma Edwards limped. Was wondering if you knew why?" He was pleased at the casual tone to his voice.

"Not my story to tell, Mark," Lily replied in a guarded tone.

"Which means you do know."

"Not my story to tell," she repeated in a no-nonsense way.

"Here's the deal. I know something is physically wrong. I think I can help. However, I do respect that it's not your story to tell." He paused, took a deep breath and exhaled. "So, would you relay a message to Jocelyn for me?"

"It depends," Lily replied still cautious.

"Ethan really liked Emma and you know what a big deal that is. Give her my phone numbers, personal cell and office. Ethan doesn't have many, if any friends and he really liked Emma. I'm good with just meeting up at the park again. The kids can play on the swings and teeter totter, go down the slide or just run around. Nix the running around.

"Or maybe meet at the ice cream place? I'm open to other ideas. And, I've got this weekend free. I'm on call the next one. You know how it is, I still could be paged if I'm needed at the last minute. Will you do that for me?"

A hint of humor in her voice, Lily said "I'll talk to her and give her your message."

"And Lily." He waited a heartbeat. "It won't hurt to put in a good word for me. I don't know everything that's happened to those two but they both seemed uneasy around me."

"Mark, I'll call her this evening and give her your message. And, I'll let you know by call or text what she says."

"Thanks, Lily." He swung his feet to the floor and tapped his fingers on the desk. "I can't explain it right now. I only know it's important for Ethan to see Emma again." A spike of anxiety shot to his head where a throbbing began. "And, especially if it will ease Jocelyn's mind, you and Jackson might tag along?"

"Mark, all I can do is pass on your invitation to Jocelyn. I'll do that and then let you know what she says." He heard her smile along the phone line. "Thanks for the invitation, I'll talk to Jackson also."

"Thanks, Lily." He hung up, gathered his office and car keys and headed out to the parking garage, Emma Edwards still on his mind.

MARK PULLED his car into the driveway of his parent's single story ranch. He'd spent his high school years here and it was home base while he was at college. His room, which was little changed in the intervening years, had been claimed by Ethan. Gratitude that he had the support of his mom and dad flowed over him. He shook his head at the overwhelming idea of finding another childcare arrangement for his little boy. Another year and he'd be in Kindergarten. Time enough to make changes then.

Getting out of the car, Mark studied the house, noting the white trim needed a coat of paint. He liked the contrast of the dark grey house with the white trim and green door. Walking up the front steps, he smiled at the mongrel house that had caught his mother's eye. Not quite in the Craftsman style, the blending of natural wood and stone suited the Parker family.

Tonight he was On Call and would spend the night here just in case. On nights like this he slept in a guest room across the hall from Ethan. When he wasn't On Call, he picked up Ethan and they went home to his condominium, fixed a simple dinner, read stories and went to bed.

Weekends were Mark's favorite time because he had a full forty-eight hours plus with his son. He'd been considering how he might shift to a four day work week so he'd have more time with Ethan. For now this arrangement worked well. Ethan loved his grandmama and grandpapa and they adored him. Both of his partners were understanding, supportive and covered for him when there was a court hearing or other appointments regarding Ethan's custody and potential adoption.

Mrs. Fester, their child welfare worker, was suspicious of a single man wanting to adopt. Up to now the courts had allowed Ethan to stay with him. It helped he was a professional man, had impeccable credentials and Ethan clung to him like a barnacle whenever the social worker was near or they were in court.

"Papa, Papa, Papa," Ethan's shout accompanied the clatter of boots on the tile floor as he raced to the door.

Mark braced himself for the hurtling bundle of energy as Ethan launched himself into his papa's arms. Small arms seized his neck, short legs wrapped around his waist and a smacking kiss landed more on his jaw than his cheek. What would he do if this tiny tike was taken away from him?

"You're home!" Ethan wriggled away and, with more than a little reluctance, Mark set him down. Grabbing his hand, they walked down the hall, past the stairs leading to the daylight basement, to the great room where his parents sat. The aroma of pot roast filled the air and his stomach rumbled, reminding him he'd had nothing since lunch.

"How was your day?" Peggy Parker asked as she rose and turned toward him.

"Busy." He gave his mom a hug and kissed her cheek.

"Papa fixed everybody today." Ethan proudly reported.

Mark's father, Peter Parker, laughed, a bemused smile on his face. "Never had quite that good of a cheering section when I practiced medicine. Does a body good to know someone has total faith in you."

"And how was my boy today?" Mark tossed the question out generally so either of his parents could answer.

"Mr. Ethan was a busy boy," his mom replied, a smile on her face. "He helped me dust, change beds and do the laundry. And he helped his grandpapa in the yard. He most likely will s-l-e-e-p well tonight."

"Grandmama spells words so I won't know what she's saying, Papa," Ethan explained.

"Yes, she does and you're learning to spell so fast, pretty soon

Grandmama won't be able to do that without you knowing what she's saying." Mark tousled Ethan's brown hair.

Ethan wrapped an arm around Mark's leg. "E-T-H-A-N—that's my name. I'm going to learn how to write it down too."

"Grandpapa will help you do that tomorrow, remember?" his mother said. Turning to the stove she added, "I better get this pot roast out of the oven."

Seeing his father taking plates out of the cupboard, Mark rested his hand on Ethan's shoulder. "Let's wash up. Looks like dinner is about ready and I'm hungry."

"Can you eat a horse?" Ethan awkwardly skipped down the hall to the half-bath.

"Not a horse but I can eat a pot roast." Mark grinned and pulled the step-stool out from under the counter with his foot. He steadied Ethan as he stepped up.

Hand washing was no longer a struggle nor was the bathroom half-flooded when it was over. In the past nine months they'd made good progress. His son had caught up intellectually but he was still behind physically and emotionally. Given the progress he'd already made, Mark was confident, in time, Ethan would catch up to his peers.

The routine at his parents' home was similar to the one he maintained at his condo. Dinner, clear the table, dishes in the dishwasher and no television. Games and books were the entertainment of choice. Ethan could choose what they would do for the hour or so before it was bath and bed time.

Later, they cuddled on Ethan's bed. Mark just held his son and waited. Something was on Ethan's mind. And this was the time of day when he talked about what bothered him, what he feared and what he hoped. He was system-savvy enough to know that when the social worker came by, he could be taken away. He was naïve enough to believe Mark powerful enough to prevent that from happening.

As he waited, Mark stroked Ethan's arm and back, long caresses meant to soothe.

Ethan's breathing slowed. Mark held his own breath. Maybe he was wrong something bothered his son. Maybe he was quiet because he was tired.

"Hey buddy? Let's get you tucked in, okay?" Mark shifted off the bed and tugged the covers around Ethan's shoulders.

"Papa?" Ethan managed around a yawn.

"Yes?" Mark bent over, rested his hand on Ethan's shoulder.

"Will you fix Emma? Please? When I was broken, you fixed me."

Mark's throat tightened hearing the plea in Ethan's voice and seeing the hope in his sky blue eyes. Perched on the edge of the single bed, Mark brushed Ethan's hair back from his forehead. "It's different with Emma, Ethan. She has a mom and her mom would have to want me to help Emma. And, I don't know what's wrong with Emma so I might not be able to fix her."

"She had a mean dad just like me." Ethan sat up, his hands gripped Mark's arm. "He broke her but she couldn't go to the doctor like I did."

His gut absorbed the words as he fought to remain calm, to keep his voice steady. "How do you know that?"

Ethan's blue eyes were round and guileless, his voice earnest. "Emma told me. I asked her why she walked funny. She got scared. I told her I'd been broken and the police came and you fixed me. She said when she'd been broken no one came and helped her."

Mark's stomach lurched and tears stung his eyes as memories of the small, helpless battered body that was his Ethan rose in his mind. Where was Emma's mother when all this was happening? Why hadn't she gotten help? Why hadn't she called the police, left—done something?

He willed himself to be calm, leaned over and kissed Ethan's forehead. "No promises, but we'll see if there's something we can do."

CHAPTER 4

𝒥ocelyn hung up the phone. Anxiety sped through her nerves settling in her stomach. She'd written the two numbers Lily had given her on the notepad she kept on the battered kitchen counter. The numbers blurred as she stared at them. Grasping the scarred countertop with both hands, she blinked. Her vision cleared. Before her were Mark Parker's phone numbers–his personal cell and his direct office number.

Pulling herself together, Jocelyn knelt down and wrapped Emma in a hug, grateful to see the worry lines easing from her daughter's face. "Well, Pumpernickel, Lily called to tell me that Ethan would like to play in the park with you again."

Jocelyn watched a light spark in Emma's eyes although her face remained neutral. "What do you think of that idea?"

Emma reached out and touched Jocelyn's cheek. "We don't have to move?"

"No, Emma. We're okay here. Lily was checking in to see how we're doing. And to let us know that," Jocelyn took a deep breath determined to keep her promise to always tell Emma the truth. "Well, it seems that Ethan's papa wants to find a time when you and Ethan can see each other again."

Jocelyn's head ached, her shoulders hunched forward as the stress of the situation weighed her down. Ever since meeting Ethan at the park, Emma could not stop talking about him. While she talked about Ethan, she never mentioned his papa directly. It was always 'Ethan said his papa this or that'. Even when Jocelyn had been right there at the ice cream parlor, Emma never said Mark or even Ethan's dad said. It was always further removed—Ethan said his papa said.

What she wouldn't give for a moment or two, well, maybe a couple of minutes of that neck massage. At the ice cream parlor she'd been on her way to a massive headache. A minute or two of gentle pressure by knowing fingers rubbed away the pain.

Even though they'd moved to the well-worn brown couch, Emma watched her just as she had during the entire conversation. Even after she knew it was Lily she was talking to her eyes never left Jocelyn's face. Now, however, Emma sat next to her on the dilapidated sofa, her hands clasped in her lap, her shoulders rigid as if something good happening couldn't be true.

Jocelyn knew if she said they had to move, Emma would immediately go to their bedroom and get out her non-descript dull yellow small suitcase. Within five minutes she would be packed, her bag by the door. Then she'd help wrap up the few belongings they always took with them. In less than an hour, everything would be packed, in the car and they'd be off to a new place. She pulled her thoughts away from previous scenarios to the serious little person beside her.

"Would you like that, Pumpernickle?"

This time joy flashed across Emma thin face.

Jocelyn waited, knowing that Emma would have questions first.

Emma turned and looked up, her dark blue eyes searching Jocelyn's face. "Do you want to, Mama?"

Jocelyn smoothed her hand over Emma's head, bent down and kissed her forehead before tugging her onto her lap. "Only if you want to see Ethan again."

"Where would we go?" Emma sat rigid on her lap.

"Where would you like? The park? The ice cream parlor?" She

tossed those suggestions out because Lily had mentioned them as possibilities.

Emma's anxiety, her need to have the right answer was painful to see. Jocelyn wrapped her arms around her and gently rocked. "We don't have to decide now, Em. We can take all the time we need. And, it's okay to say 'no' or 'not now'."

Emma relaxed against her, not quite snuggling but certainly not holding herself away. "Why does Ethan's papa want to?"

"You want to know why Ethan's papa wants you and Ethan to have time to play together?"

Emma nodded.

"I imagine it's because Ethan wants to see you again. What do you think?"

Emma snuggled closer. "I like Ethan. He doesn't yell or hurt anyone."

"So is that a 'yes'? Do you want me to call Ethan's papa and see what kind of a plan we can make?"

Another nod.

While one part of her rejoiced that Emma had a friend, someone she wanted to see which meant it was someone she felt safe with, another part of her quaked at the idea of seeing Mark Parker again. Without Lily as a buffer, she'd be required to interact with him. Her inner protection meter was registering mild anxiety about this meeting.

Emma slipped off Jocelyn's lap. She got her mama's cell phone and notepad from the kitchen counter. With an expectant look on her face, she held them out.

Jocelyn's chest tightened with love for her brave little girl. "I'll call, Em, but I need to see what my work schedule is first. It won't be posted until morning."

Emma's blue eyes remained focused on Jocelyn's. "Okay, but you won't forget?"

"No, I won't forget," Jocelyn said with a smile. "Now how about dinner?"

Jocelyn was keenly aware of little eyes following her through the routine of making dinner. She heated up a can of chicken noodle soup on the old electric stove while Emma got out two plastic bowls, two spoons and saltine crackers. After the simple meal, together they cleaned up. Emma's deliberate concentration while putting the two bowls and spoons back on the shelf tore Jocelyn's heart.

Would she ever see Emma comfortable when she couldn't see her mom? Would she ever be comfortable going into the next room without telling Emma where she was going? What she was going to do? She wished there was something she could say or do that would ease the fear in her step-daughter's eyes.

Jocelyn stifled the sigh that surged in her chest. Emma was even more watchful and fearful when she heard the sighs. Giving herself an internal shake, she did a final wipe down of the kitchen counter and hung the cloth over the sink's faucet.

Turning to Emma, who was on the chair next to the counter, she said, "What'll we do this evening?"

Emma scrambled off the chair and took her hand, leading her to the couch. "We got new books."

"So we do," Jocelyn sat down in her spot. Emma remained standing. Excitement gleamed in her eyes but she remained still. "What are the books about, Em?"

"We got the doctor one with the cat and the elephant one." Emma picked the books up from the table in front of the couch and held them out.

Jocelyn smiled at the bright covers of Dr. Seuss's *The Cat in The Hat* and *Horton Hears a Who* held up for her to pick. "Hmm." She peered at the books, her head tilted to one side. "I wonder which one is best." This was another part of their nightly routine.

Emma played her part. "You have to choose, Mama. It's your turn to choose."

"Hmm, do I want to know about a cat or an elephant?"

This was as far as she'd go with the game because Emma's ability to handle suspense was dramatically limited. "Okay, my little Pumpernickel. I see the clock and I think we can read both of them tonight.

One here on the couch. Then bath and teeth and all that. I'll read the other when you're in bed. How's that for a plan?"

"That's a good plan, Mama. That's a really good plan." Emma scrambled up on the couch and thrust *The Cat in The Hat* into her hands. She pulled Jocelyn's arm around her shoulder and opened the book. Pointing at the first page she directed "Read."

And Jocelyn did read, different voices for the various characters, relishing this time when Emma slipped into the story and laughed at the antics of the cat. The story finished, bath time was a happy event. It wasn't a long soaking bath like Jocelyn longed for, but when it was done, a clean and happy Emma jumped on the bed and pulled the covers down.

"I have some work to do tonight, Em, so after we read the next book, you need to snuggle down by yourself. I'll leave the door open so you can see the light and hear me. Remember, we've already locked the door so we're safe."

The worried look that crossed Emma's face was quickly followed by her resigned one.

Jocelyn's own worry-meter rose a notch. Would there ever come a time when this little girl was comfortable sleeping by herself?

The second book finished, Jocelyn kissed Emma's forehead and turned away. At the door, she blew a kiss in Emma's direction. Emma reached up to catch it and after pressing her hand to her heart, blew a kiss back to Jocelyn.

"I love you Pumpernickel." Jocelyn walked down the short hall, leaving the door wide open. She curled up on the end of the couch where Emma could see her if she ventured out of bed.

Picking up the notebook from the end table she began to leaf through the pages. She'd volunteered to be the Intercessor for the next Women of the 14th Moon Gathering and she had no idea what she was supposed to do. Lily had given her this notebook and encouraged her to read it over and ask questions if she had any.

A few pages in and her brain shut down.

What was she doing? She had no business being the person to hold the focus, the sacred energy, so other women could participate in safety. She didn't even know how to keep herself and Emma safe. The Intercessor brought her spiritual practices or spiritual path. Panic raced down her spine. What spiritual practice? What had she done?

She closed the notebook, clutching it to her as tears flowed silently down her cheeks. Another *gift* from Tony, she'd learned to sob without making a sound.

The ticking of the clock registered. It was late and she had work tomorrow. Her brain foggy from crying, she struggled to her feet and put the notebook back on the end table.

In the bathroom she looked at the unfamiliar face in the mirror. This face was thinner, the eyes duller and the spark of life missing. As she washed her face and brushed her teeth she resolved to call and talk to Lily tomorrow. She'd be firm and let her know she'd made a mistake. She couldn't be Intercessor.

Crawling into bed next to Emma, the tears welled. Jocelyn burrowed in the pillows and willed herself to remain motionless as the first drops ran down her face.

CHAPTER 5

Mark pressed two fingers to his temples and glared at his phone as he unplugged it from the charger in the car. He rested his head against the back of the seat, eyes closed. Dreading what awaited him once inside the door, Mark literally shook himself before going inside.

"Papa, you're home!" Ethan barreled through the main floor and leapt into Mark's arms. Barely had he given his son a squeeze and kiss on the top of his head when Ethan wiggled to get down. "When can I see Emma?" Ethan gripped his hand and the thought that his son was getting stronger flashed through his mind. Sky blue eyes stared up at him. Eyes filled with expectation and hope.

Mark shook his head. "I don't know. Emma's mom hasn't called me yet."

The excited light in Ethan's blue eyes disappeared, replaced by a crease that furrowed his forehead.. "Why don't you call her?"

"I don't have her phone number." Mark tamped down the irritation that always accompanied admitting to Ethan he couldn't do something. Not that he probably couldn't track down a phone number. But, he wouldn't do that. Too much like stalking and while he didn't know the particulars, he'd bet she'd been or maybe even was being stalked. That would explain a few things.

Ethan, his earnest, 'you can do anything look,' said, "Lily does."

So his son had been figuring things out. Good for his problem solving skills and bad for Mark. How to handle this one?

"You're home." His mom bustled up, already in her coat, purse over her arm and car keys in hand. "We've had dinner. Your plate has been in the refrigerator less than an hour so you can easily heat it up in the microwave. Salad is also in the fridge." She reached up and kissed his cheek. "Take care of yourself."

Bending down she hugged Ethan. "See you tomorrow champ. Grandpapa will be ready to play darts with you again so get a good night's sleep."

"Papa, I beat Grandpapa at darts today!"

Mark reached out to his mom as she passed him and brushed a kiss on her cheek. "Thanks for everything."

"My pleasure," she said as she breezed out the door.

Turning to the bundle of energy dancing before him, Mark swooped Ethan up in his arms. "So you are the Dart Champion?"

Ethan's thin arm pumped the air, his high-pitched giggle lifted the gray cloud that had accompanied Mark on the drive home. With this little boy in his life, it could only be good times ahead.

JOCELYN'S FEET HURT, her shoulders hurt, not to mention her neck and head. Where didn't she hurt? Pity party! *You're lucky to have a job and tips enough to pay rent and keep food on the table.* She dug in her purse and pulled out a small box and popped a couple of the white tablets inside.

Jotting down her schedule for the week, she noted she could pick up a couple extra shifts if Audrey could watch Emma. Maybe she'd be able to put a little aside for those rainy days that seemed to happen even when the sun shone bright.

Jocelyn hesitated before signing up for the extra shifts. True, they would ease the always tight budget, but they were on the weekend. Emma, in her quiet way, asked about seeing Ethan. The disappointment when Jocelyn said she hadn't called was heartbreaking. Taking a moment, she leaned against the wall, her gaze fixed on the schedule, mentally calculating the additional income if she worked one or both shifts.

The internal debate was not a new one but the answer was not a given. Money was always tight but for Emma, money was not time. When she worked too many extra hours, Emma became withdrawn and anxious. And Audrey gave her worried looks when she picked Emma up. Like it or not, she was still Emma's main source of security.

Two of her co-workers ambled down the hall. Jocelyn stepped forward and wrote her name on the Sunday shift. She'd call Mark Parker and arrange a play date for Saturday between Emma and Ethan. That should help Emma deal with her being gone the extra hours.

Striding was beyond her but she walked as briskly as her sore feet would allow to her car. As she was manually unlocking the door because the key fob wasn't working again, she noticed a blond woman getting out of a car parked three slots away.

Lily! OMG, she'd totally forgotten she was supposed to meet Lily —a glance at her watch informed her thirty minutes ago.

"Lily, I'm so sorry!" Jocelyn rushed to meet Lily halfway.

Her friend smiled and gave her a hug. Stepping back Lily said, "Don't worry. I always have notes to write, calls to make and if all else fails I've a lovely romance novel to delve into."

"But... ." Jocelyn stopped mid-second apology. Lily was not upset. No need to grovel, beg, plead—much less duck.

Lily gestured toward Jocelyn's car. "Why don't we drop your car off at your place? We'll take mine to pick up Emma. That way we can talk on the way. If we still need more time to sort things through, we'll figure something out."

"I-I-I... ." Jocelyn stammered, the fear that had charged through her when she realized how late she was, that she'd totally forgotten the meeting with Lily eased. It was a sensible idea and obviously Lily thought there was something to talk over. "Okay."

"I'll follow you," Lily said. She headed back to her car and, without turning, waved over her shoulder.

All the way home, Jocelyn rehearsed what she would say to Lily about being Intercessor.

Pulling out of the parking lot of Jocelyn's apartment complex, Lily glanced at Jocelyn as she turned onto the street. "Now what is it you want to talk about?"

All those carefully chosen words flew out of Jocelyn's head. "I made a mistake when I volunteered to be Intercessor." The words rushed out followed by a sharp intake of breath. Jocelyn waited for the verbal lashing.

"And you believe that because?" Lily asked, her voice curious yet neutral.

Jocelyn breathed out, tension ebbed from her shoulders, her hands now rested in her lap. "I looked at the notebook. I can't do that. I don't have a spiritual practice. I can't hold energy. I don't—." Despair stopped her words. She swallowed and looked out the passenger window at the sidewalks filled with people, some with packages, some with children, some window shopping or browsing. The silence in the car was deafening. The urge to fill the silence overwhelming. "I'm not the right one to do this," she whispered. "I'm not capable of leading anything. I'm barely surviving my own life."

Lily pulled the car to the curb and put it in park before she shifted to face Jocelyn. "Here is a truth for you to consider. Every woman who has volunteered to be Intercessor has been challenged at some point. We've all had some issue that was imperative for us to come to terms with. And each of us have found our way to move forward toward our highest good."

She placed her hand on Jocelyn's arm. "Hearing me say that, what do you believe is the issue you face?"

Jocelyn felt the support in Lily's touch and heard the assurance and acceptance in her voice. The knots in her stomach unwound. "I'm not sure. I feel so lost, so unworthy." She shook her head. "I know I'll fail.

Let everyone down. Meredith was a fantastic Intercessor last year. I can never be as good as she was."

"Of course you can't. You aren't Meredith." Lily gave her arm a gentle squeeze. "I know this year was your first 14th Moon. Because I've been to many, I can testify that every year the Intercessor is wonderful. And that is because she brings her unique authentic self to the circle. Trying to emulate someone else doesn't work."

"But I have no spiritual practice to share."

Lily's eyebrow rose as she said, "Are you sure?"

"I don't belong to a woman's circle like you do. I don't go to church. I don't—"

Lily interrupted with a wave of her hand. "So tell me what you do do? How do you deal with the challenges you face? Where did you find the strength to leave an abusive relationship and take Emma with you? How do you manage now?"

Jocelyn stiffened, her flight instincts at the ready. "Are you psychic?"

A soft smile played across Lily's face. "No, not psychic but I am observant. For one, Mark Parker is one of the kindest gentlest men I know and yet you are uncomfortable around him. Then there is Emma who has all the behaviors of a traumatized child. With her limp I'm fairly sure she's a physically abused traumatized child. You have skills, if not a formal education, yet you work as a waitress in a bar, live in an out-of-the-way apartment, drive an old car. All signs of someone trying to disappear."

Jocelyn focused on her jaw, willing the tightness away. She checked her inner self and confirmed she trusted Lily. "I'm listening."

"All I'm suggesting is for you to consider my questions—especially where did you find the strength to leave and take Emma with you? How do you manage now?"

Jocelyn choked out a laugh. "I cry a lot."

"But that isn't what got you out of your situation," Lily pointed out.

"No it wasn't." Jocelyn sighed and gazed out the passenger window to the world outside. "Tears weren't enough. Begging, groveling sometimes worked. But if I misjudged and did it too soon, Tony just got madder and the beating lasted even longer." She turned back to Lily. "I just try to block that all out."

Lily gave Jocelyn's arm a comforting pat. "What do you think about making a plan? A plan for you to have a safe place and time to sort out how you managed?"

Safe? The tension in Jocelyn's neck eased. "What about Emma?"

"Of course Emma would be included. You remember Ashley?"

A knot in her stomach unwound. Jocelyn nodded. She'd met Ashley Kenner at the 14th Moon.

"She has a daughter a little older than Emma but Amanda is wonderful with other children. Setting up a play date will allow you, Ashley and me time to talk while the girls have fun together."

Jocelyn sighed. "That might work. Emma would enjoy meeting a little girl more her own age."

Lily shifted, her hands again on the steering wheel. "Trust that being Intercessor serves you in ways you cannot imagine at this point in time. Always know you have not just my support but the support of all of the women who've been Intercessor before you. And don't forget, there were four of you who volunteered."

Starting the car, Lily signaled and moved out into the traffic. "Now let's get Emma and get you home. You look like you've had a very long day."

Jocelyn let the thoughts flow. She trusted Lily because of her core of honesty. If Lily believed Jocelyn could be a successful Intercessor, maybe she could.

THAT NIGHT after putting Emma to bed, Jocelyn sat at the breakfast bar, a pad of paper in front of her. At the top of the list was Mark Parker's name and phone numbers. Before her courage deserted her she picked up her cell and dialed his office number. The office was closed which was why she'd waited to call. While she was ready to set up a play date, she wasn't ready for a phone conversation.

She chose the "leave a message for Dr. Parker option" instead of having the call forwarded to the answering service. After the beep, she left a short message. "Dr. Parker, this is Jocelyn Edwards. Please give me a call about a possible meeting on Saturday." She added her phone number before hanging up and sagging against the counter.

Would she take Lily up on her offer to come along? She might. It wasn't that she thought she or Emma would be harmed by the good doctor, but would they feel safe?

CHAPTER 6

Mark sifted through the stack of messages his receptionist handed him as he strode down the hall to his office. He absentmindedly nodded to the staff who were already preparing rooms for afternoon patients. Especially after he'd spent a morning in surgery, messages were always organized by importance. His habit was to glance through to see what awaited him.

"Dr. Parker?" He turned to see Anne hurrying after him, a message in her outstretched hand. "This message was left on your direct line."

He glanced at the brief message, grateful he'd have good news for Ethan tonight. "Thanks, Anne."

So Jocelyn Edwards had finally deigned to call. *That's a bit harsh.* He closed the door to his office, putting messages on his desk. *At least she's called.* Being able to ease Ethan's insistence to see Emma curbed the growing throb at his temples. That was the good news. The not so good news? *I'm on call.* Mark massaged his neck.

His hand dropped at the soft knock on his door. Kent, his nurse, stuck his head in. "Patient ready in one."

Mark picked up the chart and glanced through the most recent notes on his way to the exam room. By the time he walked through the door, he was ready. A smile on his face, Mark extended his hand in greeting.

It was almost six when the last patient left. He ran long because he made two calls to protective services. One was to child welfare because x-rays showed old breaks even though the current one definitely fit the explanation of a fall off a swing set at the park.

The other call was to adult protective services for an eighty-year-old man with a re-injury to a newly healed break. The patient kept looking at his caregiver to give answers and the caregiver was all too ready to step in and speak on his patient's behalf. Something wasn't right. He scheduled a follow-up x-ray at the hospital for tomorrow and alerted APS of the time and place. Hopefully they'd have someone there to talk to his patient without the caregiver in attendance.

As Mark strode to his car he checked his watch. Ethan would still be at his parents', which was a good thing. Except it added another hour or two to a very long day.

Plugging in his cell phone, he put it on speaker and called Jocelyn. Having a play date with Emma would ease Ethan's distress over his being so late—again. And they weren't even into winter sports season, his busiest time of the year! He rubbed a hand over his neck massaging the pressure points to stave off the threatening headache.

No answer. He decided to leave a message. "This is Mark. Got your message. Will call again later."

Brief, to the point, that was all he could muster after a long draining day.

In some ways the thirty minute drive to his parents' home was a good thing because it gave him some space to morph from Dr. Parker to Papa. By the time he pulled into the driveway, he was in full or almost full "Papa-mode."

He'd willed a call back from Jocelyn to no avail. Debating on whether to say anything to Ethan at this point or whether it was premature, he knocked once and opened the front door.

Alerted when no charging-papa-yelling-bundle-of-little-boy-energy pelted toward him, Mark closed the door and walked toward the back of the house and the great room.

Relief coursed through him when he heard voices. A high-pitched familiar one followed by an equally familiar deeper one. There on the floor in front of the fireplace sat his dad with Ethan in his lap. The dart board was leaning against the glass doors and they were taking turns throwing darts. Mark was amazed to see how close Ethan was coming to hitting the bulls-eye. And ninety percent of his throws at least hit the target.

Leave it to his dad to find fun ways to help Ethan's nervous system recover from the abuse he'd sustained.

"Hey, looks like you two are having fun." Mark crossed the room and perched on the hassock near them.

"Grandmama is sick so Grandpapa and I are being quiet, aren't we?" Ethan announced.

Mark's brows rose, concern laced his voice. "Mom?"

"Your mother fell. While nothing is broken, it shook her up. She's resting, hopefully sleeping."

"How'd she fall?"

His dad's worried look had alarm bells ringing. "She doesn't really remember. She was checking the flower pots on the patio, you know, snipping off the dead blooms. Ethan was with her and came running to get me." He gave Ethan a bit of a squeeze. "Our boy here is fast on his feet. He came right away to get me because Grandmama had fallen asleep when she fell and Ethan couldn't wake her up."

Possible scenarios flew through his mind. Fainting? Stroke? Maybe a seizure? "Did you take her to the ED?"

"She refused. She wasn't going and that was that. She can be quite obstinate when she wants." His dad ruffled Ethan's hair. "So instead of calling the EMT's to check her out—Ethan and I did it ourselves. No signs of anything serious. And, she agreed to stay in bed.

"This boy of ours checks on her every fifteen minutes or so and reports back whether or not she's still asleep. He's very good at checking on his Grandmama. Couldn't do better myself."

Ethan straightened on his dad's lap. He looked over at the clock. "When the big hand gets to the three, I go see her," he said, his expression serious.

The three of them sat in silence watching the time crawl by for four minutes until the big hand was on the three. Ethan jumped up but then quietly walked out of the room and down the hall.

Before Mark had a chance to say anything, his dad spoke. "I've already called and made an appointment with her doctor. They'll work her in tomorrow at noon. Just bring Ethan by like usual. We'll drop him off at your office. It'll be your lunch hour and he can hang out with you for a time."

Mark's mind whipped through his schedule tomorrow. Booked full as usual. But what else was he to do? There were toys and books in the waiting room. Anne could keep an eye on him. And if Mom's appointment ran longer—which it most likely would. Between them all, somehow they'd work it out.

He nodded. "That'll work. What's most important is Mom being seen. I'll see to Ethan."

The pinched, sour face of the social worker, Mrs. Fester, popped into his mind. *If you had a wife, Ethan wouldn't be at risk. Without a wife, you can't provide him with a safe placement.*

Right now he almost agreed with her. What he needed was a back-up plan. That was something he'd thought about and talked about and planned to do but had not yet done. The biggest problem would be finding someone Ethan trusted, someone he felt safe with.

He took a turn at checking on his mom on the quarter hour. She was adamant that Ethan needed to come the next day. They would manage. She was already feeling better. He shouldn't worry about her or Ethan. They'd both be find.

That evening Mark made sure everything was set up for the next day. He had Ethan help him so his son would understand that tomorrow would be different. His concerns about his mom and about Ethan being with his parents circled around in his head until Ethan was in bed.

Once his son was tucked in, Mark headed past the living room for the kitchen. Head in the refrigerator, his hand on a cold beer, he decided against alcohol. Perched on the stool by the kitchen counter, he pulled his phone out from his pocket and hit speed dial.

"Montgomery residence." Mark recognized Jackson's voice.

"Hey, Jackson, Mark Parker here. Is Lily available?"

"She's had a long day, but I'll check."

The distress hit him in his temples. The throbbing beat spread to his neck as he waited.

A few minutes later, Lily came on the line. "What's going on, Mark?"

He quickly explained what had happened to his mom, the cobbled-together plan for tomorrow. "You know Ethan is slow to warm up to people. I don't know how to find suitable child care for him on short notice that won't set him back. Thought you might have some ideas."

Lily yawned. "Sorry about that. One of those long days. You have tomorrow covered?"

"Pretty much."

"I'm really exhausted, Mark. Let me think on it and we'll talk tomorrow. I've a client who is seeing a doctor in your building. If it's okay with her, we'll stop by your office and have Ethan come with us."

A spasm streaked across his back, more evidence of unmanaged stress. "Tomorrow is covered, Lily. It's Friday and then this weekend. I'm on call and I heard from Jocelyn Edwards. She's open Saturday. Ethan has been hounding me to see Emma again."

"Call me after your last patient tomorrow. If it's okay with my client, I'll stop by earlier and check on how things are going with Ethan. I'll have some ideas for you to pursue by the end of the day."

Her stifled yawn whispered across the connection. The ever-present tension that had stalked him since he'd walked into his parent's home eased. "Deal."

"I'm not saying I'll have answers." Lily reminded him.

"Maybe not answers but you'll have ideas. Right now that's more than I have. Talk to you tomorrow. Thanks again, Lily." He huffed out a breath and then sucked air into his lungs. Another layer of stress ebbed.

His phone on the charger, his pager next to the bed, Mark checked on Ethan one more time before calling it a night. Sleep did not come easily as he tossed and turned, trying relaxation technique after relaxation technique. Worry about his mom and Ethan crept into his dreams. There were blessings and curses to being a doctor–in this case, the curse was he knew too well what could have caused his mom's blackout.

CHAPTER 7

Jocelyn grabbed the phone from the pocket in her purse, answering it while she literally ran with Emma in her arms through the rain to Audrey's door.

"Hello?" She gasped as she set Emma on the porch.

"Jocelyn? Are you okay?"

Recognizing Lily's voice, she quickly responded. "I'm dropping Emma off at Audrey's. They called me in to work a few hours early."

The door opened and Audrey's welcoming smile and outstretched arms were a clear invitation to enter.

"There's my Emma-girl." Audrey enveloped Emma in her ample arms while holding the door open for Jocelyn with her hip. "Come in out of the rain, dear."

"I'll be right there. Go on ahead, Emma. I'm going to finish talking to Lily and then come in to say goodbye before going to work."

Emma speared her with wide blue eyes. "Promise?"

"I promise to come in and say goodbye before I go to work. In fact I'll sit right here in this chair where you can see me out the window.

Jocelyn perched on the chair, her phone in a death grip as she struggled to find the calm in the chaos. "Are you still there, Lily?"

"I am."

"What's going on?" Jocelyn shifted and shrugged in an effort to release the iron bars in her shoulders.

"Two things: I'd like Audrey's contact information. Mark Parker's parents are not going to be able to take care of Ethan for at least several days if not much longer. I thought it might be easier for Ethan to be with Emma since the two of them get along so well."

"I can take a few minutes," Jocelyn said. "You can just ask Audrey about Ethan when I go in to say goodbye to Em. What else? You said two things."

"Mark is On Call this Saturday. He doesn't want to cancel the play date because Ethan is looking forward to it. Just wanted you to know that I'll be there in case he is called in."

"Okay," Jocelyn welcomed the news Lily would be at the park. The death grip she had on her phone relaxed. "I'm going inside now so you can talk to Audrey."

"So here's the plan, Mark." Lily pitched her voice to a low confidential tone. Her client was in the waiting room, being entertained by Ethan who was playing zoo. Mindful that she'd caught him between patients, she hurried on. "Ethan can go to the same day care that Emma goes to. And, I've talked to Ashley. She and her children will also come to the park on Saturday if her husband has to work. That way Ethan can get to know her and her kids, especially Amanda who is close in age to him."

Relief, unfettered, unrestricted relief and gratitude flowed through him. He restrained the urge to hug her, instead he put his hand on her shoulder. "Thanks, Lily. I owe you and then some for this. Mom's doctor is running several tests and I know long term Ethan and waiting rooms aren't a good match."

"He's doing well now," Lily observed.

Mark smiled. "He is because I'm here and pop in to give him a hug between patients and I've promised pizza for dinner."

Her brow quirked. "If he's good?"

"No conditions. We've both had a long week and it's time to treat ourselves to our favorite dinner. Healthy eating is always a good thing but every now and then a loaded pizza hits the spot."

Lily laughed as she handed Mark the piece of paper with Audrey's name, address and phone number. "She's expecting a call from you."

MARK WAS grateful the weather held and this play date didn't start until eleven. He was also grateful his pager hadn't gone off. Maybe he'd make it the entire weekend without being called in. His dad had assured him that Ethan could come stay with them if that happened. He really didn't have any other option right then. Mrs. Fester's voice rang in his head admonishing him that Ethan needed a mother as well as a father.

"There they are!" Ethan tugged on his hand, pointing toward Emma, Jocelyn and Lily when they were at least a city block away. The slim blond woman must be Ashley Kenner. A young girl, who looked a bit older than Emma, with blond hair and wearing jeans and a long sleeved pink top must be Amanda. She sat with Lily, Jocelyn and Emma while two boys played on the swings.

Lily waved.

Letting go of Ethan's hand, his son took off, his short legs pumping. When they'd first met, Ethan was literally a broken little boy. Chest swelled as he sucked in a pride-filled breath of fresh air. *Look at him now.*

A few minutes later, Mark joined the group and introductions were made. The adults settled around a picnic bench to watch the children. Ashley's boys were older. Artie, who appeared to be about ten, watched out for Ethan, Emma and Amanda while Anthony, maybe a year younger, grumbled about being with 'little kids.'

Lily had thought ahead and brought sandwiches which were immediately devoured. An hour or so later, they headed to the ice cream parlor.

Ethan, Emma and Amanda sat together at one of the child-size tables. Artie and Anthony sat at a table next to the adults. While he and Jocelyn got the ice cream order, Mark asked some casual questions about Audrey. She was out of town this weekend so he'd meet her for the first time Monday morning when he'd drop Ethan off.

It was comforting to hear Jocelyn describe Audrey as down-to-earth, comfortable yet not quite grandmotherly whose affection for children was her biggest asset. She warned him to expect a messy, cluttered yet under-all-that-clean house.

The ice cream orders had just been delivered when his pager went off. The 111 read out had him on his feet in seconds.

Ethan's anxiety was palpable. "Papa?"

Mark crouched beside his son so they were eye-to-eye. "Remember, Lily's here with you. She's going to stay with you until I'm done." Precious seconds were ticking by. The urge to rush off was strong.

"Mama, Ethan can stay with us." Emma piped up.

Ethan clung to him.

"Lily?" He was desperate to go and desperate to stay. 111 meant major accident and multiple injuries piling up in the E.D. He really had to go.

Lily stood next to Ethan, her hand on his shoulder. "Go, Mark. I'll text you what we work out. Ethan will be fine because he's with friends, right Ethan?"

Mark noticed Ethan did not respond to Lily as he ruffled his son's hair before turning and jogging out of the ice cream parlor.

JOCELYN WATCHED Ethan curl into himself. Her heart ached for the little lost boy. Her pride in how far her daughter had come swelled. A soft smile on her face, she watched Emma hold his hand and offer him bites of her ice cream. If it was Emma, she knew what would soothe, but Ethan? She had no idea. Helplessness settled in her gut and tears filled her eyes as she watched Lily made every effort to reassure Ethan everything was going to be okay.

Ice cream finished, it was time to leave. Emma clung to Ethan's hand and Jocelyn steeled herself for the battle ahead. Having Ethan come home with them would solve everything, except she didn't get paid until tomorrow and they were down to virtually no food. She could go without dinner, say she was full from sandwiches and ice cream but...hopelessness washed over her like a tidal wave and she grasped the back of a chair to steady herself.

"I've an idea," Lily said. "Let's go to my place. Jackson is making spaghetti and the kids can watch a movie. Mark can pick Ethan up when he's done at the hospital.

"Ashley? You can invite Art to come when he gets off work. And, if I know Jackson, there'll be enough so I can invite everyone else."

Lily had her phone out and was talking to her husband before they were out the door. "It's all set then," she reported when she hung up.

Jocelyn thought Lily had a bit too much brightness in her voice. She looked tired again. And, Emma's death grip on Ethan's hand looked like it was returned.

"We're gonna need to take a rain check, Lily." Ashley had buttoned up Amanda's jacket. "Got some chores that need to get done before Art gets home."

She turned to Jocelyn. "Pleasure to meet you, Jocelyn. I think my Amanda and your Emma could be friends." She leaned down and spoke directly to Emma and Ethan. "One of these days we'd like for the two of you to come to our house and play with Amanda. Not too many more days of clear weather before the rains come in earnest." Ashley and her brood waved and took off at a faster pace. Soon they were over a block ahead.

Emma and Ethan held hands and trudged on.

"I think they need to be together right now," Lily said in a lowered voice, nodding her head in the children's direction.

It was hard to know which hurt more, her head or her stomach. One hand rested on her stomach, her head searched the kitchen's contents for something for breakfast. She forced a calm note in her voice. "We can take Ethan with us."

Lily glanced at her. "Are you sure?"

"Of course." Jocelyn waved a hand in the kids' direction. "You're right. Those two need each other right now."

"Before we make a final decision, I'll check in at the hospital and see what's happening with Mark. I know a couple of the nurses in the ED and they'll get a message to him if I can't talk to him directly."

They'd almost reached the cars when Lily's phone rang.

Listening to one side of the conversation, Jocelyn knew it was Jackson calling. "My husband said he has enough spaghetti for an army and a half. The least you could do would be to stop by and take a bucket of it home."

Jocelyn heard the fatigue in Lily's voice and saw the tiredness in her posture. "I'm not sure—."

"Please, just follow me. I'll call Jackson back and have him put the food in containers. He'll bring it out. You don't even have to get out of the car. He is, by the way, an excellent cook." Lily's smile warmed her eyes and some of the tiredness faded.

While Jocelyn dealt with moving a car seat from Lily's car to her own, she heard Lily's phone ring again. When she'd won the battle with the car seat, she called to Emma and Ethan to come get in the car.

"That was Mark," Lily said in a quiet voice. "Major accident. He'll be there for hours. I told him Ethan could stay with you. He said he didn't want to impose. Asked me to call his parents and see how things were there. I will call to check in with them, let them know Ethan will be with you and that he is fine."

She smiled. "Now about that spaghetti. It also comes with garlic bread and salad. Afraid no dessert but then we've already had ice cream." Lily patted Jocelyn's arm and then leaned over to talk to the children. "Who likes spaghetti?" They must have nodded because she added, "You're going to follow me to my house and Jackson is going to give you a big sack of food."

And so it was. Jackson came out with a large grocery sack with a gallon-size container of spaghetti sauce, a package of noodles with an apology they weren't homemade, and another container of salad. The bread was still warm from the oven and the aroma of fresh yeasty bread filled the car. Jocelyn's stomach growled on the drive across town to her apartment.

When Mark called, it was eleven o'clock. He'd been at the hospital for over ten hours and still had another surgery. She woke Ethan so he could hear Mark's voice. He and Emma slept in the bed, she curled up on the couch.

"I'm working tomorrow," she told him. "My shift starts at noon."

"I'll be by before that to pick Ethan up. Who's watching Emma? I thought Audrey was out-of-town this weekend."

"She is." Jocelyn heard the defensiveness in her tone before the words were uttered. "It's a shorter shift and Emma just goes to work with me. She takes a coloring book and paper to draw on."

"She can come home with us," Mark offered.

"I don't want to impose." The war between feeling defensive and protective raged. She hated taking Emma to work but she didn't want to admit she couldn't take care of Emma herself.

"You won't be. Not arguing with you. Got to go. Thanks for taking care of Ethan for me."

CHAPTER 8

A knock on the door woke Jocelyn from a restless sleep. She missed having Emma's small body curled next to her. Or at least that's what she'd told herself as she shifted multiple times during the night for comfort. Staggering to her feet, she shuffled to the door and peeked through the security peephole. A coffee cup was held up so she couldn't see who it was.

Tremors shook her from head to toe as her brain wrestled with the idea that Tony had found them. She didn't answer, didn't move as she struggled to figure out what to do. This apartment didn't have a back door. Then she remembered she had Ethan with her.

OMG raced through her panicked brain as she stood so still the only movement was in her chest as she fought for oxygen.

"Jocelyn? It's Mark. I've got coffee."

Mark? Mark? His voice filtered through her fear and her body slumped against the door.

"Just a minute." Her voice was shaky, as were her hands as she worked the chain and deadbolts loose and opened the door.

On the other side stood an unshaven Mark Parker, dressed in worn jeans, a University of Oregon sweat shirt and tennis shoes that had seen better days. "May I come in?"

"Oh, of course." Jocelyn stood aside until Mark stepped into her place. She shut the door behind him.

When she turned, he held a to-go cup of coffee in his outstretched hand. "Missed my boy. Mornings aren't the same without him. Thought I'd take us all out to breakfast, drop you off at work, keep Emma and Ethan with me. We can pick you up after your shift and plan from there."

"I thought you were on call all weekend?"

"I was, but I worked about fifteen hours yesterday, I've only had four hours of sleep. At that stage I'm too wired to sleep but not alert enough to perform surgery. Another orthopedic practice was called in to cover the rest of the weekend."

She took a sip from the cup in her hand. "Oh." The bitter taste wrinkled her nose.

Mark, took the cup from her and set it on the counter. "What do you drink?"

"It's that obvious?" She scrunched her nose and her eyes narrowed.

He grinned, not a boyish one but one tinged with mischief. "Didn't see your eyes close in rapturous pleasure or hear a deep felt sigh of joy."

"No, you didn't. I don't think there is anything that elicits that reaction from me." She ran a hand through her hair realized it was in a snarled mess. An image of the picture she made standing in her apartment in her baggy sweat pants and t-shirt with her rat's nest hair popped into her mind. She blushed a bright red.

"I'll check on the kids. Take a seat, I'll be right back." She dashed from the room. A glance in the bedroom showed Emma and Ethan were curled together and still sound asleep. Looking into the bathroom mirror, the look of horror on her face was laughable. The fact Mark Parker hadn't run screaming into the morning said something for his character. She marveled he hadn't even seemed repulsed by the sight of her.

After attempting to put herself to rights, she shoved her hair back from her face and marched into the living room. Mark sat on the couch, his head back and eyes closed. She didn't think she'd made any sound but he opened his eyes and smiled. "Catnap."

"I'll just fix my tea and take a quick shower if you don't mind. The kids are still asleep. It's been about twelve hours. Can't ever remember Emma sleeping this well."

While she was talking, Jocelyn went into the kitchen, which was really the appliances and sink set along one wall, and fixed her tea. She turned back to the living room to find Mark watching her.

"Ethan often wakes with nightmares so I say take your shower, let them sleep until you're ready. Then we'll head out to breakfast."

It may not have been the fastest shower she'd ever taken but it was a close second. Dressed in her waitress uniform with a skirt and blouse over it, she opened the door to see Ethan dancing from one foot to the other.

"It's all yours," she stepped quickly out, hiding the grin on her face.

He dashed in and the sounds of a little boy peeing were clearly heard because the door didn't shut tight. "He had to go really, really bad," Emma said from the bedroom doorway.

"And you?"

Emma scrunched her face. "I'm waiting really hard."

Jocelyn looked up to see Mark at the beginning of the short hall. She startled, she reached for Emma before realizing he was no threat. Water ran. Ethan must be washing his hands.

She knocked on the door. "Ethan, can you finish washing your hands at the kitchen sink so Emma can use the bathroom, please?"

The door opened almost immediately and Ethan's concerned face brightened when he saw Mark. Throwing the door wide, he sprinted for his papa whose face had lost the lines of exhaustion.

Emma rushed in as Ethan raced out.

Surreptitiously Jocelyn checked the bed. It was dry. She'd wondered if Emma would have an accident because their routine had not been held to yesterday.

Bodily functions taken care of, little bodies dressed, they trooped out to Mark's car after Jocelyn gave up protesting she should take her own. The clincher was when it wouldn't start.

Mark had pronounced the battery dead. He was probably right.

They moved car seats and once the kids were strapped in. Jocelyn climbed into the passenger seat, the problem of the dead battery foremost in her mind. She'd ask her neighbor for a jump start tomorrow. A new battery wasn't quite in her budget. Did they do used or reconditioned ones? She'd have to check.

"Jocelyn?" Mark's voice pulled her out of her thoughts about batteries and budgets. "Any place special you like to go for breakfast?"

"No, we don't go out for breakfast very... ." Her voice trailed off as she registered her body cradled in the luxurious leather passenger seat of a what? She spied the "L" on the steering wheel. A Lexus! Very different from her twenty-year-old Honda Civic with close to two hundred thousand miles on it. Cheap had been what she'd needed when she and Emma had run away from Tony.

"Ethan?" Mark looked at his son through the rear view mirror. "Where shall we take these ladies for breakfast?" He turned the key. The engine purred in response.

"Cora's! She does really good pancakes."

"Cora's it is." Mark backed out of the parking spot. He turned toward her, catching her eye he said, "Cora's is a little place not far from the hospital. Great food but always crowded. Where do you work so I can make allowances for drive time? Don't want you to be late."

Jocelyn gave him the name and address. She looked for a raised eyebrow or some sign that he knew of her place of employment or was in judgement of the part of town in which she worked but his face remained neutral.

Eyes on the road, Mark pulled out into traffic.

Jocelyn turned once just to see for herself that her quiet, reserved daughter was happily engaged with Ethan before settling in and enjoying the smooth ride.

Mark Parker was a hard man for her to read and that meant he was dangerous to both Emma and her—except the vibration of danger wasn't in the air.

A table miraculously opened up when they walked into the small restaurant. Cora, a tiny African-American woman, ran a tight ship with humor. Jocelyn noticed how her diverse wait staff (she employed a wide variety of ethnic and racial men and women of varying ages to serve customers) treated everyone—with attention and respect. Food was served hot. Ingredients were top quality. Prices were also, but Cora's was an exclusive venue.

And, after tasting her veggie omelet Jocelyn didn't think the prices were that excessive. Cooked to perfection with organic ingredients. Not a chemical taste anywhere. When their waitress, Maisie, checked back in with them she asked the young brunette, "Free range chicken eggs?"

Maisie's smile lit her dark brown eyes. "We only use sustainable, organic ingredients so you'll see our menu isn't as extensive as some other places."

"You can tell the difference between free range and caged eggs in an omelet?" Surprise colored Mark's question.

"I can," Jocelyn replied. She leaned on the table and continued. "Well, it's more that I can't taste any chemicals, additives, that kind of thing. I'm fairly sensitive to them so it's more that I notice they aren't there."

Before they left, Cora came to their table. It was obvious Mark and Ethan were regular customers. Mark introduced Emma and Jocelyn, and Cora's welcome was warm. Her "any friend of Mark and Ethan's is always welcome here" registered with Jocelyn as genuine.

"Well, you made a hit here." Mark said as they left. He carried breakfast leftovers in recyclable boxes in a brown paper bag.

She must have looked confused because he continued. "Cora doesn't always stop to have an actual conversation with customers. More of a "how is everything". I'm sure Maisie said something to her about you knowing about the eggs. She was sizing you up."

Jocelyn had no idea how to respond to that so she busied herself securing kids in car seats while Mark put leftovers in the trunk and helped finish up with Ethan's seat.

He maneuvered his car through traffic while keeping up a steady conversation with the children. What did they want to do while

Emma's mom was at work? What about lunch or dinner? Jocelyn didn't have the energy to intervene, especially hearing Emma's excited responses.

She still had fifteen minutes before her shift started when Mark stopped his car at the end of the alley. Leo poked his head out the alleyway door, no doubt looking for her. Something was wrong. Waiting until straight up noon would only bring her grief. Better to go in now and deal with it. She needed this job working in this hole-in-the-wall-dive. She hated the skimpy costume he called a uniform, the costume that invited butt patting and pinching.

But Leo let her bring Emma when she didn't have day care. Of course Emma stayed in the employee's lounge. What a laugh. Peeling paint, bare fluorescent lights, cracked linoleum flooring, a dilapidated couch where Emma could doze – but she could duck in every ten or fifteen minutes and check on her. When she had a little cushion in her bank account, she'd have the energy to look for work outside this neighborhood.

"You can let me out here," she said at the end of the alley. "It's narrow and I don't want your car to get scratched." She already had her seat belt unbuckled and her bag which included her high-heeled shoes and purse in hand.

Mark looked down the alley and put the car in park. "If we don't hear from you, we'll pick you up at five. You've got my number if you get off earlier."

Jocelyn nodded and bolted from the car. She walked backwards waving madly to Emma. Hearing Leo bellow, she turned and jogged the rest of the way. Breathless when she reached the backdoor, she smiled at Leo, who held the door open, and ducked in.

The employees' lounge was to her right. She stepped in and opened the old athletic locker with her work name on it. Slipping off her jacket, blouse and long skirt as she toed off her shoes, she pulled out the high heels before stuffing her everyday clothes in her bag. She shoved her feet into the stilettos. Five hours of agony awaited.

Once her belongings were safely stowed in the locker, she tucked the key in her bra and turned, knowing Leo had watched her the entire time. She saw lust in his eyes. He never came on to *his girls* although he obviously got something out of watching them change.

"One of the regulars been asking for you. And you'll need to work Ester's shift. She called in sick. I'm short-handed."

Jocelyn placed her hands on her hips and kept eye contact with Leo. "So you'll pay me time-and-a-half for these extra hours? I already worked forty-five hours this week." Why wasn't she saying 'no' to working eleven hours? Her car needed a new battery, that's why.

"We'll see," Leo said. "Maybe a little bonus for you if business is good." He patted her butt as she passed him in the doorway and headed for the bar.

Leo's was called a restaurant bar and grill cause there was a kitchen attached and they did serve more than snacks—hamburgers, hot wings, fries and nachos. Food that went well with beer and booze.

Jocelyn pasted on her welcome to Leo's smile and went to work. She'd have a break in three hours. Time to make some calls and see what arrangements she could make for Emma until she got off work.

CHAPTER 9

Mark's feet dragged as he did a couple loads of laundry and changed beds. He stifled yawns while glorying in the reality that Ethan and Emma got along well. They played with Ethan's trucks, watched his Little Mermaid movie and each picked out a book to be read later.

As he smoothed the clean sheets on Ethan's bed, his smile ended in another yawn. He scrubbed his hands over his face and rubbed his neck to increase blood flow and get more oxygen into his system. A grin spread at the picture of his son's serious face as he announced the bed was dry this morning. And at Emma's house.

Progress!

Mark caught the call from Jocelyn on the second ring. Both children were immediately at his side. After listening to Jocelyn's plan for coping with her schedule change by having Emma wait in the break room, Mark schooled his voice to speak calmly. "The change isn't a problem. We'll pick you up tonight. No, it won't be difficult, Jocelyn."

"But Mark, I know my getting off so late is a hardship for you," Jocelyn said. "If you bring Emma by here, she can sleep while I finish my shift and I'll take her home."

"I am not bringing Emma there tonight except to pick you up from work. Ethan and I will take you both home. Or Emma can spend the night here with us and I'll take her to Audrey's when I take Ethan in the morning.

"Call me back when you've decided." Mark ended the call. Knowing he'd overstepped his authority, he blamed it on being so tired. Another rub of his hands over his face, he looked at the little girl stiff and unwavering two feet in front of him.

Emma's voice quavered and her eyes widened. "Where's my mama?"

Mark expected a protruding lower lip and tears but Emma remained stoic. "Your mama is at work. We're going to have dinner, bath time and stories."

Ethan put his arm around Emma, "My papa will make sure your mama is safe."

Mark's stomach plummeted and bile rose in his throat. How many other children wondered about their parent's safety?

He crouched in front of the two little ones. "Here's what we're going to do. We're going to call a taxi and have them go to pick Emma's mama up from work. They will go early and stay as long as they need to. Then they will take her home or maybe bring her here. We're going to call and leave a message for her on her phone so she knows someone is waiting to make sure she is safe going home. How is that for a plan?"

Doubt registered on each child's face. His mind scrambled to come up with another idea.

"Okay, we're going to call her work and see when she has a break. We'll go and see her so Emma can get her hug and kiss good-night. We'll make sure she has a safe way home. Then we'll come back here and get a good night's sleep because tomorrow you two get to go to Audrey's."

Although happier with that plan, Emma was still worried. How did he know? She had a death grip on Ethan's hand.

Mark stood and looked up the phone number for Leo's. He called and asked to speak with Leo. Unimpressed with the growling, gruff voice that finally came on the line, he was more impressed that Leo called Jocelyn over to the phone.

"Just checking on the timing of your next break. Emma would like to give you a hug and kiss tonight. Thought we'd come down so she could see you."

"I can talk to her instead."

Mark fought the urge to pace with two sets of eyes watching his every move. "I don't think that's enough tonight. She's quietly upset by all the changes."

"Okay, my break's in forty-five minutes." Her tone was brisk but not hostile.

He relaxed the hold he had on the phone. "We'll be there."

"I'll meet you at the end of the alley where you dropped me off."

He countered. "No, we'll meet you out front where there are street lights. It's not safe for you to be walking up and down the alleyway in the dark."

"Mark, please." He heard the exhaustion in her voice and wondered again why Jocelyn Edwards worked in a dive like Leo's. While not movie star beautiful, she was attractive, smart and could easily work at a high-end place where she'd make better money in a better environment.

On a hunch, he agreed to meet her at the end of the alleyway as she asked.

Next he called his parents and asked if his dad was comfortable leaving his mom for an hour or so. "Need to run an errand and kids need to be with me but I don't want to leave them alone in the car."

"I'll be ready when you get here." His dad's availability made his impromptu plan work.

There wasn't much time left in that forty-five minutes when Mark pulled into a space along the street two car lengths from the end of the alley's opening. "I'll be right back." He handed the car keys to his dad and headed down the alleyway to what he thought was Leo's back entrance. He waited only a few minutes under the cage-encased light bulb before the next door down opened and Jocelyn came out.

"Jocelyn?" Mark said her name as he stepped towards her. He saw her startle, her hand pressed against her chest. Thankful she didn't scream, he held out his hand. She didn't take it. She'd also been in a hurry to put her clothes on. In the dimness, he saw her top's buttons weren't in proper order and her skirt was askew.

"May I?" he said holding out his arm to escort her.

"Dear God in heaven. What are you doing here?" she hissed.

"Walking you down a dark alley to the street where Emma awaits."

"I told you—,"

Not sure why she was so mad, he kept his tone light. "Yes, you did but I believe I said something in return. Come. We don't need to waste your break time arguing when you could be spending it with Emma."

When she didn't taken his offered arm, Mark almost reached for her elbow. He held himself back because she'd been seriously startled. Suspicions turned to certainty. Jocelyn Edwards had been subjected to physical abuse.

He escorted Jocelyn to his car while playing a few scenarios in his mind. He'd love to get his hands on the lowlife who had hurt Jocelyn and Emma. More importantly, he'd love to make the report, make the case to the police and child welfare so the rat bastard never touched them or anyone else again.

Emma's face lit up when Jocelyn opened the backseat door and leaned in. She tugged at the straps holding her in her car seat, wanting out. Jocelyn fumbled with the different seat buckling.

"Let me help," Mark offered.

She stood back and as he deftly undid the car seat straps he said, "Jocelyn, I'd like you to meet my dad, Peter Parker."

Jocelyn stepped back as an older version of Mark rose from the front seat.

"I'm pleased to meet you, Jocelyn. Your Emma is a delight."

"Thank you, I think so too."

Finally free, Emma ran to her mom. Small arms wrapped around her knees. Jocelyn picked Emma up and holding her close, walked down the street.

Mark saw Emma shake her head. When Jocelyn stopped talking,

Emma laid her head on her mom's shoulder and hugged her. Leaning against a car parked about ten feet further along the street, Jocelyn and Emma blended in the shadows so he couldn't see where one ended and the other began.

A man strolled by, the fumes of hard liquor strong. When he slowed and then stopped by Jocelyn, Mark was on the move, jogging the short distance. "Thought you'd decided to finally meet me, Jackie," the drunk guy said. "Quickie?"

Mark wedged himself between Jocelyn, Emma and the man. "Hey, babe, this guy bothering you?"

The man swayed as he peered over at him. "Who're you?"

"I asked first."

"Mark, don't." Jocelyn's terse words fractured the air. "Emma."

"Take Emma back to the car," Mark said. He crowded the guy back a step, his eyes never leaving the slightly glazed ones glaring at him. Jocelyn slipped by him and headed back to the car.

"Wife, stay away," he said.

The guy staggered when he shook his head. "She ain't married. Can't be and work at Leo's."

"Back off." Mark leaned forward and emphasized the words.

Mumbling, the drunk headed back down the sidewalk toward the corner. Mark kept pace and blocked Jocelyn and Emma from any contact. When he turned the corner, Mark released a pent up breath of relief and started back to the car.

"My break's over." Jocelyn said to Emma. Her daughter was frightened. Nothing she said helped. Emma was hanging on to her neck for dear life.

"Emma, your mom's okay," Mark said. Other than prying Emma's hands from Jocelyn's neck, which he would not do, he had no idea how to handle this predicament. He shoved his hands in his pockets in a gesture of helplessness and stepped back a few feet.

His dad joined him.

"Ethan's upset but can see that everyone is okay," Peter reported.

"Thanks, Dad."

A heavy set man barreled out of the alley way. "Your break's over. What the fuck are you doing?"

Mark recognized Leo's voice from the phone.

Jocelyn faced him and in a steely voice said, "Saying good night to my daughter, Leo. You knew she was coming down to see me."

"And what's this about you being married? You know I don't want any angry husbands showing up."

"You must be Leo," Mark strode the half-dozen steps until he stood next to Jocelyn and offered his hand. "We spoke on the phone a short time ago.

Leo ignored his outstretched hand. "You married to her?"

"Afraid there was a bit of a misunderstanding. Ms. Edwards came out to see her daughter, not to have an assignation with a half-drunk guy. He had a hard time hearing her say 'no'."

"So who are you?" Leo's tone was belligerent.

Jocelyn piped up. "He's a friend. Our children are best friends and he was kind enough to offer to watch Emma when you asked me to work extra hours."

Taking Jocelyn's cue, Mark added. "You know kids, they have their night time routines. Emma just had to give her mama a good night kiss. We'd already be on our way if that dude hadn't interfered."

Jocelyn kicked him with the side of her shoe.

Mark ignored it. "Any chance you can let her off now or in the next thirty minutes or so? We'd just wait here so she'd have a ride home."

"Where's your car?" Leo looked around as if noticing for the first time her vehicle wasn't parked in the alleyway.

"Battery." Mark offered.

Leo glared at Jocelyn. "That pile of crap you call a car. It's one thing and then another." His face softened for a moment when he focused on Emma, still clinging to her mom. "The whole thing hard on her, was it?"

Jocelyn nodded.

Leo huffed and puffed. The glare softened. "Go ahead and take off.

We'll manage. Could use you to work tomorrow night. Don't think Ester will make it in for a couple of days."

Mark knew that working a double shift would mean no time to get a new battery. And no time with Emma.

He put his hand on Jocelyn's shoulder grateful and surprised she didn't shrink away. "Can she let you know in the morning? Child care arrangements and all that."

"Kid can always stay in the employee's lounge. She's done it before," Leo pointed out.

Mark peered around Jocelyn's neck until he met Emma's eyes. Terror and defiance in her gaze, she hung on to her mom for all she was worth.

"Hey, Emma, Ethan is lonely and needs you to come sit with him. Mr. Peter will help you into your car seat while I walk with your mom back to her work so she can get her things. She's going to come home now. Okay?"

Emma whispered in Jocelyn's ear. When her mom nodded, the death grip Emma had on her eased. She allowed Jocelyn to put her in the car seat, give her a quick kiss and pull away. His dad took up the space and chatted while he worked the buckles and straps into place.

Mark took Jocelyn's hand and walked with her down the alley, Leo leading the way. He stepped inside the back door just as a scantily clad woman came out of the restroom.

She shrugged at her boss. "I'm sorry, Leo. Couldn't wait any longer."

Mark leaned against the doorway to the employees lounge while Jocelyn opened a locker with the name *Jackie* on it. She took her purse and bag from inside. She slipped high heeled shoes from the locker floor into the bag before shoving her purse inside. Slinging it over her shoulder, she turned toward the door.

He stepped into the hall. As Jocelyn passed by Leo, his hand rose as if to pat her butt. Mark caught his eye and raised a brow. Leo, hand now at his side, headed back to the bar.

Saying nothing and with a light touch to her elbow, Mark escorted her outside. Once in the alleyway, he dropped his hand but kept pace beside her. "Do you get anything to eat when you work?"

"Do you mean are meals included?"

"Yeah."

"Not usually." She sounded tired and demoralized. "Leo really is shorthanded tonight so he threw in a hamburger around five."

"Hungry?"

Her stomach rumbled.

Mark chuckled. "Guess that was an answer. Why don't we call ahead? I can order a pizza and we can pick it up on the way."

"You don't have to feed me."

"I know I don't *have* to, but maybe I *want* to. Any objections to someone else purchasing food for you?"

She stopped. "Obligations."

"Consider this pizza obligation-free. You need something to eat and I predict morning is going to come very early.

"By the way, how are you getting Emma to Audrey's?"

"One of my neighbor's will give me a jump and I'll leave the car running while I take Emma in to Audrey's. If it won't start when I get off work, Leo will see that I get a jump."

So Leo wasn't a total asshole. "Looks like you've got it covered."

She nodded. At the car, she slipped into the backseat between the two car seats. Very cramped but she assured everyone she was fine and refused his dad's offer to change seats.

Before they pulled away from the curb, Mark called in a pizza order.

He walked Jocelyn and Emma to her apartment door. Jocelyn was still protesting his paying for their pizza. Mark gave the folded bills to Emma. Enough for the pizza, a tip and a bit more.

As luck would have it, when he reached the parking lot, the pizza delivery guy was pulling in. The driver had the insulated bag in hand when Mark approached.

"Delivering the pepperoni and extra cheese?"

"Yeah," the young man said, warily looking around.

Mark handed him a twenty. "Here you go. Tell the lady some guy in the parking lot already paid you, okay?"

"Sure." A grin on his face he headed up the stairs.

Slipping behind the wheel of his car, Mark glanced back at Ethan. His son, looking a bit forlorn and a tad lost, stared out the window towards the steps leading to Emma's.

Mark caught his son's gaze and said softly. "Missing Emma?"

Ethan nodded. "She needs me, Papa."

"And you'll see her in the morning at Audrey's. Remember? You get to go to a new place and spend the day with Emma."

Mark swallowed the lump that had formed in his throat. He reached back and patted Ethan's knee knowing that the need went both ways.

"Remember? You get to spend the whole day with her." He forced a cheery note to his voice.

"That's right, Ethan," his dad said. "You'll have a fun day tomorrow."

Mark was grateful Ethan fell asleep on their way to his parents' home. He didn't stir as he and his dad talked quietly about the reality of them taking care of Ethan as they had been. Nor did he wake when they pulled into their garage. He did stir when released from his car seat. Ethan's head on his shoulder, Mark relished the weight of his son as he carried him into the house and tucked him into his bed.

Going through his own nighttime routine, Mark let his mind wander and shift through the conundrum that made up Jocelyn Edwards. Was that even her real name?

She shadowed his thoughts as he pulled the covers up over his shoulders. She was prickly and prideful. Persnickety and penurious—well, not the later by choice. Pretty, pleasant, purposeful, protective. Positively memorable.

CHAPTER 10

Jocelyn found the next week full of surprises. A benefactor installed a new battery in her car, her shifts were eight consecutive hours and she was always able to pick Emma up by six. Mark was picking Ethan up at the same time on two of the days. She accepted an offer of dinner expecting to pay for hers and Emma's meal but another surprise awaited.

After dropping her car off at the apartment, Mark drove to his condo and fixed a simple dinner: scrambled egg sandwiches and a slice of cantaloupe. Milk with a dash of chocolate syrup completed the festive meal. She helped clean up the kitchen while Ethan and Emma picked out a story they wanted read.

At eight o'clock they pulled into the parking lot at her apartment complex.

"Let's go, Ethan," Mark said getting out and opening Ethan's door.

"You don't have to—," her protest was cut short.

"Manners. My mom's big on them and has been teaching Ethan basic manners."

Her apartment door unlocked and standing wide, Jocelyn turned and took Ethan's hand. "Thank you for your escort, sir."

"What about my papa? He ested you too."

"Yes, he did." She shifted so she caught Mark's gaze. "We are grateful for your assistance. Dinner was delightful as was the company."

"We had a really good time," Emma told Ethan.

"Good night," Jocelyn guided Emma inside and, with a last look at Mark and Ethan, smiled and waved as she shut the door. Dead bolt, chain and knob locked, she took Emma's hand and headed toward the bedroom.

"Did we have a good time, Mama?" Emma asked, still holding Jocelyn's hand.

"What do you think? Did you have a good time with Ethan?"

Emma had climbed up on the bed and was pulling her top off, her head nodding vigorously. "Ethan has lots of toys and books. And they're his. He doesn't have to take them back or anything."

Jocelyn heard the wistfulness in Emma's voice but said nothing. What would be appropriate? He's lucky. Wish you could have all that too? But even though wistful, if given the choice, Emma would choose to get books from the library or borrow from Audrey. Being able to pack quickly was imperative. As young as Emma was, she knew the truth of that.

JOCELYN CHECKED the directions again as she navigated in unfamiliar territory. She was in a part of Fremont new to her. The ranch with the right numbers was on a street with similar houses. She recognized Lily's car and pulled in behind. A glance in the rearview mirror gave her a glimpse of Emma's tense wistful face.

Her stomach unsettled, Jocelyn reminded herself this playdate with Amanda Kenner was for Emma. *And you.* Startled at the small voice in her head, her foot slipped off the brake. The car lurched forward. Jocelyn squeaked but got the car stopped before hitting Lily's rear bumper.

"Are you okay, Mama?" Emma was worried.

Hearing that tone helped Jocelyn calm. "I'm okay, Em. Just startled myself. But everything is okay." She unbuckled her seat belt, catching Emma's gaze in the rear view mirror. "Ready to go see Amanda?" She saw her nod and start to undo the car seat buckles.

The door opened and Ashley and Amanda stood welcoming them before they made it to the front steps. "We've been watching for you," Amanda announced, reaching out to Emma. "We can play in my room while they all talk."

Emma didn't resist although she didn't chatter along with Amanda as they went down the hall. Jocelyn made note of which doorway they turned into.

"Bathroom is the next door down from Amanda's room." Ashley pointed in the general direction. "We're here in the living room." She gestured for Jocelyn to go ahead of her into a well-used room with a bright multi-colored throw over a well-worn couch.

Lily, who was in a rocking chair near the picture window, rose and crossed the room. "I'm so glad you could make it." She slipped her arm around Jocelyn's waist and hugged.

"Tea?" Ashley asked from the doorway. "I'm fixing a fresh pot. This time it's a lavender black tea."

"Yum, do you need help carrying things?" Lily asked.

"I've got it. Ya'll get comfortable." Ashley headed to the kitchen.

"Sit where you're comfortable," Lily said waiting for Jocelyn to settle. "If you'd like the rocking chair, please sit there. I've one at home."

"Sometimes rocking chairs give me a headache, so you go ahead. I'll sit here on the couch." Jocelyn settled on the end closest to the doorway.

When tea mugs were filled and the cozy back on the teapot, Lily began. She leaned towards Jocelyn, care and concern in her eyes, a slight wrinkle between her brows. "Ashley's been to several 14th Moons but has not been an Intercessor, however, she's been instrumental in some of the other aspects of ceremony."

"So what seems to be ya'll's problem?" Ashley asked reaching over and patting Jocelyn's hand.

"I don't—that is I think—the truth is I'm not able to be Intercessor.

I don't know how. I don't have any spiritual practice or path to bring to the group. I don't know how to hold energy. I don't know... ."

"We all'd only been to a couple of 14th Moons when Lily and then Sophia volunteered to be Intercessor so I think we pretty much know what ya'll are worried about."

Ashley's words in her soft Southern accent soothed. The incipient panic receded.

"Whatever you need, I know with a certainty it will show up," Lily said, scooting the rocker closer to the couch. "When we started this journey, we had each other and a desire to deepen or widen or perhaps just find a spiritual path."

"That was part of the adventure." Ashley grinned. "We hadn't a clue what we were doing, only knew we wanted something different than what we had. And you have Carol, Meghan and Molly on this journey with you."

Jocelyn was entranced and appalled. They both, well, everyone at the 14th Moon seemed so, well, self-actualized. "I volunteered because I wanted to be like everyone else." The words were out before the hand she clapped over her mouth could stop them.

Lily leaned back in the rocker, a smile on her face. "Not realizing you already were like everyone else because you were there. That was all it took."

"I remember being mesmerized by the Crone's part of the ceremony. I wanted to crawl up and sit literally at their feet so I wouldn't miss a word. Ya remember our first 14th Moon, Lily?"

"I do. One hundred women singing, drumming and praying together. The first place I really understood the concept of unconditional acceptance. All that mattered was that I was there."

Jocelyn wrapped her arms around her middle, held herself close. "I felt that way. And I don't know how to make that happen for everyone."

"Ahh, yes." Lily smiled and nodded. "How does that happen? Ash, what do you think creates that unconditional acceptance?"

Jocelyn watched Ashley, who with no hesitation answered, "It's because it's sacred space. The altar, calling in protectors and guides or whatever your spiritual path is. Maybe angels? It's always a bit different. But what is the same is that the circle becomes a sacred space."

"How?" Jocelyn's curiosity engaged.

"What do you remember happening when you first arrived?" Lily, now leaning back and gently rocking, asked.

"You mean like when I signed in?"

Lily nodded.

"Oh, I got a flyer about how to treat the land, you know picking up all trash, etc. And even before that I got a list of what to bring and expectations. So I knew everyone who wore yellow was a Matron like me. I could tell who the Crones were and who the Maidens were also."

"What else," Lily prompted.

"Just, well, everyone was so happy and helpful. It was contagious. I remember two Crones called out for help with their tent and at least ten other women showed up. In minutes that tent was up and all their things moved from their car to the tent. It just happened—almost like magic."

Lily leaned forward and added, "It happened because expectations were communicated to everyone who attended. Crones are to be honored, supported in all ways. No one had to wonder what to do when those Crones asked for help."

Jocelyn remembered the looks on their faces. "They didn't really believe they would be honored. I'm not sure they needed help putting up their tent. Asking for help was more of a test. But when their tent went up, they were grateful. They'd never been to a 14th Moon before and I could tell watching them over the weekend what a difference it made as they were repeatedly honored."

"So what did Meredith, the Intercessor, have to do with that?" Lily asked.

Jocelyn's brow furrowed in thought. "I hadn't even seen Meredith at that point."

"Because she was isolated and doing the energy work that she'd decided she needed to do before ceremony began."

"But—."

Lily stopped Jocelyn's words with a wave of her hand. "Answer me this. What part of the ceremony from opening to closing, did you feel deep inside you?" She put a hand over her heart and one over her abdomen.

Jocelyn stopped to consider before answering. "I felt things more like here," she demonstrated by waving her hands over her shoulders and head. "When we went through the cleansing with sage and feathers and drum, my whole body relaxed but I noticed it most in this area.

"The drumming I felt in my bones, my entire body, and I sometimes had pictures flash through my mind."

"Do you remember them?" Ashley asked.

"Now that you bring it up, I do remember most of them. It was strange because they had nothing to do with Emma or me. Not really anyway. I was, well, Emma and I were in a family. We were flying a kite on the beach. We were flying somewhere—well, I don't remember Emma in that one."

"Why do you think they had nothing to do with you and Emma?" Lily asked, her face neutral.

"Because there was a man and a little boy in them. I've no intention to ever get involved with a man again. And Emma is terrified of men."

"Were there any other visions?" Lily's head was tilted to one side, her hand propping her cheek.

"Only one," Jocelyn's gaze strayed beyond Lily out the front room window. "I was holding a new baby. Emma was smiling and there were two other children with us. A hand was on my shoulder in support. It felt like whoever was there supported me."

CHAPTER 11

Mark rubbed his forehead in an effort to chase away the burgeoning headache. His dad, stoic as ever when the news wasn't to his liking, stood stock still. His mom? Well, he didn't even want to think about what the news was going to be for her. The fact that the tumor on her brain was operable wasn't enough to dispel the chill that now crept from his insides out.

To top it off, this temporary child care arrangement would have to become permanent. Audrey's was further away from the condo so that meant adding an hour to the beginning and end of his days. Who would watch Ethan when he was On Call? It had been easy for Ethan to accept staying with Grandmama and Grandpapa, but someone else? He'd done better than expected at Audrey's but Emma was there and he'd been told it was "for a little while."

He laid his hand on his dad's shoulder. "We'll make it through this. Mom's strong and determined. We can be strong and determined with her."

His dad reached up and patted his hand. No words because there were no words. Nothing could describe the devastation they felt. Peggy Parker was the heart and soul of the family. Being a Parker already felt different just because of his mom's diagnosis and with it the knowledge this wasn't a minor thing.

Thank God Dad is retired and able to be home. Mom would hate having a care- giver come in. He'll need breaks. Time to play golf or work in his shop. Or just go for a walk.

His mom came out of the exam room, a frown on her face. "You both look like I'm half dead. That will not do."

Mark summoned up a smile. "Is this better?"

"It will have to do until I see Ethan. He'll have a big smile and hug for me."

His dad wrapped his arms around his mom. "Am I getting too old for you? Taking after those younger guys now?"

His mom melted into his dad's embrace. "Right now you're tops in my book."

"Glad to hear it. Now, what we need to do is—."

His mom kissed her husband's cheek and interrupted. "What we need to do is pick up Ethan, go home and have pot roast for dinner. Everything else can wait until tomorrow—oh, until Monday. Nothing drastic is going to happen between now and then. Dr. Norton assured me the tumor is slow growing so we have some time to figure our way forward, make plans and all that."

Mark observed his mom's demeanor. She was cheerful for them, mainly for his dad, but … . "Are you up to coming with me to pick up Ethan? Or I can drop you off at home so you can rest while I go get him."

"Let's go together to pick him up. That'll be a surprise and I'll get my Ethan fix a little sooner. I've missed him." She tucked her hand in her husband's elbow and leaned.

Pulling his mini-van into Audrey's driveway, Mark recognized Jocelyn's car. Thankfully his mom was managing and didn't need her seat reclined. In fact she looked better in anticipation of her "Ethan fix".

Just as he got out, Jocelyn came out with Emma who was still holding Ethan's hand.

"Hey, buddy. Look who I brought with me to pick you up?" He gestured to the van.

Ethan's face remained stoic when he looked over at the van. He kept hold of Emma's hand.

His mom and dad must have noticed Ethan's distress, because they got out and walked around the van.

Ethan frowned. Then straightened his shoulders, tilted his chin up and Mark saw the beginnings of a full-fledged battle coming on. Instead of a tantrum, in his polite voice, Ethan said "Emma this is my grandmama. Grandmama this is my very bestest friend, Emma. Oh and her mama." His mouth turned down and tears welled.

"Why Ethan what a wonderful job you did in introducing me." Mark's mom stepped forward and crouched down in front of Emma. "I'm so pleased to meet Ethan's bestest friend." She rose and with her warmest smile added, "and her mama. You can call me Grandmama but if you'd rather not, please call me Peggy."

"Grandmama, aren't you supposed to shake hands?" Ethan said, a frown on his face.

"Why yes, Ethan, that's usually how it's done. But sometimes the other person doesn't want to shake hands." She looked over at Emma. "Do you want to shake hands, Emma?"

Emma shook her head.

Mark knew something was wrong. Ethan always raced to greet his grandmama and grandpapa. He felt Jocelyn's gaze. When he glanced in her direction, she raised her left brow.

Stepping into the growing silence, Mark said "Mom, this is Jocelyn Edwards, Emma's mom. And Dad, I'm sure you remember Jocelyn and Emma from the other night."

Jocelyn smiled at Peter before turning to Peggy, her hand extended. "I'm pleased to meet you, Peggy. Ethan has said so many things about his grandmama," she glanced over at his dad, "and grandpapa, I expected an Amazon."

Peggy shook the offered hand while saying, "Do you have plans for dinner, Jocelyn? I may call you that, might I?"

"They have sandwiches for dinner on Friday night," Ethan piped up. "Emma said."

"We'd love to have you and Emma join us tonight." Peggy went on without a hitch. "Pot roast with all the trimmings. And, we may even convince Mark to stop at the ice cream parlor and get some for dessert."

Jocelyn smiled. "Thank you for the invitation, Peggy. Emma and I don't want to intrude."

Peggy looped her arm through Jocelyn's and walked a few steps away. "Your intruding as you call it would be a blessing, dear. I had some difficult news at the doctor's this afternoon. The men in my life tend to be over-protective. Right now I'm out numbered. With you and Emma, the numbers will be even.

"And while I don't know what's happened," she gestured to Ethan and Emma who were still holding hands, "those two seem to still need more time together."

Jocelyn, who had kept Emma in her sight except for the few minutes of introduction, smiled. "You're right. They do need a bit more time together. Do you think you could talk to them a minute while I let Mark know what happened today?"

"Of course," Peggy said then walked the few steps back to where Emma and Ethan stood clinging to each other. She nodded in Jocelyn's direction before ushering the children toward the van.

Mark, his heart beating the-what's-happened-to-Ethan tattoo, took Jocelyn's elbow and half-turned them away. He leaned down to better hear her. "What happened?"

Jocelyn looked up into brown eyes clouded with worry. "Audrey took on two new children today. A brother and sister. They came with social workers with notebooks and paperwork. Audrey said both Ethan and Emma immediately regressed. The new children were taken into protective custody this morning. When I saw them, they looked lost. What's even worse is bruises and bandages are still evident."

"Thanks for letting me know." Mark ran a hand through his hair, before stuffing both hands in his pockets and rocking back on his heels. He let his gaze rest on Jocelyn's upturned face. Her worry for the children was visible in the slight frown between her hazel eyes.

He took a deep breath and plunged on, his words coming out in a rush. "Mom has a tumor on her brain. She'll need surgery soon. So I'm going to have to figure something out about child care. Ethan's done okay here because Emma's here."

"We're all buckled up and ready to roll," his dad called out.

Jocelyn turned toward the van. "I can follow you."

Mark gestured toward her car. "Or we can follow you home and you can leave your car there. With the van, we've room now. And, Ethan and I can take you and Emma home. Do you work tomorrow?"

Jocelyn's chest tightened as she absorbed the news about Mark's mom. He was close to his parents. Peter Parker had been so good with both Ethan and Emma the other night. "For now I'm working Monday through Friday and have Saturday and Sunday off. Oh Mark," she laid her hand on his arm. "I'm so sorry to hear about your mom. You must be so worried."

Her touch comforted. In that moment he didn't feel so alone, so distraught about his mom's diagnosis. What the future might bring. "If things haven't dramatically improved between Ethan and Emma by the end of the evening, maybe we can meet up at the park tomorrow around eleven?"

CHAPTER 12

The next morning, a few minutes after eleven, Jocelyn buckled a distressed Emma into the swing's seat. Her daughter had had a fretful night including wetting the bed, something she hadn't done in well over a week. Emma kept looking around for Mark and Ethan. Jocelyn's shoulders ached and the headache she'd already taken two aspirin for knocked at her temples. She knew as soon as Emma saw Ethan, she'd settle down.

"Where are they?" Emma whined.

"They're coming," Jocelyn said. "We were out pretty late. Maybe they slept in."

"Nuh uh." Emma's chin quivered and tears welled.

"Let's swing a little while we wait, okay?"

Jaw set, Emma held tight to the chains. "No, I want to wait for Ethan."

Even with the headache looming, a lightness settled in her chest. Strange to feel lighthearted when your child was being defiant.

Jocelyn refrained from rubbing the back of her neck instead keeping her hands on Emma's swing.

In the distance she spotted a couple with a little boy. At first she was sure it was Mark and Ethan, but the woman threw her off. It couldn't be Peggy. Even on this beautiful bright fall day, she wouldn't be walking in the park. Yesterday's news and then everyone for dinner had taken its toll. She'd been so gracious when they'd left, thanking them for coming, holding both Jocelyn and Emma's hands a bit longer than necessary as if she didn't want them to go.

The threesome drew closer. The man let go of the little boy's hand and waved him forward but the child stayed close, reaching for the man's hand again.

It was Mark and Ethan. She was sure of it. But who was the woman with them? Girlfriend? She frowned and shook her head. No, not a girlfriend. Colleague?

The briefcase in the woman's hand suggested attorney, or maybe social worker. Jocelyn's heart lurched at the mayhem she knew was going on inside Ethan if the woman was a social worker. She struggled to tamp down her emotions before clearing her throat and waving in their direction. "I think that's Ethan and his dad."

Emma shook her head and pronounced, "Ethan doesn't have a dad, Mama. Dads are bad! Ethan has a papa."

Startled by the vehemence in her daughter's voice, Jocelyn looked down at Emma who stared at Ethan.

Jocelyn called out to Ethan now that they were closer. "Good to see you this morning. Emma's been waiting for her bestest friend to play on the swings with her. What about it Ethan?"

His mulish look on his face, Ethan shook his head and said nothing. The grip on Mark's hand telegraphed his fear.

Jocelyn smiled at Mark's jovial tone, noting the rest of him was not pleased. "Mrs. Fester's making one of her unannounced visits today. She was gracious enough to let us come to the park so Ethan and Emma could have their play date."

Stepping forward, Jocelyn said, "Mrs. Fester, I'm Jocelyn Edwards and this is my daughter, Emma. Thank you for coming along. Emma was so looking forward to seeing Ethan today." Her senses on high alert, her intuition running rampant, she stepped closer to Mark and leaned to whisper in Ethan's ear. "Emma really wants to talk to you. I will stay with your papa if you go see Emma since she can't get out of the swing. Okay?"

Ethan stared at her with his sky blue eyes, searched her face for what felt like minutes before nodding. He walked over to the swing and took Emma's hand. They watched the group of adults ten feet away.

Mrs. Fester pinned Jocelyn with a suspicious glare. "Are you a close friend of Dr. Parker's, Miss Edwards?"

Jocelyn forced a smile and casual tone. "It's Ms. Edwards, Mrs. Fester. And to answer your questions, we've become friends through our children. They've become close friends or as they describe it the bestest friends." She glanced up at Mark. The lighter energy she associated with him was missing. In its place tension radiated under the pleasant façade.

Brittle was the word that came to mind. So tightly wound he was brittle. Brittle enough to break. She didn't stop to consider whether her actions were wise or not. She touched his arm, felt the steel of control as he kept his voice calm. Her shoulders relaxed in relief. He didn't, of course. Break that is.

Jocelyn slipped her arm through Mark's and leaned close. Her body recognized him as if he was the home roost and she the homing pigeon. Enveloped in lightness, the sensation of floating while her feet were on the ground, she heard what everyone was saying. She followed the conversation even though she didn't respond. And she even heard birds chirping in the background. *I'm dissociating.* She surreptitiously pinched the inside of her arm, the point of pain bringing her back in her body.

Dr. Mark Parker had a lot on his plate with his mom's diagnosis, daycare issues and now the threat of losing Ethan. He was stretched thin. A glance toward the swings showed her Emma was just fine. Intently watching the drama unfold with Ethan. It looked like both children were doing better than Mark.

Determined to support him as best she could without jeopardizing Emma, Jocelyn focused back on Mark and Mrs. Fester.

Mrs. Fester zeroed in on her. "And how long have the two of you known each other?"

"You know I'm not sure." Jocelyn looked up at Mark with a warm smile. "It's been several months I think. Mark and I pay more attention to the children than counting the number of days we've known each other. Wouldn't you say that's true, Mark?" Jocelyn patted his forearm.

Mark looked down at her, a grimacing smile on his face. "Right. Kids come first." Then he slipped his arm around her and snugged her closer.

"And how serious is your relationship?" Mrs. Fester had a gleam in her eyes that struck Jocelyn as feral. "Are you sleeping together?"

Jocelyn choked and sputtered.

Mark answered. "No, Mrs. Fester, Jocelyn and I are not intimate. We enjoy each other's company and especially enjoy the bond that's grown between her daughter and my son.

His brows drew together and an earnestness infused his voice. "You didn't know Ethan when he first came to live with me. He was afraid of everything. He had nightmares every night and he wet the bed. Ethan's made great progress, especially since becoming friends with Emma. For that alone I'd hold Jocelyn in high esteem. As it is she has many traits to recommend her."

The gleam in Mrs. Fester's eyes sharpened. "For example?"

Jocelyn was taken aback by the social worker's hostile tone. Her worry meter ratcheted up several notches when Mrs. Fester took out a notepad and pen and was now writing.

Mark drew a deep breath. His hand covered hers which was still resting on his arm. "Jocelyn is kind, considerate and puts the needs of children above her own. She is selfless and compassionate. She is a hard worker and does what she must to see that her daughter is provided for. Never one to take advantage, she gives back to others. I believe she is highly regarded by her friends. She certainly has my respect and appreciation for all she does for Emma and Ethan and, by association, me."

"She sounds like wife material," Mrs. Fester's beady eyes zeroed in on Mark and then shifted to Jocelyn before switching back to Mark.

The warmth that had settled in her chest at Mark's words turned to ice upon hearing Mrs. Fester's. Jocelyn carefully kept her stance casual and her features neutral, totally aware that she was in Mrs. Fester's peripheral vision even when she appeared to be looking only at Mark.

Speaking into the growing silence, Jocelyn was surprised at how calm she was. "We aren't the kind of people who rush into things, Mrs. Fester." She struggled against the light, the floating, the urge to detach from these events. "It's too soon to know what will develop at this point, but we will always be the best of friends. We both know how important it is for Emma and Ethan to have time together."

Mark cleared his throat. "As Jocelyn says, we are friends, good friends outside our connection through the children."

Lily's voice came from behind them. "There you all are!" Jocelyn turned to see Lily and Jackson coming toward them, hand-in-hand, smiles of welcome on their faces. "Jackson and I were driving by and thought we saw your car, Jocelyn. We haven't seen you for several days so we decided a walk in the park would be lovely."

Hand outstretched, she approached the social worker. "You must be Phyllis Fester, Mark and Ethan's adoption worker. I'm Lily Hughes. This is my husband, Jackson."

And just like that the mood shifted. Lily commented that those children needed swing time which gave Jocelyn and Mark the excuse to leave.

As they strolled to the swings, Mark leaned toward her saying "Lily is magical, isn't she?"

Jocelyn nodded and looked up at him. The tension gone, his eyes remained riveted on Ethan who waited rigid with expectation. Looking over her shoulder, Jocelyn saw Jackson with an amused grin on his face. Lily was still talking. Before she turned back, Lily paused. Jocelyn assumed Mrs. Fester would respond but they were at the swing set and two worried children awaited.

Ethan wanted to be on the teeter-totter. Jocelyn noted it was the furthest playground equipment from the social worker. Holding her breath, Jocelyn waited for Emma's meltdown. It never came.

Mark set them both on one end of the teeter-totter and wrap his arm around them. She pushed the other end down and climbed on. Mark controlled their up-and-down motion for a slow, smooth ride. He talked to them the entire time. They listened intently. Jocelyn wished she was close enough to hear what he was saying. Every once in a while, Ethan nodded. Emma didn't nod. And throughout it all, she never saw any of the three of them smile.

After the teeter-totter, everyone's focus was back on Mrs. Fester, Lily and Jackson.

"Is there anything else you need, Mrs. Fester?" Lily asked as the four of them neared. "Of course you are welcome to join us at the ice cream parlor a couple of blocks away. That's become a tradition." Lily chatted and subtly moved Emma and Jocelyn out of Mrs. Fester's line of sight.

Grateful that Lily was continuing to deflect Mrs. Fester's interest, Jocelyn held Emma's hand and hung back but not so far back that she didn't hear the next question.

"Do you come on these play dates often, Mrs. Montgomery?"

"Not often," Lily replied. "But with our background, you will admit that it is delightful to see children doing so well."

Mrs. Fester grimaced. "I would expect them to have disagreements."

"They are friends, Mrs. Fester, not siblings," Jackson said. "Having had both, I can attest the dynamics are very different between friends than between siblings. I think these three," Jackson gestured to Lily, Mark and Jocelyn, "don't have that experience. Were you an only child?"

Mrs. Fester bristled. "That's an inappropriate question, Mr. Montgomery."

"My apologies. It's been my experience that when we've had similar experiences ourselves we see things differently from those who've not. Nothing meant by it," Jackson said in a casual tone.

Jocelyn battled the warm feelings of gratitude and thankfulness for

Lily having materialized with the undiluted fear in her belly that without Lily, she and Emma might be in Mrs. Fester's crosshairs.

It was a perfect day to kick the multi-hued fall leaves as they walked across the park to the ice cream parlor. But no one, not kids or adults, even shuffled their feet in the dry crisp colors. In fact, Ethan kept looking back at Emma. Jocelyn kept a smile on her face and winked when she caught his eye.

Mrs. Fester decided to join them for the ice cream. With Lily's maneuvering, the two women walked together followed by Jackson. Mark dropped back and when Ethan grabbed Emma's hand, he let go and the children, heads together, held tight to each other.

"We're right here," Jocelyn said.

"Two steps behind," Mark added. He reached out and tousled Ethan's light brown hair. "See, I'm really close."

Ethan ignored him.

"It's okay," Jocelyn said sensing the tension coiling. "You know he heard you and felt your hand on him."

Mark sighed. "I know. It's so hard to have him ignore me."

Jocelyn laughed. "I know. It's hard when they act like children with happy pasts but wonderful also."

At the ice cream parlor, Mark held Jocelyn's chair out for her. Jackson held a chair out for Mrs. Fester and then Lily. The social worker sat with the adults, her notebook open.

Emma and Ethan did not eat much of their favorite flavors of ice cream.

Conversation was somewhat stilted between the adults. At the end of the interminable ordeal, Mark took Jocelyn's hand, leaned over and whisper his thanks in her ear.

Jocelyn squeezed his hand in acknowledgement as her body relaxed with his closeness.

When they left, Mrs. Fester reached her car first. Waving goodbye, a palpable sigh of relief filled the air.

Next closest car was Mark's. As Mark fastened Ethan into his car seat, Jocelyn's heart went out to Emma, who bounced from one foot to the other trying to keep her friend in sight.

To her surprise Jackson took charge. "Okay, here's the deal. All of you are coming to our place for a couple of hours. The kids can take a nap or watch a Disney movie while you two," Jackson nodded to her and Mark, "chill."

He turned and pulled Lily into a hug. "I can't believe you were civil to her the entire time."

Lily pulled away after kissing Jackson's cheek. "Phyllis is not a bad person. She just has the belief all children need a two parent family to succeed. Because of that she's confused because it's obvious Ethan is doing very well. And in her mind, he shouldn't since he is living with a single dad. So, she's hypervigilant thinking she's missing something."

"Jocelyn," Mark said. "Is it all right if Emma rides with us?"

Lily held up her hand. "Another option. Jocelyn, give me your keys and I'll drive your car to our place. You can ride with Mark and the kids."

Jocelyn gave Lily a hug. "Thank you. Last night was rough for both of them." She dug her keys out and handed them along with five dollars to Lily. "And here's money for gas. I'm almost on empty. Emma was in a hurry to get here today."

Lily tucked her arm in Jackson's and beamed. "Not to worry. Jackson and I'll meet you at our place in thirty minutes. That way you can stop and get a change of clothes or whatever you need to spend the afternoon with us."

CHAPTER 13

Mark and Ethan waited in the car while Jocelyn and Emma gathered a few things for an afternoon at the Montgomery House. Mark watched his son in the rearview mirror. Ethan's head was turned so he'd see Emma as soon as they reached the bottom of the stairs. Glancing at his watch, Mark figured they'd be several more minutes.

He took his cell phone from the clip on his waist band and checked for messages. Surprised there were two of them, he checked and saw the sound for "notification" was on mute. One text was from one of his partners informing him there was a major accident and asking if he could come in for a couple of hours. The other message was a similar one from his other partner relayed through his answering service.

Tension settled across his shoulders. So much for 'chilling' at the Montgomery's house.

He waited to tell Jocelyn until they were inside Lily and Jackson's house.

He waited until the children were settled in front of the fire.

He waited until the adults were gathered in the great room. He cleared his throat, his gaze traveled between Jocelyn, Lily and Jackson.

"I know this isn't fair of me, but there's been a major accident. Both of my partners have been called in. They've asked me to come in if at all possible."

Lily stepped forward, rested her hand on his arm. "Of course you can leave Ethan with us. And we'll keep food for you. Jackson has started a pot of his chili so you know there'll be plenty."

He turned to Jocelyn, a worry line between his eyes. "Are you okay with this?"

She started to step toward him pulled by the deepening worry line, the slight narrowing of his chocolate brown eyes. She gestured to Lily and Jackson and then herself. "If you're needed, you're needed. I'm sure we can cope."

"I'm sure you can do more than cope," Mark said and smiled. Crouching down, he took in Ethan's grave face. "Papa has to go to work."

Ethan nodded. "Lots of people get hurt. You'll fix them, Papa." He dashed into Mark's outstretched arms and clung. Warm little boy snug in his arms, warm little arms wrapped around his neck, warm little legs clamped around his waist—a mix of love and pain spiked through him.

When he reached the door, he set Ethan on the floor. "Be back as soon as I can." He tousled his little boy's light brown hair and left.

CHAPTER 14

A lump the size of Mt. Hood lodged in Jocelyn's throat and tears welled, shimmering on the rims of her eyes. While her own family hadn't been abusive like Tony, they'd not been particularly demonstrative. The love Mark felt for Ethan was palpable, visible, a visceral feeling that lodged in her bones.

Losing Ethan would be Mark's worst nightmare. Devastated, shattered, destroyed were not strong enough words to convey what his life would become. Add to that the worry about his mom and the brain tumor. And rightly so his father's attention was on her. In many ways Mark was as alone as she was. Alone and facing the possibility of losing a child.

Small hands tugging her pants brought Jocelyn out of her thoughts. The pull on her pant leg wouldn't stop until she paid attention to her daughter, so Jocelyn leaned down and picked Emma up.

"What do you want, Pumpernickel?" She nuzzled Emma's cheek with her nose and then kissed her temple.

Emma held her mom's face with both hands. "I don't want to go home. I want to stay here with Ethan."

Jocelyn's gaze found Lily talking to Ethan. The little boy's lower lip trembled. How frightened he must be with everything so topsy-turvy. Her chest tightened and more tears threatened. "If it's okay with Lily and Jackson, I think it's a good idea for us to stay. You can keep Ethan company until his papa comes to pick him up."

CHAPTER 15

Eight hours later, Mark half-stumbled out of his car and staggered to the front door of Montgomery House. He knocked and seconds later, Lily opened the door and pulled him into the house and into a warm hug. She led him to the couch in front of a glowing fire, pushed his shoulders down until he sat.

"I'll get you a bowl of chili or do you want a sandwich?" Lily asked.

He leaned forward, elbows on knees. "Ethan?" he asked, his voice laced with concern and exhaustion.

"Ethan and Emma are asleep downstairs. Jocelyn's with them."

Jackson appeared with a thick sandwich, a small bowl of chili and a cold beer. "Rough day?"

Mark nodded. The spicy aroma of chili pricked his senses. He was ravenous. He grabbed half the sandwich and bit into the varied flavors and textures of a BLT. Swallowing, he managed "Thanks."

Jocelyn came up the stairs. "I thought I heard you come in."

Chewing another bite, he motioned to her and patted the seat beside him.

Swallowing, he called out, "Great sandwich, Jackson. Would you be my personal cook?"

"He's already got that position," Lily said from the kitchen, laughing. "But I do loan him out for special occasions."

Mark looked over his shoulder and caught Jackson's gaze. "It doesn't bother you she married you for your kitchen skills?"

Jackson waggled his eyebrows. "Kitchen skills and other things, right Lily, my love?" He pulled Lily to him in a tight hug and rained nibble-kisses over her face.

Mark leaned toward Jocelyn, "That will keep them busy while you fill me in on how things went?"

She searched his face. "First, how are you?"

He dredged up a tight smile. "Tired but satisfied. We didn't lose anyone. No amputations either although three are in serious condition.

"I can eat and listen at the same time so tell me about the kids—please?"

"Very needy and clingy, but otherwise they did okay. Your text messages for Ethan really helped him. That was very kind of you."

"When he stayed with my parents, my dad could keep Ethan informed as to what was happening because he's also a doctor. Figured none of you would have anything specific to say about what was going on. Ethan does better with concrete information in times of stress."

"He asked after Mrs. Fester several times. I let Lily answer those questions. She told him that Mrs. Fester had a job to do, and part of that job was to make sure he was healthy and happy." Jocelyn chuckled. "He'd then make muscles and ask Jackson to see how strong he was." Her voice serious, she added, "He asked Jackson to tell Mrs. Fester and the judge that he was really strong so he could stay with his papa. Of course, Jackson said he'd certainly tell them how strong Ethan is and how he was much stronger since coming to live with his papa. It was quite touching."

The sandwich sat like a lump of coal in Mark's gut. "How long did that reassurance last?"

"Initially it was every fifteen to thirty minutes but then it stretched to between movies. The Montgomery's have a wonderful selection of children's movies. I figured today the kids would not be harmed with a movie marathon. I hope you don't—."

"Perfect plan." Mark washed the last of his sandwich down with a swig of beer noticing Jocelyn tense as he did so.

"So Emma's father was a mean drunk?" he asked. He set the bottle back on the coaster.

Jocelyn wrapped her arms around her middle, locked her hands on her elbows and hunched forward. "When everything went his way, he was charming. When anything didn't go his way, he wasn't. Alcohol might or might not be involved."

Although he was fairly certain he knew the answer, Mark kept his tone casual and asked, "Do you know what happened to Emma?"

Jocelyn's knuckles turned white and she stared at the fireplace. "Tony said it was a congenital condition when I asked why she limped." She shook her head. "I was so naïve! He said she took after her mother who was quiet by nature.

"It wasn't until after we were married and he flew into one of his rages that I realized what must have happened before. Emma was brushing her teeth and some droplets of water splashed on the counter." She turned to Mark, tears glimmering at the memory. "They were droplets. Hardly visible," she whispered. "Tony went into a rage. He picked her up and threatened to flush her down the toilet." She shivered and held herself tighter. "I screamed, pulled on his arm and begged him to stop. He pushed me so hard I hit the wall and almost got knocked out.

"Emma? Emma didn't even cry. He dunked her, head first into the toilet and then tossed her at me. I was so shocked, so terrified. I held her and rocked her. Eventually I gave her a bath and washed her hair and put her to bed. She never said a word, no tears, nothing. In some ways that was scarier.

"That night as I held her while she went to sleep I realized what must have happened. She was just a baby, Mark. A toddler when he-he-he did that to her. When he b-b-broke her. I couldn't always protect her but I knew I couldn't leave her."

Mark fought the urge to smash something. Fought the urge to take her in his arms. Fought the urge to make promises he couldn't keep. He unclenched his fists and reminded himself she needed a friend, needed him to listen.

"So, I rationalized—he hadn't hit me, just pushed me into the wall." She looked up at Mark, a sad smile on her face. "I did the same thing the first time he slapped me. But then he hit me with his fist. I had no way to rationalize that away. Except I'd made a promise to myself that I'd never leave without Emma. It took almost a year to put enough money aside, to make a plan for us to actually get away. Chicago is big but you still have to have a place to stay."

He risked touching her arm. His fingers met hard muscles with a shimmer of a quiver. Using his best bedside manner voice he asked. "Domestic violence shelters?"

She nodded. "We did stay in one for a few weeks. One day I peeked out the window. Tony stood across the street. Emma and I moved with the help of the staff to another shelter. He found us again. That's when I knew we couldn't stay in the Chicago area. We moved to Wisconsin. He found us there but the front door had a dead bolt and we escaped out the back.

"The DV advocate program gave us money to move farther away. I chose Fremont thinking we'd be far enough away, that he'd never look for us here. But, I can feel him still trying to find us. Emma and I have an escape routine. We practice every few weeks so we know we can escape if we think he's nearby."

Mark's gut churned with indignation and anger. "What about the police?"

Jocelyn's knuckles were no longer white but she still clung to herself. "What about them?"

"You can get a restraining order. I'm sure the shelter staff told you to get one, right?"

She nodded. "On what grounds?"

He blinked. "So you never called the police or went to the Emergency Department? Neither you nor Emma?"

She shook her head. "Tony wouldn't permit it. I think he'd learned with his first wife just how far he could go without causing permanent injury. He never hit me in the face. As long as I wore long-sleeved-tops and slacks or jeans, no one could see the bruises."

Mark relaxed his jaw before he broke a tooth. *That sonofabitch.* "What about Emma?"

"I did my best to protect her. I could usually get him to redirect his anger on me instead. I think he found holding power over a grown woman more—more." She shivered at the memories. "I learned quickly how to cower, beg or plead—not too soon, not too late. When I failed and he went after Emma, if he left marks on her face, I had to keep her inside until they healed or deal with the consequences which would be even worse."

Jocelyn's gaze rested on Mark's hands. "When I asked her why she limped, she told me Tony had broken her. I suspect Tony went a little too far with Emma's mom. She died after a fall down a flight of stairs. There weren't any stairs in the apartment but there were stairs from their second floor apartment to the parking lot."

"Again, no witnesses?" Mark kept his voice just short of casual not wanting Jocelyn to stop talking until he'd hear the entire story.

"Tony said it was at night. He even teared up when he told me why he needed me to marry him. His sweet little girl needed a mommy and he needed a wife. I fell for the whole story."

Mark paused before commenting. "So you married him." He heard the note of incredulity in his tone and took a deep breath, releasing some of his frustration on the exhale.

Pale and shaking, she looked away. "I think so."

Confused, Mark shook his head. "You think so? Why wouldn't you know?"

"Tony wanted a private ceremony. Just a Justice of the Peace, Emma and me. The JP was one of Tony's friends. He brought his wife and adult daughter as witnesses."

Mark started to rise, to pace off the nausea settled in his gut. Halfway to his feet he changed his mind and sat back down. "Does Lily know any of this?"

Jocelyn shook her head. "I don't even know why I've told you, Mark. It's so embarrassing and you've had a long and difficult day."

Exhaustion faded as adrenaline pumped. He shifted to look directly at her. "I think she needs to know because you need legal advice before Tony finds you."

Jocelyn shivered and whispered to herself. "Emma and I won't stay here long enough for him to find us."

Mark reached for and held Jocelyn's hand. He turned toward the kitchen where Jackson and Lily were talking. "Lily? Need your advice here."

Jackson trailed behind Lily. "I'll just take these." He leaned over and picked up the empty plate and bowl.

Lily settled in a chair next to the fire but across from the couch. "What's going on?"

Mark turned toward Jocelyn. "How do you feel about just putting it all out there for all of us, including Jackson?"

Her hand gripped his so hard, he felt a stab of pain. Gently she shifted her grip to his palm from his fingers.

"Okay," she said her voice child-like.

Lily motioned for Jackson to join them. He perched on the arm of Lily's chair.

It took Jocelyn twenty minutes to share the life she'd survived from the moment she met Tony until the last time she and Emma snuck out the back door in the dark of night from the apartment in Wisconsin, everything they owned in a suitcase and backpack. She'd always parked the car a block away from where they lived so once they made it to the vehicle, they'd be able to escape.

Those minutes of walking with Emma, her backpack strap clutched in one hand the other clinging to Jocelyn's pant leg, were sheer terror. Her heart pounded and her hands shook the entire time it took to get Emma buckled into her car seat and everything they owned stowed in the pitch dark. Pitch dark because she'd made sure no interior lights came on when the doors open.

"You want my advice?" Lily asked Jocelyn.

Jocelyn nodded.

"You need to see an attorney and you need a private investigator."

"Why an investigator?" Mark figured Lily would recommend an attorney but an investigator?

"Because we need to know where Tony is, what he's doing to find Jocelyn and Emma. Jocelyn can change their appearance to some extent with hair dye and glasses but she cannot change Emma's limp. And Emma does more than just limp, she has a different way of moving her body."

Jocelyn's grip on his hand tightened. "I don't have—."

Mark cut her off. "Do *not* say you don't have the money. I'll pay for a consultation with an attorney."

"You can't!" Jocelyn started to rise but Mark did not let go of her hand.

Lily kept her gaze trained on Jocelyn. "Mark doesn't have to pay anything. I know a very good attorney, Ms. Lawford. She will gladly talk to you for up to an hour at no charge. That, I think, would be your first step."

"How long have you lived at that apartment?" Jackson asked, a serious look on his face.

"Since we arrived. So it's been four months."

"Do you have friends in the complex?" Jackson continued.

Jocelyn shook her head.

"Then I think you and Emma should move. The longer you are in one place, the easier it will be for the bastard to find you. Same thing goes for your job."

Jocelyn stiffened. "But I have to work. We don't have any money if I don't work."

"I've an idea," Mark said. "I need to make a couple of calls in the morning before I can tell you about it, but if it works out you'd have free room and board."

CHAPTER 16

Jocelyn and Mark spent the night at Montgomery house rather than wake up Ethan and Emma to take them home. Since both children shared one bed, the other single bed was available. After a short argument that ended with them both agreeing they needed to be downstairs with the children, and because Jocelyn emphasized he'd had the longer, harder day, Mark agreed to take the bed.

Curling up on the couch, Jocelyn snuggled under a multi-colored throw. She fought sleep afraid she'd wake in the throes of nightmares, scaring everyone in the house with her screams. She didn't wake at all. Neither had Ethan and Emma. Not only did they sleep through the night, the bed was dry. She waited by the door as Ethan checked on his papa, who was still fast asleep.

Of course she watched Ethan approach the bed. Saw him frown and start to touch his papa's face, saw him pull his hand back, his shoulder hunch. He looked over at her and she smiled, thankful she'd already talked to him about Mark needing his sleep. And as she watched the little boy, she saw the man. Mussed brown hair against the white pillowcase, dark shadows of bristles on cheeks and chin, his mouth slightly open and his breathing that of someone dead asleep.

Herding the children up the stairs, she was delighted to see Jackson up.

"What do you want to do after breakfast?" Jackson asked the group sitting around the kitchen island. He already had a skillet heated and was whipping eggs with a bit of milk and spices.

"Park!" Emma and Ethan bounced on their seats.

"They've had enough sitting and movies," Jackson observed in a dry tone.

Jocelyn nodded. "Park it is! What has to happen before we can go to the park?"

Ethan just looked at her but Emma jumped down. "Where's my coat? Where are my shoes, Mama?"

Jocelyn laughed. "First my little Pumpernickel, you need your breakfast."

Emma's stricken gaze took in Lily and Jackson. She ran to her mama and scooted behind her.

Jocelyn squatted down, her hand on Emma's arm, her gaze steady. "It's okay, Emma. You aren't in trouble. No one is mad at you. We're going to finish our breakfast and then we'll go to the park, okay?

"And look, Jackson is fixing French toast. That's one of your favorites."

As Jocelyn helped Emma back in her chair, she saw Mark at the top of the stairs. Ethan bounced out of his seat and dashed to his papa. Mark swung him up and gave him a loud, smacking kiss. "You were going to the park without me?" he playfully growled making chomping noises.

Ethan took Mark's face in his hands. "Nuh uh, Papa, I would come and get you first."

"Good to know," Mark said, plopping Ethan down at the table.

Mark passed close by her to get his plate of French toast. "You did that very well," he said softly.

Jocelyn tensed as his breath drifted across her neck. An involuntary shiver followed. It took her a second or two to realize he was complimenting her on how she'd dealt with Emma.

When he looked her way, she smiled and mouthed "Thank you." He nodded and tucked into his food.

At the park, Mark excused himself and walked a short distance away, his phone to his ear. It was hard not to wonder who he was talking to, especially if this was the call about a free room and board situation. Jocelyn returned her attention to the swings. Who Mark Parker was talking to was none of her business.

"More Mama," her daughter urged.

Tears choked her throat as Jocelyn pushed the swing in a short arc. Was it only a couple of weeks ago that Emma had been terrified if the swing moved at all?

Gratitude softened the tension in her shoulders. Gratitude they were in Fremont. Gratitude they were both healing. Here at the park or at Lily and Jackson's, her own body was less stressed.

Jackson's advice to move was sound. Where to and deposits were the problem. Of course if the Montgomery's offered her a place to stay, she'd have to turn them down. They had too many beautiful things and Emma was still a little girl. She wouldn't mean to break anything but... ."

Mark strode over to stand beside her. Together they watched their kids allow Lily and Jackson to take them out of the swings. Holding hands, Ethan and Emma confidently walked toward the ice cream parlor.

"I'm told this place has pretty good stuff," Jackson said to Lily as he ambled along. "Emma says their strawberry is the bestest. But Ethan disagrees. He says the chocolate is bestest."

Lily laughed. "And you will have a scoop of each to see what you think."

Jackson chuckled. "Lily love, I know I make the bestest vanilla. I think it's time to spread my wings and try some other flavors."

After handwashing and ordering, Emma and Ethan went directly to the smaller children's table and waited expectantly for their ice cream.

The adults sat nearby. Jackson did have two scoops, one strawberry and one chocolate. Mark had a double scoop also, one of

Marion berry and one of vanilla. She and Lily had single scoops of peppermint.

Marked leaned forward and lowered his voice. "Here's the offer."

Jocelyn's heart beat faster and her breath caught in her lungs. Her grip on the plastic spoon half-way to her lips tightened when Mark's unwavering gaze trapped hers.

"My mother does not think she needs someone with her 24/7, but both Dad and I do. She blacked out once. It could happen again. She's also facing surgery. My dad is stressed out and needs a break but is afraid to leave her alone.

"You've seen their place. There's a whole suite of rooms downstairs. Bedrooms and bathrooms. One of the bedrooms can become a play area for Emma. Free room and board in exchange for you being there to help dad with mom when needed and to be there so he can leave sometimes. Also, I can leave Ethan there when I'm On Call or get called out on an emergency."

A pent up breath escaped. Automatically she shook her head. It was too good to be true. For all intents and purposes, she and Emma would be invisible. Her spoon slipped from nerveless fingers, clattering back in her bowl.

The crestfallen look on Mark's face registered. Her heartbeat rapid, her breathing stilled. Whirling words rushed through her mind. Confused she clutched her cup of tea in silence.

"Let me get this clear," Lily said, leaning toward them her voice also pitched low. "Your parents are offering Jocelyn and Emma free room and board, a safe place to live in return for her being available when they need her. And that's all?"

Mark straightened and turned including Lily in the conversation. "That's the agreement. I'm sure Dad would appreciate help fixing meals but that's not a requirement. They already have a service that comes in once a week and cleans so that isn't an issue. Laundry? I think he's on top of that right now."

Jocelyn's heartbeat slowed, her breathing normal as Mark's litany of expectations registered. She shifted and reentered the conversation. "So there may be other things I'd do in order to free up your dad and help lower your parent's stress level?"

Mark's gaze swung from Lily back to Jocelyn. He smiled.

"And mine. I'm worried their concern for each other is putting even more stress on their health. Dad can follow up on all of Mom's medical care, medications, appointments, etc." He waved his hand in a dismissive gesture. "He's in his element and can sit down and talk options over with her. But, doing that and remembering to go to the grocery store, at times, have been too much for him. He knows he needs to go but is so anxious about leaving Mom, he puts it off and they run out of something. Or he goes but forgets his list and half of what he was going to get."

Jocelyn closed her eyes to better see what it would be like if she agreed to this arrangement. "So I'd go to the store or stay with your mom while your dad takes a break and goes grocery shopping, runs errands or whatever he needs to do."

"That's about it," Mark said and nodded. "What do you think?"

Although she hadn't spent much time with either Peter or Peggy Parker, she'd liked them. And what was more important, so did Emma. But she and Emma came with problems. What if Tony found them? What would that do to the Parker family? I'm not sure... ." Jocelyn started and stopped.

"What are your concerns?" Jackson asked.

Jocelyn turned to him. "If Tony finds us at the Parkers' house, it will be nasty and stressful and could even get dangerous."

"Is that it? That's your main concern?" Jackson pressed.

Jocelyn focused on Jackson, intensity infused her tone. "I know none of you think he'll find us. But me? I'm not so confident."

Jackson turned to his wife. "Lily, can you arrange for Jocelyn to talk to Ms. Lawford?"

Lily patted Jackson's hand. "Jocelyn is perfectly capable to make the call. I'll make sure she has the number. I can watch Emma if Ms. Lawford can see her right away. Or if she wants to talk to her in more detail over the phone before setting something up I can distract Emma so she doesn't overhear."

Jocelyn felt little eyes focused on her. She shifted and look directly at Emma. "Mama's okay, Emma. We're just talking about grown-up stuff."

Lily laid her hand on Jocelyn's arm. "Let's go back to our place, okay? I'm concerned you'll worry. At our home, you'd at least have someone to talk to."

"And, you'll have my world-famous spaghetti for dinner," Jackson added. He wagged his eye brows and thumped his chest.

Jocelyn laughed at his antics. "World-famous is it?"

"You can judge for yourself. And, if everyone is very, very good, you can have a dish of my private reserve of vanilla ice cream."

"With lots of toppings so you can make a marvelous sundae." Lily leaned into her husband and kissed his cheek.

"Ethan and I'll take a rain check on dinner," Mark said, relieved that Lily and Jackson were there. "I want to stop by and see my parents. They're anxious to see their grandson. These past couple of weeks have been hard on them because they're used to Ethan being with them almost every day."

Jocelyn walked with Lily, Ethan and Emma in the lead, Jackson and Mark behind.

"Are you thinking you're imposing?" Lily asked her.

She nodded.

Lily shook her head. "Well, you aren't. If it was an imposition, Jackson and I wouldn't offer."

Jocelyn's chest tightened. Her voice quivered when she said. "I've done nothing to deserve all this kindness."

Lily slipped her arm through Jocelyn's. "Of course you have. You are."

Jocelyn shook her head. "I don't know what that means."

Lily's gesture swept an arc in the air before coming back to rest on Jocelyn's arm. "Just that. You are in my life. Why would I not want to treat you with kindness? One of my women's circle's tenets is "And Harm To None." If I'm not harming anyone or anything, I'm being kind."

Her breath shaky, Jocelyn swallowed the lump in her throat. "I've imagined being in a place like this where Emma and I are accepted and supported."

Lily gave her a knowing smile. "Even dreamed about it? Or had visions of your life in that place?"

"I have." Tension drained as Jocelyn looked ahead at her daughter still walking hand-in-hand with Ethan. "I know I can confess to you I've had visions, premonitions and you won't think I'm crazy."

Lily patted her hand and gave it a gentle squeeze. "Far from it. I see you as a spirit sister."

CHAPTER 17

That night Jocelyn visualized the future she wanted for Emma and herself. In her mind's eye, they laughed and ran through a park. Not just any park but the park here in Fremont. The sun shone catching her daughter in a stream of light as Emma jumped across an imaginary puddle. As she raced on there was no sign of her limp. In the distance a man and a boy appeared, waving to them, urging them closer. Emma dashed forward, her arms flung wide, straight into the embrace of the man.

Jocelyn turned over, hugged her pillow and began the descent into sleep. Her last conscious thoughts wondered who the man and boy were. Mark and Ethan? She'd never aspire that high, but someone like Mark or Jackson. A man who was kind and caring, who'd love Emma and show her that some men can be safe.

THE NEXT MORNING, with Lily nearby for moral support, Jocelyn called Ms. Lawford's office. The attorney answered the phone herself. Her brusqueness was off-putting. Thankfully Lily had mentioned that

Ms. Lawford's manner was one of the things that made her so formidable.

When Jocelyn hung up five minutes later, she had an appointment to have lunch with Ms. Lawford at the courthouse. Lily assured her all would be well, offered to go with her and sit nearby or just drop her off and then pick her up because "parking is such a hassle."

Emma was at Audrey's compliments of Jackson, who had charmed her daughter and promised she see Ethan. Jocelyn, with too much time on her hands, made the bed, and after shaking out and folding, secured the change of clothes they'd brought in their backpacks. That done she still had time. Lily was writing a report but had assured her she'd set a timer so they'd have plenty of time to get to the courthouse.

Standing in front of the great room's windows with a view across the valley to the mountains beyond, Jocelyn let her mind drift. Her gaze unfocused. In the distance the mountains pierced the bright blue sky, but an expanse of green lawn filled her near vision. She stood higher than the yard. On a deck? Laughter and the buzz of happy voices sounded in her vision.

"Jocelyn?" Lily's voice seemed so far away. "Jocelyn, it's time to go. We don't want to be late."

Jocelyn pulled herself from the dream back to the Montgomery's great room. She turned and hurried toward the short hall and the door to the garage. "I'm sorry. I-I guess I was daydreaming," she stammered.

Lily waited for her by the door. "Well, I hope it was a good one. They are the best kind. Like a window into what our future can be."

Jocelyn's stomach churned the entire thirty minute drive to the courthouse. As they approached the building, Jocelyn's palms sweated and her breathing fractured. A silent mantra repeated in her head. *I can do this. For Emma I can do this. I can do this. For Emma I can do this.*

"Oh my goodness, the parking gods are smiling on us today," Lily said. She backed into a spot a block from their destination. "And there is time enough on the meter to cover us. This is a good omen!"

Jocelyn fell into step beside her friend as they made their way to the courthouse, through security and to the cafeteria.

"I don't see Ms. Lawford. Let's get something and grab a table," Lily suggested. She picked up a tray and turned back toward Jocelyn.

"There you are Ms. Hughes."

Jocelyn recognized the voice from the phone, turned to see the owner and stared into the intense blue-eyed gaze of a woman of indeterminate years.

"And you must be Ms. Edwards," the woman said, her hand out in greeting.

Jocelyn had the presence of mind, just, to shake the woman's hand. "I am, and you must be Ms. Lawford."

The attorney's genuine smile softened her face and shone from her eyes. "That I am. That I am."

Jocelyn's initial concern faded away.

Ms. Lawford gestured to the rack of trays. "Let's get something to eat and see what we can do."

As the three of them made their way through the cafeteria line, they spoke of mundane matters. Lily, who was first, indicated to the cashier she was paying for all three of their meals. Ms. Lawford picked up her tray and turned, scanning the room for a table.

Lily leaned toward Jocelyn. "I think it best if you talk to Ms. Lawford alone. What I don't know may be in yours and Emma's best interest."

Ms. Lawford nodded. "The decision is yours, of course, but Ms. Hughes has a point." She gestured with her head. "There are two tables fairly close to each other. If we sit there and you need Ms. Hughes for moral support or to jog your memory, she'll be nearby."

Jocelyn was in a daze as she and Lily strolled back to the car. Ms. Lawford would represent her. She had an appointment in three days in her attorney's office. In the meantime, she had a list of tasks to complete.

The most daunting? Write down everything she could remember about Tony from the day they first met until she last saw him.

Why would it be daunting? Thinking about it only exacerbated her fears, heightened her hypervigilance and increased the frequency of her nightmares.

Writing down everything she remembered Emma telling her about her mommy and Tony and what happened to her before Jocelyn came on the scene would be painful, but doable.

She also needed to detail, as best she could, the beatings. When, where, precipitating event if any, results.

And last but not least, she needed to have Emma evaluated. Without medical records, an expert witness would be needed to testify that Emma's awkward gait was from old injuries that were not properly treated.

Ms. Lawford also encouraged her to move again and do it soon. And, in the best of all possible worlds, to find another job. When Ms. Lawford left, Jocelyn called Lily over and read off Ms. Lawford's homework assignment.

"I know this is important," Jocelyn said, her hands gripped around her purse as they walked to the car. "I only hope I can do it without upsetting Emma."

Waiting at the car for Lily to unlock it, Jocelyn noticed Lily putting coins in the parking meter. "Paying it forward," Lily said as she unlocked the passenger side door.

"Paying it forward?"

"Didn't you ever see that movie?" Lily asked before starting the car. "The one about the young boy who gave to people he didn't know?"

Jocelyn smiled and buckled her seatbelt. "I do remember that. I'm going to talk to Emma about that. Maybe if we look for ways to pay it forward, looking back at our past won't be so scary."

"How are you doing?" Lily asked as she pulled out into traffic.

"I'm relieved yet overwhelmed, elated yet cautious and frightened yet hopeful."

Lily smiled. "That means you're normal. May I offer a bit of advice?"

"You may if you aren't going to wave a magic wand and fix everything."

Lily reached over and patted Jocelyn's hand. "If I had a magic wand, I would've already waved it so you never needed to see Ms. Lawford."

A bone deep exhaustion drained Jocelyn's elation. "What would you do, Lily?"

"I'd do what she said. I'd move first and then start on the assignments."

Jocelyn gulped down the panic and rested a hand against her stomach now in revolt. "As I dredge up the past and write it all down, I'm afraid I'll have worse nightmares and scare Emma."

"Emma won't be as afraid if you tell her what's going on."

"I know you're right." She sighed. "I just wish there was another way...."

"And, you don't have to think about money. You have an offer of free room and board with the senior Parkers."

Jocelyn shook her head. "I don't think taking all this baggage there is what they have in mind," she said in a firm voice.

"True," Lily said. They'd stopped for a red light. Lily tapped the steering wheel. When the light turned green, she started forward. "So another idea," she said picking up the conversation again, "is you and Emma come and spend this week with Jackson, Eleanor and me. We'll coordinate with Mark to see that both Ethan and Emma are at Audrey's for a few hours during the day. When Jackson and I are gone, you know Eleanor will be there. She's an excellent listener, gives commonsense advice and loves supporting people in finding their way forward in their lives."

Jocelyn turned that idea over. *It might work.*

Lily went on. "Emma likes Eleanor enough to have read stories with her and helped her in her apartment without you right there. I do realize the door was open and she could turn her head and see you but—." She paused to make a turn.

Caught up in Lily's excitement, Jocelyn smiled. "But Emma went right along into Eleanor's apartment without any hesitation."

Watching the road as they took the last of the curves to the Montgomery's House, Lily nodded. "I'll check with my circle and see who has space in their garage for your car. That way it's out of sight if Tony does figure out you're in Fremont."

Muscles tensed and adrenaline flowed. "It takes Emma and me less than an hour to pack everything and get it into the car."

They pulled into the driveway and on into the garage. Lily reached over and squeezed Jocelyn's hand. "Let's hope you never again need to do that."

LILY WAS RIGHT. Telling Emma what was going on was best. Jackson and Lily followed them to their apartment. While she and Emma packed, Jackson complemented Emma on how smart she was and what a good job she did in packing. "I've never ever seen anyone so quick about it," he'd marveled.

Emma's shy smile blossomed and she stood a bit taller.

"I'll come back later and clean," Jocelyn said as she put the last of their things in the trunk of the car.

"How much is the cleaning deposit?" Jackson asked.

"$200.00."

"Steep."

She nodded, her mind already tracking where she'd put kitchen supplies so she could easily retrieve them.

"Let me talk to my cleaning service. They may do this for twenty-five dollars. You'd get the difference back. And the management can't hassle you because a professional service did the work."

"But—," Jocelyn started to argue.

Lily put her arm around Jocelyn's waist. "We're thinking safety and you're thinking finances. Safety first, finances second will get you through this in the best of shape."

Jocelyn swallowed her argument and her pride. "Okay. I'll let the manager know. My rent's paid until the end of the month."

"Another reason for them to refund the full amount," Jackson continued, "is they can rent it as soon as it's clean."

She felt a little better after hearing that truth.

That evening Mark and Ethan came for dinner. Jackson fixed steaks for the adults and hamburger patties for the children. Before dinner was over, Gabriella and Hunter came by. Neither had a garage, but Hunter had parking space next to her own car behind her dance studio.

Jocelyn thought she saw disappointment in Mark's eyes when she told him she would not be moving into his parent's home. Maybe when this next week was behind her? Doubts about the living situation with Mark's parents popped up. The one doubt that didn't? She and Emma would be physically safe there.

Lily's elbow nudged her side and Jocelyn tuned back in.

"What?" she mouthed.

"You have something on your list that Mark may be able to help with."

She shook her head. "I don't think so. Emma's insurance coverage is...."

Mark interrupted, "Emma's insurance coverage is what?"

Jocelyn heard the defeat in her voice. "I don't think you take Medicaid insurance."

Mark grinned. "And you think wrong. We do take Medicaid."

"Great," Lily chimed in. "Then you'd be able to assess Emma to find out if her physical problems are congenital or from abuse."

"I already know they are not congenital," Mark replied. He help up his hand, palm out to stop further questions. "Bring her to my office tomorrow—. No, wait, I'll pick up Emma when I get Ethan tomorrow. We'll stop by my office and take x-rays before I drop her off here."

Lily put her arm around Jocelyn's waist. "Call or text when you're on your way to your office and we'll meet you there."

She was a piece of asphalt with duo-steamrollers bowling over her with Lily and Mark taking charge.

Gabriella leaned in from Jocelyn's other side. "You're not a victim. This is called "hovering." We all dread being the focus of it, the hoveree, but—," she smiled, her hazel eyes sparked with humor. "We all love being the hoverer. If it gets too bad, don't be afraid to speak up. I can promise you it will pass and you'll find your life may be better because of it. Ask Lily."

"I heard that, Gabby," Lily said and laughed. "As a hoveree survivor I can attest that it is survivable and life can be better as a result."

CHAPTER 18

Mark, with Ethan at his side, held Emma in his arms as he walked into his waiting room. It had been a bit difficult to get the x-ray he needed because Emma was terrified of being alone. He'd moved a chair so Ethan could stand on it and Emma could see him through the small window.

As they'd talked about it before, Ethan ran ahead and opened the office door to let Jocelyn and Lily in. And, as he'd expected, Emma reached for her mama. With no hesitation, Mark handed the child to Jocelyn who wrapped Emma in a tight hug.

"She was a very brave little girl," he reported to Jocelyn who was now smoothing Emma's hair.

"She was a champ!" Ethan fist pumped the air. "That's what Papa said, didn't you?"

"She was a brave champ and has certainly earned a treat." He turned toward Lily. "What she wanted more than anything else was some of Mr. Jackson's basetti and ice cream with lots of whipped cream and nuts and... ." He looked over at Emma. "What did I miss?"

"Cherry," was muffled against her mama's neck.

Lily had her cell phone out but stepped away before speaking.

"Why don't we sit down here to see if Emma's treat will be tonight or maybe another night? We've already talked about maybe Mr. Jackson won't have time to make his special sauce for tonight so Emma and Ethan need to have a back-up plan."

"Hmm, I wonder if that would mean waffles." Jocelyn pressed a kiss to Emma's head and stroked her back.

Emma and Ethan shook their heads.

"Pancakes with blueberries?"

"Nuh uh" Ethan said.

Mark noticed Jocelyn holding Emma's hand now and holding out two fingers.

"I've got three more guesses, right?"

Emma nodded. "Guess the right one, Mama."

Jocelyn soft laugh was filled with love. "Okay, I was going to guess liver and onions—."

"Eww!" Emma and Ethan said in tandem.

"But I'm not going to guess that. Instead I'm going to guess hamburgers."

Lily had joined them. "Hamburgers on the grill tonight and Mr. Jackson's special spaghetti tomorrow night. How does that sound?"

"Yeah!" Ethan jumped in the air and ran the few steps to Emma. "We get hamburgers and then basetti." He turned toward Lily. "What about the ice cream?"

Lily crouched in front of him. "Let's see if there's any room after dinner and what your parents have to say, okay?" Standing, she rested a hand on Ethan's shoulder. "Why don't you help Jocelyn and Emma? You can hold the door open for them and push the elevator button. I'll help your papa lock up and we'll be right behind you."

As Mark set the alarm, Lily turned off the lights. "Wanted to clarify what's going on. Emma and Jocelyn are staying with us for the next week," she said as Mark turned his key in the lock. "Mrs. Lawford's assignment is that she write everything down that happened that she remembers as well as whatever Emma told her. She's afraid she'll have nightmares and Emma will be worried.

"Jackson and I helped them pack and move everything out of the apartment. A couple of suitcases and boxes contain their entire life."

Mark closed and locked the office door. "In time?"

Lily smiled. "In time she's grateful for the opportunity to support your parents and you and Ethan. Right now she believes she'll be more of a hindrance."

He looked down the hall toward the elevators and sighed. "What do you think?"

"I think she's very wise. I'd be surprised if she didn't have nightmares, if Emma wasn't upset because she'd know. And I recommended she tell Emma what's going on which will both reassure her but also throw Emma into her own nightmares."

"What about Audrey's?"

"I think Emma needs to go to Audrey's although perhaps not for the entire day. Something to talk about tonight is how to work the child care out, etc. I'll have my calendar available. I think Diana, Elizabeth and Ashley may be able to help out as they have some flexibility in their schedules. Jackson has offered also. I think both Emma and Ethan have been around him enough that they'd be okay with him, especially if he is picking them up and bringing them back to our place."

A dinging sound let Mark know the elevator was being held open beyond its normal time frame. "Let's finish this after dinner."

Lily nodded in reply. "We're coming."

Jocelyn still held Emma but was leaning against the back of the elevator.

"Hey Emma," Mark said making eye contact with her. "May I hold you until we get to the car?"

"My papa's strong," Ethan said with surety.

Emma shook her head but when they walked out of the elevator, she whispered in her mama's ear and Jocelyn put her down, keeping hold of her hand as they walked to the car.

Mark still had two car seats in his vehicle so Jocelyn climbed into the front passenger seat once Emma was secured. Lily, not encumbered with seeing children strapped into safety seats, had already left.

In the rearview mirror, Mark saw Ethan reach out and take

Emma's hand. Every time he glanced back, their hands were still clasped.

At one point he caught a glimpse of Emma, her eyes closed, tears slipped down her face yet she made no sound. His lungs seized, his chest tightened and his throat closed. Dear God—

LILY MADE a few phone calls while Jackson grilled hamburgers and steaks. Child care, meals and Jocelyn's follow up appointment with Ms. Lawford were taken care of. Mark would pick up Emma and take her along with Ethan to Audrey's in the morning. Lily would pick them up in the afternoon and bring them back to Montgomery House or drop them off at Ashley's house for a couple of hours to play with Amanda.

Once off work, he'd come to Montgomery House and have dinner before taking Ethan home. His plan was to see what appointments he could have his partners take on or reschedule so he'd have time to check in on his parents.

It's only a week he reminded himself. You can make it happen for a week. Don't make it more difficult than it already is. He chuckled as he replayed the mantra: *Nothing lasts forever.*

When he stopped to consider Jocelyn and Emma's situation, he had the easiest piece. Or he did depending on how Ethan handled his friend's distress. Another mantra popped into his head. *Time will tell.*

CHAPTER 19

Trapped and sweat soaked, Jocelyn struggled toward the light.

"Mama, Mama," Emma's high-pitched whisper pierced the dark.

The bedroom nightlight now aided by the bedside lamp being turned on, her eyes hurt. She squinted against the brightness.

Small hands patted her shoulder. "It's okay, Mama. I'm here. It was your bad dream."

Jocelyn untangled her limbs from the confining covers and reached for her daughter. "I'm sorry I scared you, Pumpernickel."

"That's okay, Mama. I membered where we are. Mr. Jackson won't let anything happen to us. Member he showed us he turns on the larm so nobody can get to us?"

She snuggled Emma close, brushed her hair away from her face. "I think we need to try to go back to sleep."

Emma yawned and nodded and cuddled closer. "I like it here, Mama. Mr. Jackson said I can help him make basghetti tomorrow."

"You do know we can't stay here for very long."

"Just until the bad dreams go away and then we go to Ethan's Grandmama's."

"I love you, Pumpernickel." Jocelyn squeezed the slight frame and kissed her forehead. "Let's straighten the bed so we can get some more sleep."

Another practice they had developed since leaving Tony was remaking the bed. Thankfully with fitted bottom sheets it was much easier to straighten out the top sheet and blankets. Jocelyn fluffed the pillows and they crawled in. Gathering Emma close she asked, "Did I hurt you?"

"No, Mama. I woke up right away and turned on the lights."

"Good girl. I'm so very proud of how smart and brave you are."

She turned off the bedside table lamp, the soft night light gave enough illumination so she could see around the room. Their clothes were in the closet and dresser. Emma had the bottom drawer and Jocelyn the top. The two in-between drawers remained empty. Special items like her glass wizard and Emma's unicorn were on top of the dresser for safety. Emma's favorite stuffed toy, a rabbit, was on the bedside table on her side. He was facing the door so he could protect them from any intruders. On her side were two books they'd read tonight before going to sleep. In the bottom of the closet were two boxes of towels, bedding and kitchen items and their suitcases.

Jocelyn closed her eyes and willed dreamless sleep to return. Emma relaxed in her arms and her breathing and dead weight confirmed when she went under. If she shifted Emma onto her side of the bed it would be easier for her to sleep but letting this precious bundle go was not something she could make herself do.

If this is what happens and I've not even begun to write anything down. She shuddered at what the rest of the week would bring.

You aren't in this alone. You have a safe place to live. You have a safe job in your near future. Count your blessings instead of your worries.

Emma still in her arms, she turned on her side and closed her eyes. A picture of how she wanted her life to be burned bright in her mind's eye. Parts of that life were indistinct but the feeling state remained the same. She and Emma were together, they were safe. Emma smiled and laughed and slept in her own room without fear. There were expanses of green grass, flowers and trees in this picture. She knew they were important because they were some of the first details in this 'dream-come-true' vision she'd built.

Holding the vibrant picture in her conscious mind, Jocelyn hoped to keep the nightmares away. "That's not how it works," she muttered as her vision faded.

CHAPTER 20

Mark's head throbbed and his fingers tapped the corner of his desk to the same beat. Ethan was unhappy if Emma wasn't with him. His nightmares and bedwetting proof of his distress. Last night he'd relented and approved of Ethan spending the night at Montgomery House—without him. Ethan and Emma shared one of the two beds in the downstairs room. Jocelyn slept in the other one. Lily's text that everyone slept the night through was good news but, and he knew he was being petty, it hurt to know he wasn't enough.

To top it all off, and since he was being petty, he might as well go with it. Jocelyn had the redoubtable Ms. Lawford as her attorney. The court had appointed an attorney to represent Ethan, but that jerk had never met with either Ethan or him. It didn't matter that he'd petitioned the Court so Evan, his son's legal name, could be called Ethan. He was being petty and small-minded and these petty and small-minded thoughts were adding to the pain now pounding in his head. He rubbed the back of his neck and massaged his forehead and temples.

Yesterday's mail included a notice of a court hearing to be held in forty-five days. It was called a regular review hearing but Mark was positive Mrs. Fester's report would recommend Ethan be removed from his home and "prepared for adoption." Pain stabbed behind his eyes and his vision blurred.

Was there a bright-side to this nightmare? He could be grateful she wouldn't recommend he do the "preparing." That small piece of gratitude was lost in the reality that this tight-assed, thin-lipped, throwback to another era adoption worker was in the picture at all.

Today, nerves on edge after another restless night, he'd been too brusque with staff and partners, reserving the little patience he had for his patients. He was finishing up the report on Emma's injuries—adding an extra hour to an already killer day.

With the report completed and tucked in his briefcase, he left the office to pick up Ethan. He'd make time to talk to Jocelyn and Lily to see what they wanted him to do with the report: send it to Ms. Lawford, child protective services or just give it to Jocelyn.

At Montgomery House, he took a minute to stuff his depressing thoughts back in their hole. *Don't need them with me.* Before he went in, he put the report in the inside pocket of his jacket. Getting out of the car, the strange compact also in the driveway registered. No children's car seats so it wasn't Ashley. He didn't see a sticker about adoption so that left out Elizabeth. He knew Sophia's car and that wasn't it.

"Just go in and see who it is," he muttered heading to the door.

Before reaching Montgomery House's front door, the door to Eleanor's apartment opened. Jackson's mother was an elegant woman he'd gotten to know when she fell almost a year ago. "The children are in here," she announced in her British accented voice, "but you are to go on into the main house."

He saluted, contained his confusion and need to see his son and continued on toward the front door. Something was up and the sooner he went in the front door, the sooner he'd know what.

Mark knocked once and opened the door.

Lily greeted him with a broad smile and waved him into the great room where she, Jocelyn, Jackson and another woman sat.

"This is Ms. Lawford, Mark." Lily said and gestured to the other woman.

"I've heard only good things about you, Ms. Lawford," he said and shook her outstretched hand.

"I could and will say the same about you."

Her handshake was firm, her blue gaze steady. Mark once again wished he had her on his side.

"We're discussing options," Lily said and gestured him to a vacant chair.

"Want a beer or something stronger?" Jackson asked as he rose and headed toward the kitchen.

Ms. Lawford spoke up. "Unless you get drunk, I've no problem with your imbibing a bit at the end of what looks to be a challenging day."

"Week," Mark corrected. "Something stronger would be welcomed, Jackson."

"Preferences?"

"Whatever is easiest." The urge to see, touch and smell the bundle of energy known as Ethan surged. He popped up from the seat, ignoring the flash of intense pain in his head. "If you'll excuse me for a few minutes, I really do need to see my son." His rapid steps had him at the French doors into Eleanor's apartment in seconds.

"SORRY ABOUT THAT," Mark said, taking a sip of the mixed drink Jackson had put on the table in front of his chair. "Needed my Ethan fix. Haven't seen him since last night and that's way too long." He took another sip and set the glass down. "Now what's going on?"

Lily said, "In summary, in order to file for a divorce, Tony will know where Jocelyn and Emma are. In order to file for custody, he will have to be notified. Not her actual address, but that she is in Oregon. He'll most likely figure she's in Fremont because it's the largest city. He has connections and has reported Emma as being kidnapped so once he can confirm they are no longer in Illinois, he can contact the FBI who can then check social security records, etc.

and track her to here. They could take Emma from her and return the child to Tony."

When Lily's recitation of the facts ended, she looked at him. "Unless your report shows that Emma's condition is not congenital and how old she was when it happened. Otherwise, it's Jocelyn's word against Tony's."

Mark pulled the report from the inside pocket of his suit jacket and handed it to Ms. Lawford. "The injuries are not congenital. The x-rays show badly healed breaks not naturally twisted bone. She was two years old. Maybe a few months younger."

Jocelyn gasped. "Her mother died when Emma was 25 months old."

"How?" Mrs. Lawford asked.

Jocelyn's hands twisted together. "The story was she'd fallen down the stairs. I never saw an official report but that's what Tony told me."

"I can request a copy of the police report," Ms. Lawford said, making a note on her legal pad.

"Police report?" Jocelyn parroted.

Ms. Lawford nodded. "And maybe a coroner's report. Most states have laws that require the police to look into any at home deaths as well as a coroner's investigation."

"Would Tony be informed?" Lily asked.

"Not unless he had a friend working in records who told him." Ms. Lawford looked at Jocelyn.

"I don't think he has friends like that." She visibly straightened. "He did always tell me how clumsy she was, how she was always bumping into things and falling down. The first time he hit me, it was more of a shove into the wall. He glared at me and said 'Guess I've married another clumsy bitch.'"

"We'll move slowly and cautiously," Ms. Lawford said, her gaze sweeping the small circle. "I know a couple of judges on the domestic relations court and I'll get their take on this. I don't want to file a petition for a protective order unless I know I'll get one. With that, Tony may find you," she waved her hand in dismissal, "but he won't have any recourse to regain physical custody other than appearing in court.

"Is this my copy?" she asked, waving the report toward Mark.

"I can print out another one."

"And the x-rays?" Ms. Lawford asked as she skimmed the report.

"I can get copies of them for you if you need them." He didn't feel great but the pain in his head eased.

Ms. Lawford speared him with her sharp gaze. "What I want is this report and the x-rays in my bag when I have lunch with my friends. That way if they ask questions, I have the information at my fingertips."

"Will Monday be early enough?"

Ms. Lawford stood and began gathering her briefcase and jacket. "Monday will be perfect. I'll call them this weekend and set something up for early next week. Can it be Monday morning?"

Mark stood. "If you'll share your home address, I'll have them to you tomorrow."

"You don't take weekends off?" Ms. Lawford asked in a no-nonsense tone.

Mark started to lean toward her. He grabbed the back of the chair when his head throbbed. "Usually I do," he said trying to sound casual, "but this is important. Why Emma didn't die from the abuse and trauma she's endured is a miracle. While these injuries we've been talking about are why she walks and moves as she does, there were other hairline fractures that occurred when she was much younger.

"This child has survived systematic abuse over and over. My son has also and I know that is why they recognize each other at an entirely different level than we are even aware."

"How, may I ask, do you still have your son if you've systematically abused him?" Ms. Lawford voice was cold and precise, her brow arched in question.

Lily stepped in, her hand on Mark's arm, she said. "Ethan is Mark's foster son. He has applied to adopt him. You may know Mrs. Fester."

Ms. Lawford nodded.

"She's their adoption worker. Since you know Phyllis, you know she does not look favorably upon single parent much less single father adoptions."

Ms. Lawford took a step towards Mark. "Who's your attorney?"

Mark sighed, rubbed the back of his neck and looked at the floor before looking up into Ms. Lawford's steady gaze. "I don't have one. Ethan's attorney has only met him once when he was still in the hospital recovering from his injuries."

Was it seconds or minutes of deafening silence?

Lily spoke first. "Mrs. Fester is pushing Mark to get married."

"We hoped to put her off a bit when she came to the park with Mark and Ethan," Jocelyn gamely entered the conversation.

Ms. Lawford smiled. "So she thinks the two of you are a couple?"

Mark struggled to join in. "I'm not sure what she thinks. And I don't know that it will matter if she thinks Jocelyn and I are a couple or not. I got the notice in the mail last night that the next review hearing is in forty-five days. My concern is she'll want to remove Ethan from my home so he can be adopted by a couple."

"And that would be disastrous for Ethan," Lily put in. "Give me the date Mark and I'll be there. I saw Ethan in the hospital. I can testify as to how he has blossomed in your care and custody.

"And now he goes to Audrey's. She's gotten to know him and you. Children's Services knows and respects her opinion. She can testify as to how well he plays with others. We'll make sure he and Emma spend more time with Ashley's Amanda. So his circle is larger than you and your parents."

"The stronger and more varied his ties, the higher the chance you can keep him," Ms. Lawford added as she marched toward the door.

"If you have a recommendation of an attorney I can contact to represent me, I'd appreciate it." Mark's words rushed out, stumbling and tumbling over each other.

"Let's see what this next week brings. Forty-five days is a ways off." Ms. Lawford said over her shoulder.

Jackson had circumvented everyone as they followed Ms. Lawford to the door. He opened it and ushered her out, walking her to her car and holding the door as she got in.

Eleanor's door opened and with whoops and hollers, Ethan and Emma pelted out the door. Mark braced himself for the impact of this sturdy young boy who leapt in the air in total trust that his papa would catch him. Small arms hugged his neck, short legs tried to wrap around his waist. Mark held him tight and breathed in the sweaty little boy smell of him.

He'd lose a huge chunk of his soul if he lost him. Out of the corner of his eye he witnessed Jocelyn with Emma wrapped tightly around her and wondered if she could be his answer to keeping Ethan.

CHAPTER 21

"There's no record of a marriage in the state of Illinois with your name." Ms. Lawford's matter-of-fact recitation emphasized the truth in her words.

The room tilted and a haze dimmed her vision. Grateful she was sitting down, Jocelyn's hands gripped the arms of her chair, her knuckles white.

"Put your head between your knees," Lily said pushing gently on her shoulders. "Take slow lung-filling breaths. When your head clears, gradually sit up."

Jocelyn followed Lily's instructions, her confused mind spinning so fast she didn't even have questions. And then it began: How could you be so stupid? How could you be so dumb? How could you be so naïve?

Hands fisted on her lap, she struggled to calm the rage churning inside. Rage against Tony, rage against herself. She had wondered about that marriage, wondered if it was legal. How could she…?

An image of Emma, silent and ghost-like watching the sham ceremony, a glimpse, a spark of hope in her eyes.

"Is that good or bad news?" Lily asked, her hand now resting on Jocelyn's arm.

"A bit of both. The good news is they weren't legally married. The bad news is they weren't legally married." Ms. Lawford leaned across her desk, her steely blue-eyed gaze speared Jocelyn with its intensity. "If you are berating yourself, then stop!"

Jocelyn jerked at the harsh tone of voice. A second later tears welled. "I should have—."

Ms. Lawford grimaced. "How is blaming yourself now going to help you keep Emma? It's trite but true, hindsight is always 20-20. We can always see the signs when we look back at a situation or at least tell ourselves we see them. You've said Tony was a master manipulator. Are you?"

Confused, Jocelyn shook her head. "Am I what?"

"Are you a master manipulator?" Ms. Lawford grilled her.

"No," Jocelyn said, indignation ripe in her posture and her voice.

"So, you got scammed by a master manipulator. Scammed, beaten, terrified and although I didn't see it on your list, I imagine he raped you at least few times."

Jocelyn's face flamed. "He-he-he... ." She curled into a ball, binding her arms around her to keep the shards of herself contained. Deep racking sobs followed the initial silent tears as she slid out of the chair onto the floor.

Lily's hands stroked her hair and rested on her arm.

Shifting, Jocelyn sat up, tucked her knees under her chin. Ms. Lawford handed her tissues with which she wiped her face, blew her nose before tossing in the wastebasket. When she spoke, her voice was raw, an echo of how her throat felt. "What about Emma?"

"I spoke to a judge I know and she concurred you have no legal right to the child." At Jocelyn's pained gasp, she held up her hand and continued. "Emma is an endangered child so your protection of her is admirable. However, the judge agreed with my suggestion you file a petition in juvenile court for care and custody.

"She also suggested Emma have a psychological evaluation so you have professional expertise as to how she would fare if returned to her biological father."

"Anything else?" Lily asked.

VISIONS OF HAPPINESS

Jocelyn kept the moan deep inside or so she thought. Lily's arm circled around her shoulders and she scooted closer offering Jocelyn the support of her presence.

"Nothing realistic." Ms. Lawford said.

Lily's hand tightened around her before she asked. "What? Realistic or not, I think Jocelyn needs to know."

"Of course if she was married, settled in her own home with a stable lifestyle that would lend credence to her being able to provide for Emma. As it stands, she is staying with you which means she's seen as having no home, no job, therefore no means of support."

Lily rubbed Jocelyn's back. "She's been offered a position with Mark Parker's parents. She and Emma would have a place and income."

"And as Mrs. Parker's health improves, then what?" Ms. Lawford's tone was matter-of-fact.

"Emma can't go back to Tony," Jocelyn said in an intense but ragged whisper. "She can't. She'd die, if not from his hands then she'd just will herself gone."

"Think about filing the petition," Lily counseled. "That's a start and will mean, if Tony shows up, he can't just take Emma away. He'd have to show up in court and prove the allegations in the petition false or that he has changed."

"I've drawn a preliminary petition up. Preliminary because I want you to read it over and make sure that what I've included is, to the best of your memory, accurate. I concur with Ms. Hughes. Your best protection is to file the petition."

"Or leave." As soon as the words were out, Jocelyn knew she'd made a mistake.

"There could be worse consequences for you if you keep on running." Ms. Lawford's voice was kind in a no-nonsense way. "Especially now that you know you weren't married to her father."

Lily's arm tightened around Jocelyn's shoulders. "You have people here who care about you and Emma, who will support you in fighting for her. And you made a commitment to a group of women to lead them in sacred ceremony next Labor Day Weekend."

Jocelyn heard Ms. Lawford and Lily as if from a great distance. Pain and numbness co-existed in her body. Her head, her heart and her gut throbbed. Her arms, legs and brain numb.

The dichotomy of a pounding head and a numb brain and yet she could still think?

All she wanted to do was curl up in a ball on the floor in her lawyer's office and sleep until this nightmare was over. And then she'd awaken in that special place where she and Emma were safe. The house with the green lawn, flowers and trees, a swing hanging from the limb of an old oak for Emma. Emma who laughed and ran across the lawn to a man who was coming down the stairs from the deck on the back of the house.

Who was he? He was tall, long limbed with a stride that ate up the distance. He picked Emma up and swung her around. Her gleeful "Papa, Papa" was music in the air.

Who was he? He never had a face. He never had a name other than "Papa." Sometimes there was a shadow of another child. Was the child a boy, a girl, older or younger than Emma?

Jocelyn strained to see more details but as always, when she did, everything vanished. She slumped against the chair, the cold hardness of the floor registering through her jeans-clad bottom.

Time to gather herself together, get Emma and—? She was tired of running and Emma was, for the first time since they'd left, showing signs of being a happy little girl despite her past. Would Emma choose to stay and fight or would Emma turn tail and run away?

"Jocelyn?"

She nodded, realizing that Lily had never left her side, had never taken her arm from her shoulder, her hand from her arm.

"Let's get you home. I've got a copy of the petition so you can look it over later. We've sent a text to Jackson and he's picking Emma and Ethan up in an hour. That gives us time to get home and figure out what you want to say."

Jocelyn's brow wrinkled. "Say?"

Lily rubbed Jocelyn's back. "You told Emma this morning you were going to see Ms. Lawford today."

Tears welled and slipped over the rims of her eyes, trekking down her cheeks. "I did. She'll never ask but she'll watch me, wait for me to say something."

"And?" Ms. Lawford queried, now perched on the chair next to hers.

"We have a pact that we'll always tell each other the truth so if I don't say anything, I'll have broken my word. I-I-I." Her stomach clenched, bile rose in her throat and tears streamed. "How can I ever tell her that I'm not even her step-mother?"

"There are always ways to tell someone difficult or even bad news," Lily assured her. "We'll figure it out and if you want, I'll be with you when you tell her."

CHAPTER 22

"Picking Ethan and Emma up from Audrey's. Plan on dinner here." Mark, at his desk in his office, puzzled over Jackson's text. That morning's arrangement had been for Jocelyn and Lily to pick the kids up after the appointment with Ms. Lawford.

His head against the chair rest, Mark contemplated a future without Ethan. Even though he was a grown man, tears fell. And his chest? His chest had the weight of the world on it.

"Dr. Parker?" Anne, his receptionist, stood in the doorway to his office.

He swiped a hand down his face before straightening and looking down at his desk. Cleared his throat before answering. "Yes?"

She walked a couple of steps toward him and stopped. "Just got a call from Mr. Costello. He apologized for calling so late. He's down with the flu and won't be in tomorrow. That's the third cancellation. Do you want me to see if I can reorganize your appointments so you have the morning free?"

"If you can make that work, yes. Let me know." Mark took a deep breath before looking up at his secretary. "You can text me."

"I'll make the calls right now if you can stay another ten minutes," Anne said before turning back to the door.

He nodded at her retreating form. His elbows on his desk, head resting in his hands, Mark stared dumbly at the report in front of him. Words on the paper seemed to drift in the air. Nothing made any sense.

Five minutes later Anne popped back in. "Everything's set. Your morning is clear. Afternoon starts at one-thirty. Last patient at four. Unless there's an emergency, that is. Everyone else has a full schedule."

He forced a smile. "Thanks, Anne. I'll be here around one."

"Going to spend extra time with your little boy?" She watched him start to stand.

"Never have enough time with him these days," he said, putting the report in his desk drawer.

"And they're predicting an early snow this next week. Skiing season will soon be upon us." She smiled, started back down the hall, calling out over her shoulder, "No rest for the wicked."

Mark picked up his coat, grabbed his keys and headed out. He caught up with Anne as she was leaving. She set the alarm, he held open the door. Together they walked to the elevator.

"Goodnight, Doc," Anne said and waved as she trotted toward a pickup truck waiting at the curb. She jumped in and leaned over to kiss the young man in the driver's seat.

Mark watched until they'd driven off. Not roared off like he'd suspected might happen when he saw the big rig. The driver even turned on blinkers at the turns. He could see Anne, laughing and chatting through the rear window of the truck. The man nodded and when they stopped for a moment before they turned onto the street, he reached over and brushed the back of his fingers down her cheek.

A sadness enveloped him, a sense of loss for something he didn't have—a wife, home and security for Ethan. At that moment he knew with a certainty that Mrs. Fester's recommendation would be to move Ethan so he could have a *real family*. Would a judge be sympathetic and overrule the professional adoption worker?

A bone-deep lethargy slowed his steps as he made his way to his car. Emotions clogged his throat as he saw the two car seats in the back. Ever since meeting Emma, Mark had seen a change in Ethan. He was happier, more self-assured. He ran ahead instead of clinging to Mark's hand or pant leg. Fear was still there but it wasn't ever-present.

He stopped by the condo, changed into a sweat suit and tennis shoes, grabbed a change of clothes for Ethan, all the while talking to his dad, getting an update on his mom. "I've the morning open, Ethan and I'll come by."

"Of course we're always glad to see you two," Peter Parker said. "But don't think you have to come by." He'd emphasized the word "have."

"Dad—,"

"Mark, you have a life of your own. A life to live with Ethan. And, if Ms. Edwards ends up not being available, your mother and I have other options. We do not want you to feel responsible for us.

"Our neighbor, Mrs. Garity, has been coming by to visit every afternoon. She spends time with your mother and I've a break. You remember her husband recently died and she's a bit at loose ends. This week she stayed while I did grocery shopping. I picked up the items on her list for her so it was a win-win."

Mark locked the door and set the alarm, the backpack with Ethan's change of clothes hooked over one arm.

"I heard your alarm being set. You go on and get that boy of yours. If it works out to come by, great, but do not, under any circumstances, think you must, ought or have to. Your mother does not want to be a burden to anyone and if you make a duty visit, she'll know."

"If we don't come by, we'll call so Ethan can tell her about his day."

"That's a good plan," his dad said before hanging up.

MARK SAT in his car in the Montgomery's driveway gathering his thoughts and calming his emotions. Ethan would know if he walked in the door upset. No point in making things worse. Several deep breaths and a severe talking to himself, he opened the car door and strode to the house.

Lily opened the door. "Welcome to bedlam. It's been quite a day and everything is chaos. Jocelyn is sick. The kids are helping Jackson fix dinner. I'm grateful you're here." She stepped back and ushered him in.

"How are you doing?" she asked after scrutinizing him.

"It's been a lousy day." He grimaced and rubbed his forehead.

"Great, you fit right in." Lily's voice had a forced cheery tone.

Mark's brow wrinkled. "Should Ethan be here if Jocelyn has the flu that's going around?"

Lily's gaze met his. "It isn't the flu. Bad news or maybe good news from Ms. Lawford. She has to talk to Emma and is literally sick with it."

"Can you tell me anything?" Mark asked already knowing the answer.

Lily shook her head.

"I know, it's not your story to tell."

Lily nodded. "That's true. She's downstairs. Maybe you could check on her?"

"I will after I see Ethan."

His son scrambled down from the stool at the kitchen island and ran to Mark, arms raised to be picked up. Mark's throat closed, clogged with love as he hugged this precious little tyke.

"Papa, Emma's mama is sick. You can make her feel better, can't you?"

This child's faith in him never faltered. "I'll see what I can do. You know when a bad bug gets in you, it takes time before it leaves."

"I know Papa, but you check her anyway."

Emma had remained on the kitchen stool. Her eyes were huge and Mark saw fear in their depths as she tracked their conversation. He set his son on the floor. "I'll go check on your mama, okay?" he asked Emma. She nodded and her throat moved as she gulped.

Jackson called their attention back to dinner and stirring the contents in their bowls.

Mark trotted down the stairs and turned toward the bathroom. As he strode past the bedroom door, he spied Jocelyn curled up on the bed. He stopped and knocked on the door jam. She looked his way.

Her eyes were swollen and red, her face blotchy and she was surrounded by crumpled tissue and towels. One she clutched to her chest.

"May I come in? I've been asked by Ethan and Emma as well as Lily to check on you."

Her entire body deflated with a sigh. She struggled to sit up.

"You don't need to sit up on my account," Mark took a step inside even though she hadn't said 'yes' or even nodded.

Despair was the word that came to his mind as he settled on the edge of the other bed. "Anything you want to talk about? Or maybe I should say anything you can talk about? Or maybe the correct wording is anything you are willing to talk about?" His voice calm as he spoke, he watched her with practiced eyes.

She smiled. A watery smile that didn't reach her eyes even though her lips tilted upward. "I'm not—doing—very well—with words right now."

Her raspy voice was so unlike her normal tone, Mark's attention was snared. "Sore throat?"

That rueful smile flashed and she nodded.

"Something cold sound good?"

She shook her head. "I'm afraid if I eat anything I'll lose it. And I've got to talk to Emma... ." The tears started. "Where do they come from?" she whispered.

"The tears?" Mark spoke in a soft gentle voice.

She nodded.

"One of the mysteries of the body just like how can our nose create so much snot." He smiled.

Jocelyn choked out a laugh on that. "That's me. One big teary snot."

"Or maybe it's a snotty tear?" He grinned.

She took a deep breath and flashed her genuine smile. He didn't see it reflected in her eyes.

"Back to my question about talking." Mark quelled the urge to move to sit beside her, hold her in her arms and assure her everything would be okay. Jocelyn wasn't someone who got this upset over nothing.

"I was never married to Tony so I have no rights to Emma." The words spewed out, clogging the air with the acrid stench of an unpleasant, painful, terrifying truth.

His gut clenched but Mark kept his face calm and managed to ask in a neutral tone, "How do you know?"

"Ms. Lawford checked with Illinois Vital Records. There is nothing in their database with my name on it."

He thought she was hanging on by a thread when he asked. "What does she suggest?"

"That I file a petition in juvenile court asking that Emma be placed in my care and custody while the charges on the petition are investigated. Of course Tony will have to be served, he'll know where we are. I'm terrified he'll grab her or kill me because I won't easily let her go.

"I want to run but Lily said I need to stay and fight. I have people to support me here." She choked back a sob. "I don't know what to do. I know I have to talk to Emma and tell her what's happening. She'll… she'll…she'll."

Mark leaned toward her, caught her gaze. "She'll be frightened, she may regress and she'll survive because you do have support here. You do have people to help you protect Emma and yourself. You aren't alone."

Jocelyn was sitting up now, clutching a towel to her chest. "She's made so much progress since we came here, especially since she and Ethan became friends. I don't know how to tell her she can't see him anymore."

Mark shook his head and frowned. "Why would you say that?"

"If Tony saw her playing with Ethan, he'd go after your son in order to hurt Emma and me even more. We bring danger to anyone who's around us."

Mark's tone gentle, he said. "But Tony has to find you first. He has to find you vulnerable. You can protect yourself and Emma. He doesn't know exactly where you are. Even if you have to give him an address, it doesn't have to be where you actually live. At least I don't think so. What did Ms. Lawford say?"

"I'm sure it's all in the petition but I've been too upset to read it."

Mark glanced around. "Where is it now?"

Jocelyn shuddered, her gaze swept the room. "I'm not sure. Maybe Lily still has it?"

"Wash your face and change your top or maybe your entire outfit if you want. I'm going up to find that petition. We'll go over it together."

"I don't want to—."

Mark interrupted her with a wave of his hand. "If you are going to tell me you don't want to bother me, I'll scream."

She laughed. "No you won't."

"Want to bet?" He used his most serious tone of voice, the one he used when impressing upon a recalcitrant patient why she or he (well, usually it was a he) needed to follow doctor's orders.

"I'll meet you there," she gestured toward the family room.

"See you in five," Mark said over his shoulder as he headed out the door.

MARK SPENT a few minutes exclaiming over the kitchen skills of the little chefs-to-be. The kitchen was one big flour and sugar mess as far as he could see. Jackson didn't seem to mind and skillfully brought Ethan and Emma's attention back to the task at hand. Making something special for Mama and Papa.

He skimmed the petition that Lily did have as he headed back downstairs.

Jocelyn was waiting for him. She'd changed, combed her hair and attempted to reduce the puffiness in her face.

"So, let's look this over." Mark said waving the petition in the air.

They sat next to each other on the couch, settled into the plush cushions. No fancy perfumes for Jocelyn. Mark liked her fresh clean scent.

"I glanced through it and it seems pretty straightforward." His mind blanked for a second and his hand gripped the paper as he recalled a few of the allegations. "I don't know how you and Emma survived because both of you are lucky to be alive."

"I know," she whispered. "That's why it's so terrifying now. To think of Emma going back to him—I—I—I don't think I could survive that."

As devastating as it would be to have Ethan taken from him, Ethan would be safe. Jocelyn and Emma didn't have that to hang on to. He put those thoughts aside and focused on the task at hand—going over the petition with her. "Let's, unless you want to read all of the allegations again, skip to the last couple of pages where the petition asks the court to do something. It's pretty specific."

"I don't want to read the allegations and I don't want to hear you read them either. It's been bad enough remembering and writing everything down. Neither Emma nor I have had a good night's sleep since this all started."

"Here's what the petition asks: First is that you be given care and custody of Emma while an investigation is made regarding the allegations. Second is that a restraining order be put in place to prevent Tony from any direct contact with either you or Emma until the investigation is complete. Third is that if Tony or his attorney wishes to contact you, they can do so through your attorney or the Court. Fourth is that you and Emma are to have a psychological evaluation—."

"But why Emma? I don't see—." Jocelyn interrupted

"You probably don't but here's what Ms. Lawford said to me about Ethan. She strongly encouraged a psychological evaluation. I was initially upset but then I realized, with Lily's help and a bit of common sense, that Ethan loves me. He wants to stay with me. So a psychological evaluation may be just what is needed for me to be allowed to adopt him."

"You can't be serious that anyone would suggest much less recommend he should be taken away from you." Jocelyn jumped up from the couch and paced. "That is the most ridiculous thing I've ever heard.

Who would even—?" She stopped and whirled towards him. "Mrs. Fester."

He nodded.

"But why? Can't she see how well he is doing? How much he loves you and you love him?" The pacing had stopped and she stood in front of him like an avenging angel.

"I'm a single dad therefore I can't give him the best home. The best homes are those with a Mom and a Dad. I know that's what she'll recommend at the hearing next month. I'm trying to prepare myself—."

"What?!" Jocelyn screeched.

"Are you okay?" Lily called down.

"Of course I'm okay. I'm stunned with something Mark just said," Jocelyn assured her friend.

Sitting on the low table in front of the couch, Jocelyn faced him. "You have to fight. You can't just give-up and prepare for the inevitable. You have to fight for him. Both of you deserve as much."

Mark reached out and took her hands in his. "I'll fight for Ethan if you stay and fight for Emma."

CHAPTER 23

*A*t the top of the stairs, Jocelyn paused, a soft smile on her lips. Emma cut biscuits with a round glass dipped in flour and carefully placed them on a baking sheet. "What an excellent cook you are, Pumpernickel." She stepped to the kitchen island and waited while Emma moved another round piece of dough.

"I'm helping Mr. Jackson," Emma glanced up her eyes huge orbs of worry.

"And doing an excellent job," Jackson said, patting her shoulder.

Jocelyn noted Emma didn't flinch nor did she respond at all to the gentle touch.

Infusing her voice with a calm she didn't feel, Jocelyn asked, "Can Mr. Jackson spare you for a bit? I've some things to talk to you about."

Emma froze, her mouth open, her eyes wide, the biscuit in mid-air.

"I can spare her because it's her mama who needs her," Jackson said deftly moving the dough to the pan. "Do you want help getting down?"

Emma had not moved or spoken, suspended in that place where she knew something bad had happened but didn't know what.

Time stood still for a second or two while Jocelyn quelled the nausea and calmed her galloping heart. Walking around the island, she picked Emma up and held her close. "Let's sit by the fire, okay?" Not really expecting any answer, Jocelyn walked across the great room to one of the large overstuffed chairs set at an angle to the hearth.

"Ethan." Even though Emma whispered his name, it reverberated in Jocelyn's ear like the wail of anguish it was.

Jocelyn cast a helpless look at Mark who was standing next to his son, a hand on his shoulder. "She's asked for Ethan. I—I—."

But Ethan had already scrambled down and raced across the room. "I'm here, Em."

Mark followed and when Ethan sat on the floor and held on to Emma's foot, he followed Ethan down. While he didn't hold him or put his hand on his shoulder, his knee rested against Ethan's thigh.

"I think we need to invite Mr. Jackson and Lily to come and listen too," Jocelyn said softly to the clinging child in her arms.

Emma nodded.

Jocelyn extended the invitation as she secured Emma in her arms, one hand smoothing her hair away from her face, the other wrapped around her small body.

Focusing on Emma, Jocelyn took a deep breath and kissed Emma's crown. "You know I talked to the lawyer today."

Emma nodded.

"I was really upset when I came back here and—."

"You were crying," Emma's voice was muffled by Jocelyn's shirt.

Jocelyn stroked Emma's back inwardly chanting *I can do this.* "I was and probably upset you even more because I didn't stop and talk to you like we've promised to do."

Emma nodded and clutched Jocelyn's shirt in her fist.

She paused, took a deep breath to settle herself and calm her voice before saying. "There was good news and bad news. And I'm going to tell you the bad news first." She paused and blinked to contain threatening tears. "It isn't easy to talk about this Em, so know I'm doing my best.

"Ms. Lawford, that's the lawyer's name, said I'm not married to

Tony. There is no mention of me in the Illinois records. That means I'm not your step-mama and that also means I have no right to have you with me."

She kissed the crown of Emma's head and wished she could open up and let this little girl burrow inside her. Maybe then—.

"The better news is that Ms. Lawford was very happy with the hard work you and I did last week. She said you were very courageous to try to remember everything. She's taken all that we wrote down for her and put it in a letter called a petition. A petition is the way a lawyer tells the court what the problem is and asks the court to solve it. Our petition is very long because we worked so hard."

It was so hard to keep her voice calm, to speak in a soft tone. *I can do this.* "I know I said I'd tell you the bad news first and I did, but there is another part that's very bad. Tony will have to be given a copy of the petition so he will know we are here in Fremont, OR."

The trembling started. Emma pulled away and tried to scramble off her lap. "We need to pack."

Jocelyn held tight. "No, we don't need to pack, Pumpernickel, because here is the best news. We have friends here who want to help us stay together, help us fight Tony so he can't hurt us."

Emma held Jocelyn's face between her small hands, her blue-eyed gaze searching as if she could see beyond the words. She didn't move but remained rigid, waiting for a sign of what she should do.

"Mark will tell the court what Tony did to you. When he took the pictures of your bones, they told him what had happened," Jocelyn explained. "He's already written a report and will talk to the judge in person so if they have questions he can answer them. Lily and Mr. Jackson are our friends and we can stay here. You know Mr. Jackson makes sure the alarm is on every night so even if Tony found us, he can't get in."

"But Ethan?" Emma's high-pitched voice sighed her friend's name.

"Mark knows about Tony and he won't let anything happen to Ethan."

Emma squirmed on Jocelyn's lap until she'd turned around. "I can't play with you anymore, Ethan. My dad's mean and he could hurt you and your papa." With a sob, Emma turned back and clung to Jocelyn.

She held and rocked and soothed knowing Emma's heart broke because she chose to go back to being alone instead of endanger Ethan. She rested her head on Emma's and crooned their favorite silly song "Mares Eat Oats." It really wasn't a song written to be crooned but Jocelyn hoped the words and the memories of singing this song at the top of their lungs would help her daughter. A fierce energy claimed her heart. She was not going to give up this little girl because of a legal finding.

Mark perched Ethan on the arm of the chair next to Jocelyn and Emma. He stood next to him, keeping him from falling. He looked exhausted, drained and yet his gaze on her was intense.

Ethan reached out and batted at Emma's foot. "I'm not going away! You can't make me go away, Em! We promised!" Each sentence was punctuated with a shake of her shoe which came off in his hand. Arm raised ready to throw it, his frustration was so great, Mark interceded, lifting the shoe from his hand.

Mark looked at Jocelyn while saying, "Steady there buddy. I think Emma's mama has some more news to share."

"Let me know when you're ready to hear the rest."

"Now." Emma said, her voice fierce.

"Tony may know we are here but Fremont is a big city. He won't know where we are, where we're staying. The petition says no one can tell him if they know. And, it says he has to be checked out. They are going to have someone investigate, that means check out what we said. I'm pretty sure someone will want to talk to you and to me and we won't be able to be together when that happens. But we'll be brave because we know we'll be telling the truth and when they believe us, they'll let you stay with me until you're all grown up."

Emma sat up, her face red, her eyes swollen, her lips trembled. "I can be brave."

Jocelyn's heart swelled and broke all at the same time. "Yes, you can be very brave."

Emma's blue-eyed gaze never wavered. "Tony doesn't know I'm here with you at this house."

"No he doesn't know that."

"So Ethan is safe here?"

"Everyone is safe here," Jackson said. "And, unless I fell asleep and dreamed it, I had two great helpers fix our dinner."

The dark spell was broken by Jackson's words.

Emma giggled. "You didn't fall asleep Mr. Jackson."

"I'm glad to hear that. What do you two think about helping me finish up?" Jackson had stood and gestured toward the kitchen.

"I'm not going anywhere," Jocelyn said setting Emma on the floor.

"And I'm right here also. Very hungry too. It's been a long time since lunch." Mark rubbed his belly. "My stomach thinks I've forgotten it."

Ethan laughed. "You always say that, Papa."

With the two children ensconced on their stools listening to Jackson talk about how to make a berry shortcake even better, Lily sat with Jocelyn and Mark. "Both of you look half dead. Mark, you already said you don't have to go in until noon or one tomorrow."

He nodded.

Lily continued. "I'm suggesting we have a sleep over. We'll pile blankets and pillows on the floor and camp out. Everyone together. Those two need recovery time together."

"They made some kind of a pact," Mark said. "I don't know what it is but I have a few guesses."

Jocelyn nodded. "I don't know the details but it has something to do with sticking together, no matter what."

"That makes sense given their backgrounds," Lily said. "Until the two of you came into their lives, they dealt with the physical, mental and emotional trauma alone."

Jocelyn frowned. "I didn't say anything about the psychological testing Ms. Lawford requested. Better clean that up now." She started across the room to the kitchen area.

Mark caught up with her. His voice low he said, "Let's do this together. Maybe they can see the same person or something so that, while they can't be in the room with each other, they can support each other in another way."

Nodding agreement, Jocelyn said. "Good idea."

Lily neared. "I heard that. Great plan. And I've some names of good psychologists who specialize in small children. I'll give you the names after dinner."

It wasn't as hard as she'd thought it would be to talk to Emma about seeing a doctor who would only talk to her, maybe have her do some tasks like stacking blocks or coloring because the conversation bounced back between Mark, Lily and her. While not exactly happy, because they'd be together, Emma and Ethan handled the news well.

The camp out was a resounding success with a pillow fight, three stories and the novelty of sleeping on the floor wrapped in blankets.

With Emma tucked against her side, Jocelyn closed her eyes and saw the house with the green grass, flowers and trees. Emma was laughing and the man was pushing her on the swing hanging from the old oak tree limb. A small hand held hers. She looked down but saw nothing.

CHAPTER 24

Sharp pain shot through Mark's right calf as the cramping muscle seized. Slowly he stretched holding the hiss inside. Sleeping on the floor, even with blankets and cushions for padding was not conducive to a good night's sleep. Even with Ethan curled next to him, his sleep was restless, superficial. He was drained, going on fumes. Having this morning, this bit of extra time with Ethan was a welcomed pain.

With Ethan and Emma upstairs with Mr. Jackson fixing breakfast, he helped Jocelyn fold the blankets and put the cushions back on the couch. He stopped in the bedroom door after returning pillows to the beds and watched her straighten the throw on the overstuffed chair.

Aware of the tightening of his calf, he stretched tall, his fingertips reaching for the ceiling. He rolled his neck and then touched the floor with his hands. Tension still locked muscles and the ever-present-background-headache upped the beat as if to remind him it was still there.

Jocelyn now fussed with the arrangement of the pillows of the couch.

What would it be like to fear for your life? To fear for a child you loved? At least, he inwardly chided himself, Ethan would be safe if he was taken away.

Jocelyn stopped and looked at him, a question written all over her face.

"What?" he asked stepping into the room.

"You seem preoccupied or worried or something." Her tone conveyed concern. Concern for him?

He managed a rough chuckle. "'Or something' covers it."

She faced him, her forehead wrinkled, her hazel eyes were green this morning. "I'm a good listener."

Her hair had been finger combed and pulled into a messy pony tail. She still wore the old ratty sweats and her feet were covered in wool socks. His mouth opened, shut and then opened again. He didn't blink or look away. He stepped closer. Close enough to reach out and trail his fingertips along the curve of her jaw, pull her into an embrace and kiss her. *Maybe*.

Startled at that errant thought, Mark took a step back. "Bet you are a good listener. I'm not always a good talker."

"And this morning?" Jocelyn's soft voice asked as her gaze stayed locked with his. She stood in front of him, compassion in her eyes. "Perhaps more than anyone else in your life, I can understand the horror of losing a child you love."

Mark collapsed on the couch. That was true. She already understood without him even saying anything. Elbows resting on knees, head in his hands, he starred at the floor. "I don't know what I'll do if I lose him." He looked up at the ceiling. "It should be simple. All I need to do is have a wife and Mrs. Fester will back off."

Jocelyn sat beside him, her hand resting on his arm. "If I knew it would help, I'd marry you myself. Ethan—well, Ethan will be less than what he can be if he's not with his papa. You have an understanding of him and with him. Together you are an awesome team." She patted his arm and added. "And, I don't know where Emma would be if she didn't have Ethan in her life."

Mark's attention was snagged by her first words. His attention lasered on her, sitting beside him, her fresh clean scent wreathing around him, her warm hand on his arm. He shifted and took her hand as the answer hit him head on.

"You'd marry me?"

Jocelyn startled and pulled her hand away.

"That was not well done of me." Mark turned to more fully face her. "I like you and admire you. Our children are, I think soul mates of a sort. I believe we could create a safe haven for both of these children if we marry.

"Just think, you could take my name and disappear that way. And, we can work it out so Emma is not officially Emma Edwards." His mind whirred away with words and pictures that tumbled out into the air between them.

"We can buy a house. We'll get you a car—or at least a newer car?" Mark slowed the rush of words as he saw the incredulous look on Jocelyn's face.

"Or not.

"I've overstepped, haven't I?" He rubbed a hand over his face, now a bright shade of red.

JOCELYN SAT STUNNED, surprised with an undercurrent of suspicion. She scrutinized Mark's face, noted the embarrassment and chagrin. "I'm not sure 'overstepped' is the right word," she said.

Abruptly Mark stood and paced away from the couch.

She succumbed to the urge to follow. He'd stopped by the sliding door out onto the lower deck. The magnificent view of the city spread out before them. She noticed it, took in the grandeur before looking up at him. "You had an idea and you shared the benefits of your idea. You know that everything has an upside and a downside."

His head cocked toward her but otherwise he didn't move.

"What do you see as the downside of your idea?" She kept her gaze on him.

He didn't speak for several minutes. She heard the intake of air and then whoosh as he released pent up air from his lungs. He turned toward her and took both of her hands in his, interlocking their fingers.

"You didn't laugh nor did you say 'no'."

In the depths of his dark chocolate brown eyes the gold flecks glimmered. Jocelyn shook her head. She didn't resist when he stepped closer and unlocking their entwined fingers, slid his hands up her arms and back before stepping even closer and hugging her. His chin rested on the top of her head, his heat warmed a cold spot in her core and soothed.

"You did mention 'downside'. What do you see as the downside?" His voice was soft, his breath filtered through her hair to her scalp.

His sweatshirt soft against her cheek, she relaxed against his hard chest. "The biggest is that I believe marriage is or should be permanent."

She felt his smile on her scalp.

Did he sigh? He let out a breath and his arms tightened a fraction. "The fact that you can say that after having been with Tony is a miracle."

Jocelyn leaned back, knowing she pressed more tightly against him but it was important to see his face. "The Universe watches over, guides and protects me. I now can see I was sent to Tony so I could rescue Emma. My not being legally married to him is a blessing. But —" she paused for effect and because she now felt a ridge against her belly, "I'm not as naïve as I once was. Marriage takes both parties working together or—let's just say that I do not trust that abuse could never happen again."

MARK LOOSENED HIS HOLD, shifted so a bit of space was between them. An unasked question was currently being answered by his anatomy. "Let's sit down and talk this out." He stepped back but kept a hand on her elbow.

"Or we can go out on the deck?" Jocelyn gestured to the doors leading outside.

He relaxed an inch. "We can. Whichever you want."

"And is that how you envisage marriage?" Jocelyn asked, a tight smile on her face.

His brows veed. "Is what how I envisage marriage?"

"Agreeing with whatever your wife says?"

He laughed. As the sound rolled out, he knew this was a good thing. Laughing, being with Jocelyn, the frank talk between them.

"I didn't think that was a funny question." Her eyes squinted, her lips pinched, her toe might start tapping next. She was perturbed.

"No, it was a serious question that struck me funny because I know myself and I would never attribute that to me. I can be and usually am agreeable but not always. I do talk things over and hope for consensus."

Her brow arched. "But in the end it's your way or the highway?"

"No!" They'd progressed to the couch but had yet to sit down. Mark stepped away. "I'm not highhanded. I don't think I am anyway. You can ask Lily or my parents how they see me."

"Do they know you need to marry to keep Ethan?"

He gestured to her to sit and she did—at one end. He sat on the other end, the better to see her. "Lily does but not my parents. And in the interest of full disclosure, my parents, Mom especially, liked you and Emma. The offer to live there was not lightly made."

Jocelyn relaxed into the corner, a smile tipped her lips. "They are wonderful people. Emma was almost immediately comfortable with them. Not really like her at all."

He raised his gaze from her lips, her naturally rosy lips. "Probably from hearing Ethan chatter on and on about his Grandmama and Grandpapa."

She nodded.

Another layer of tension ebbed. Mark leaned toward her. "Will you think about us marrying? I'm sure there are downsides, but we seem to get along well so I'm sure we can work things out."

Jocelyn cocked her head. "Marriage is a lifetime commitment. What will we do with each other in ten years or so when Ethan and Emma are grown and living lives of their own?"

Hearing those words, he knew Jocelyn was seriously considering his offer. It was like looking at a house and talking about where certain pieces of furniture would go. She was looking at their marriage and talking about what they'd be doing years from now.

"We might have other children." The words were out before he'd thought them through.

Jocelyn froze. She leaned back against the arm of the couch, her face very still.

Cold seeped into his gut. He'd been thinking of a full-blown marriage. She'd been thinking of a marriage of convenience.

CHAPTER 25

It was late morning and Mark had taken the children with him to see his parents. The plan was he'd then take them with him to his office and she'd pick them up by one thirty when his first patient was scheduled.

Lost in her thoughts, Jocelyn startled when Lily sat down beside her on the couch in front of the fireplace in the great room. Lily didn't say anything, just kept her company.

Even with someone sitting beside her, Jocelyn shuddered with a chill as the depths of her loneliness surfaced, as she fought back the darkness and accompanying fear. While there were many things to like and even admire about Mark Parker, she'd not dreamed of being intimate with him. In truth she'd never thought to be intimate with any man again.

Tony had been brutal. Not at first but by the time she and Emma escaped, she went within and mechanically did what he demanded. Her worst fear was that he'd make Emma watch as he raped her.

Bile rose in her throat as a vague whisper of a memory fought free. Her heart raced and she held her hands to her head, pressing her fingers to her temples in an effort to stop the image from forming. "No!"

"How can I help?" Lily's soft voice and gentle hand on her knee helped Jocelyn stay tethered to the present.

Her voice was unsteady but her racing heart slowed down. "You've already done so much."

Her voice calm, Lily said. "Offering you a safe place to stay isn't really all that much from my perspective."

Jocelyn shuddered. "I bring danger with me."

Lily shifted. One hand remained on Jocelyn's knee the other on her shoulder. "Perhaps, perhaps not. Stay focused on the positive—being safe, keeping Emma safe, finding your way forward in the world. I will admit it isn't always easy and sometimes you have to stop those errant thoughts and bring yourself back to center—but it can be done."

Jocelyn's stomach churned and bands of tension crisscrossed her scalp. "So when my mind goes down the 'what if' rabbit hole how do I stop?"

Lily tapped Jocelyn's shoulder. "Say 'stop'—gently if possible, more forcefully if needed. And I've found there are times and circumstances when I need to repeat 'stop' several times before I gain the upperhand. Remember, you control your thoughts in that you can make a choice about them. You can redirect your thoughts, distract yourself from those thoughts, or do something very different, something that requires you to think other thoughts."

Jocelyn shifted to look into Lily's cornflower blue eyes and said in a shaky voice, "I took a class on meditation when I was in high school. We were told to let the thoughts go away, to dismiss them. I was never very good at that."

Lily held Jocelyn's gaze. "Perhaps taking a more active role will work for you. I know I've never been able to do a sitting meditation. Some people do a moving meditation like walking a labyrinth or a familiar path or pattern. Something that frees their mind because it's so familiar. Others dance or move in some way that helps.

"You've met Hunter. That's what she does. When she needs to work something out she's up and walking or dancing. She also drums.

From my own experiences I know focusing on the rhythm of a drum can clear my mind of unhelpful thoughts."

Jocelyn nodded, a slight smile tipped her lips. "I'll think about what you've said. Right now I need to pull myself together so I can pick up Emma and Ethan at the right time."

Lily patted her knee. "With your permission, I'll go with you. We can stop at this group home where I've got a couple of clients. They love to have children visit and Emma and Ethan will get lots of attention. You can relax while I check in with the care givers."

"I'd prefer it if you came along. My car's still behind Hunter's dance studio. I know you said I could drive your car but…well, I'm having a hard time focusing. She stood and took two steps before turning back. "I'm going to take a quick shower. I can be ready in thirty."

"Don't rush, if we leave in forty-five we'll be on time."

ALONE THAT EVENING, Jocelyn was amazed at how quickly the day had flown by. She successfully used Lily's strategy and ordered herself to 'stop' when troubling thoughts tumbled around in her mind. At one point she visualized them as stones in a rock tumbler growing smaller and smaller. But then she stopped that analogy because in real life that machine was used to polish the contents. *I just want these thoughts to go away.*

She smiled at the memory of Emma and Ethan at the adult group home. The residents had fallen in love with the children and had invited them back "any time." Because it was their request, next stop had been Audrey's. Downtime with other kids was how she framed that change in plans.

She was alone in the downstairs family room because Mark had picked the children up from Audrey's and they were spending the night at his parents. She hugged herself as she walked the perimeter of the room.

Mark hadn't said the words but she knew it was so she'd have time to herself, time to sort through the pros and cons of what he was suggesting. Marriage…and this time a real one, legal and—her breath caught—one where he'd have the same rights to her body as she'd thought Tony had.

Could she do it? Could she have a sexual relationship with Mark? Could she even tell him why she was so passive? Cold? Frigid?

She wandered the perimeter of the room, tightening the circle with each pass until she stood still in the very middle. Eyes closed, unbidden the image of the green grass with Emma on a swing hanging from the old oak tree, a man behind her manifested. She heard Emma's laugh, felt a soft breeze and the small hand holding her own. Was that Mark pushing Emma on the swing? When she looked down, she saw the brown hair on the top of a head. Light brown hair like Ethan's? And while she was there, on the deck overlooking the yard a flutter in her belly shocked her.

She staggered and stumbled forward barely reaching the couch before she fell. Fingers splayed over her abdomen. She'd been pregnant in that vision.

Resting on the couch, her hand still on her stomach, her mind spun with the reality that her vision was changing. It had started with the large expanse of green grass, the old oak tree with a swing hanging from one gnarled branch, bright flowers in well-tended beds.

And now? Emma was on the swing, laughing and happy and a man was with her, a small child held her hand and she was pregnant.

"I need to get some sleep," Jocelyn muttered as she stood. She grabbed the arm of the couch to steady herself as she swayed. "Sleep. Sleep and a stern talking to. I don't live in a dream vision, I live in the here and now."

CHAPTER 26

Mark picked Ethan and Emma up from Audrey's. Because his mom was feeling much better, Ethan and Emma were invited to a sleep over. Ethan was excited at first but then sobered and waited for Emma's response.

"You miss your grandmama and grandpapa." Emma's pronouncement had a wistful tone to it.

Ethan nodded but remained silent.

"I don't have a grandmama or a grandpapa," Emma said and sighed.

"I can share," Ethan piped up. "I'm good at sharing, aren't I, Papa?"

Clearing his throat of the pride stuck there, Mark said, "You are great at sharing."

He shared that conversation with his mom and dad as soon as possible. He stayed for dinner, supervised bath time and, as his parents were snuggling down on the twin beds, several books in hand, he gave Ethan and Emma hugs.

"Grandpapa is going to do funny voices," Ethan said, clearly okay with his leaving.

"Grandmama has a few funny voices of her own," his mother had countered, an arm around Emma.

"I'll leave you to it." He waved, blew a kiss to each child, waited until one was blown back, caught it and slapped it on his forehead and nose. It was easier and yet not to walk away with childish laughter following him down the hall.

Once home he settled down to watch television. Restless, he turned it off after ten minutes and booted up his computer to check emails and maybe do some web surfing.

When he clicked on 'Vacations in Paris' he stopped, rubbed at his forehead where a headache was gaining momentum.

What was he doing? Jocelyn didn't strike him as a Paris Vacation Girl. Actually she wasn't a girl but a very nicely put together woman. He was attracted to her. Part of it might have been because he'd sworn off physical relationships with women when Ethan had come to live with him. But, he'd been around other women in the past ten months. Not that he didn't notice attractive women but—. His time and attention had been devoted to this damaged little boy who trusted him in all things.

Was that why he was asking Jocelyn to marry him? Because Ethan loved Emma and Emma loved Ethan?

And Jocelyn was correct. In ten to fifteen years both of the children would be grown and basically gone. He couldn't imagine a life without Ethan. And that wasn't fair to her. Marrying her to keep Ethan without a thought for her needs, for her well-being was not who he was. And it wasn't entirely true. He'd keep her safe and he'd do whatever he could to protect Emma also. She'd never have to worry about material things. His income was more than sufficient to support a family.

But the basic question that kept circling around in his brain, that had him up and pacing through the condo, was whether he could be married to Jocelyn and not be intimate with her. He was attracted to her. For Pete's sake, he'd had an erection when she was pressed against him.

He scrubbed his face with both hands and then ran them through his rumpled hair. "Sleep," he muttered to himself as he headed to his bedroom. "I've got to get some sleep."

CHAPTER 27

Jocelyn shifted, trying to move, to get up. During the night a tornado had struck and now pillows were on the floor and the bedding askew. More than just a bit off. The top blanket was on the floor on one side of the bed, the next blanket off the other side. And the sheet? The sheet was twisted around her as if to strangle her limbs.

So this is what happens when I go to bed and think about being married? Not a good sign.

A quick shower and a dressed Jocelyn headed upstairs. The house was quiet. No note from Lily, she wandered to look out the window at the forlorn looking mountain in the distance. With little snow, Mt. Hood looked naked.

The sound of water running and a little shriek startled. She smiled as tears welled. Smiled because she knew Lily was okay and tearful because she'd never experienced a fun-filled shower with any man much less one who unconditionally loved her.

"Probably more than fun-filled," she said and sighed.

Jocelyn busied herself in the kitchen and by the time Jackson and Lily came downstairs she had bacon fried and the fixings for French toast ready to go.

"Who gave you—?" Jackson started but stopped with a huff when Lily's elbow connected with his side.

"What a treat!" Lily said into the abrupt silence. "We haven't had French toast for some time and it's one of my favorites."

Jocelyn jumped, then froze. Her gaze darted between Jackson and Lily.

"I'm sorry," Jackson said, worry in his tone and his eyes. "I was teasing. You are welcome to use the kitchen and anything else in the house whenever you need to."

"I over-reacted." Jocelyn said, apology in her tone, her head submissively bowed. She stepped back to the stove and started the French toast. "Bacon is warming in the oven. I wasn't sure how you liked your coffee, Jackson. But I do have water heated for tea, Lily."

Jocelyn couldn't shake off the internal tremors that had started when Jackson first spoke. Her mind knew he wouldn't hurt her, but her body? Her body had taken three steps back, catalogued where Emma was, where her car was and had started on how they'd be able to escape by the time Lily's voice registered.

This kitchen episode spotlighted why she couldn't marry Mark. As kind and gentle a man as he was, he most certainly raised his voice at times. Why, she'd heard him call across an expanse of park for Ethan so she knew he had the volume. Of course calling for Ethan there was love in his voice, nothing to fear. And, she wasn't in front of him. She'd been to the side and slightly behind him.

The devil's advocate in her argued: he'd never hurt Emma. Ethan trusted him and even Emma had expanded her circle of people she was comfortable with to include Mark, his parents, Lily and Jackson, Ashley and her children. She loved seeing Hunter's dance studio and the long-legged red-head had shown Emma a few dance steps.

"Jocelyn?" Lily was beside her.

"Oh, the French toast!"

"Is just fine. Jackson has long arms and we have more than one spatula. Do you want maple syrup or something else on yours?"

Her faced heated with shame and her shoulders hunched as she tried to turn away.

VISIONS OF HAPPINESS

"Let's get the place settings out on the table. The food is almost ready." Lily slipped an arm around her shoulders and guided her to the table. "I'll hand things to you and you can do the rest."

Conversation was general as they ate. What each was doing that day was the main topic. Jackson had work in his office that would keep him busy most of the day. He'd be home around five depending on traffic. If it wasn't raining, he'd like to grill again.

Lily had a couple of clients to see, the ever-present reports to write but there were hours open. She turned to Jocelyn. "What do you have on your agenda other than picking the kids up from Audrey's this afternoon?"

Thinking of the mess downstairs, Jocelyn's shoulders tensed. "I thought I'd clean the downstairs, maybe do laundry and change my bed. I was a bit restless last night so at the very least it needs to be remade from the bottom sheet up."

"Or, since we have a cleaning service we could pick up Emma and Ethan a little early and stop by Ashley's," Lily offered. "Or maybe go to the park?"

Jocelyn purposefully tensed and then tried to relax the steel bars in her shoulders. "I think the park would be better if the rain holds off. It will give them time to burn off some of that energy."

"Good idea. I'll text Mark so he knows where Ethan will be when he gets off work." She grinned and patted Jocelyn on the shoulder. "And while there are many things I love about Jackson, one of the perks is we kept his housecleaning and yard services.

"And the cleaning service comes today. If you want to strip the sheets, you certainly may but don't think you have to. They strip all the beds, do the laundry while they clean and then remake the beds with fresh sheets from the linen closet and put the ones just washed on the bottom. Very organized.

"I will admit I feel *very* pampered. I never was fond of housework and now when I pitch in and clean up the kitchen after Jackson has fixed a wonderful meal, I do it with gladness in my heart."

Tension still held her tight, her voice quiet, Jocelyn said, "I can't imagine not having to do housework."

"Do you enjoy it? I know some women get great pleasure in cleaning. Sophia certainly derives pleasure from baking. And I derive great pleasure from her baking." Lily laughed and towed Jocelyn along.

"We're going to have a 'go with the flow kind of day' and if you feel like talking about whatever is bothering you, we'll make time for it."

Jocelyn debated talking to Lily about Mark's offer. She was the one woman she could talk to because Lily had known Mark even before Ethan came into his life. She'd know about his character, how he thought about women, if there was a disconnect between how he treated women in public, in his office—maybe not in the privacy of his home but, when Tony turned on her, he didn't care where they were.

A picture of a time in a restaurant flashed through her mind. Tony enraged, yelling at her. He'd thrown a glass of wine in her face and pulled the tablecloth so all the food spilled in her lap. The owner had rushed over, his concern evident. But the trickster or chameleon that was Tony, flipped and he was charming. Pulled money out of his wallet to pay for any damages. So many apologies to the owner. She and Emma were invisible. But maybe they weren't as invisible as she thought. The police weren't called. Enough money changed hands to smooth those waters. But did the restaurant staff remember the incident?

"Lily, I just remembered something. May I use some of your paper to write it down?"

"Of course, help yourself."

Jocelyn diligently traced the events of that evening on paper, starting with how happy she and Emma were to be going out for Italian. Emma loved Basghetti and Jocelyn always said the word so Emma could nod and Tony wouldn't ridicule her. She used both sides of two sheets of legal-sized papers and had just finished up when they pulled into Audrey's driveway.

"I'd like you to read this." Jocelyn held the notes out to Lily who took them and started to read.

Lily turned toward Jocelyn, her gaze fierce, her voice clipped and controlled. "You need to get this to Ms. Lawford. She needs to know about this and any other incident that you can remember where there were witnesses."

"But I-I-I wasn't hurt." Jocelyn stammered.

"And when you got home, Tony was calm and even-tempered?" Lily asked in her matter-of-fact manner.

Her gut clenched, a sharp pain in her chest and a shudder rippled through her. "No," she whispered, her head in her hands, she burst into tears.

Lily leaned over and put her arms around Jocelyn's shoulders. "You're safe now. Tony doesn't even know where you are."

Sobbing, Jocelyn turned into Lily. "He-he-he r-r-raped me. It-it-it was worse than-than other time-time-times because he hurt me."

Lily's arms tightened around her and she rocked a bit within the confines of the car. "I am so very sorry that happened to you. What do you need from me right now to help you bury your past?"

"I don't know. I'm so confused. I feel safe and yet I feel more vulnerable. I am happy and yet I'm more miserable. I love seeing Emma begin to blossom but I'm terrified... ."

"Terrified you might lose her and terrified as to what might happen to her?"

Jocelyn nodded. "I'm even more afraid for her than I am for myself. I don't know how to protect her, to give her something to hang on to if Tony ever sees her again."

Her head rested in an awkward position half on Lily's shoulder and half on the back of the seat. She breathed in through her nose and out through her mouth. Her tears slowed and then stopped. Her voice a raspy whisper, she said, "I'm better now."

"Good. Let's get the kids and go to the park. I'll leave a message for Jackson about dinner. I'm thinking hamburgers with all the trimmings. Ethan never fusses about lettuce and tomato on his hamburger... ."

Shaking, Jocelyn straightened, a tremulous smile on her face. "But if he's like Emma, he isn't as happy to eat them in a salad."

Lily patted Jocelyn's arm. "Very true. Why don't I get the kids while you take a few minutes to gather yourself together? I think the fresh air in the park will be good for all of us."

CHAPTER 28

They took a round-about way to the park to stop by Ms. Lawford's office. Lily and the children walked around the block while Jocelyn went upstairs to her attorney's office to drop off the papers.

"Sit while I take a look." Ms. Lawford gestured to an empty chair.

Jocelyn perched on the seat, her feet tapping on the carpet, her fingers drumming on the chair arm.

Finished, Ms. Lawford laid the paper on her desk and leaned forward. "Anything else like this you remember, write it out like this and get to me," she said, in her no-nonsense voice.

Jocelyn quelled the urge to bolt or puke. "I don't know if anyone will remember."

"Do you know if the place has changed ownership?" Ms. Lawford asked in that same tone.

Jocelyn shook her head. "It's a family run business. Third generation."

Ms. Lawford stood and rounded her desk. "Someone will remember. Leave it to me to figure that out. Your job is to write down things you remember and get them to me." Ms. Lawford leaned against the front of her desk, her features softened. "You do know the safer you feel, the more incidents like this you'll remember."

"N-N-No, I didn't know that." Jocelyn clenched her hands into fists and pushed on her knees to stop her legs from jittering.

"In reality it's a blessing and a curse to feel safe," Ms. Lawford's briskness was gone, calm steadiness in its place. "And when the memories come, they bring with them the fear, the terror of the original incident. Some of my clients have found counseling helpful. For others writing down the memories seems to help. My advice is to get therapy or at the least find someone you trust to at least be able to listen to you."

"Where's your daughter?"

Jocelyn's head jerked up. Ms. Lawford was watching her. "Lily is walking around the block with Emma and Mark's son, Ethan," she replied and stood.

"Those two have a firm bond." Ms. Lawford remarked.

Jocelyn's stomach churned and she fought the bile back before answering, "They do and I don't know what will happen to Emma if she loses Ethan, even if she still has me. And if she lost us both?"

Ms. Lawford straightened and held out her hand. "Let's concentrate on none of that happening. Those two kids have been through enough already in their young lives. Rest assured I will do everything in my power to see that you and Emma stay together and are able to move forward with your lives."

They walked to her office door. Before Jocelyn stepped out into the corridor, Ms. Lawford said "Remember what I said about counseling or someone to talk to."

"I do remember. We've appointments for Emma and Ethan to see counselors. Lily helped set that up and she's going with us, at least for the first appointment."

"Good. I'll look forward to seeing the report on Emma."

OVER THE NEXT WEEK, Ms. Lawford's prediction came true. Memories popped up, nightmares were the norm. Jocelyn talked to Emma and told her it was normal and even a good thing when they had the nightmares and memories because it meant they felt safe.

Before going to bed, they talked and wrote down whatever it was they'd remembered that day. It was helpful, even though Lily never said anything, to have her read over the reports before faxing them to Ms. Lawford's office. Lily knew the worst things about her and yet, still welcomed her. And even invited Jocelyn to go along to visit clients. Twice she stayed and read to a woman on Hospice while Lily left to see other clients.

Being of value, being useful and being appreciated for something as simple as reading was a new experience. Even before Tony, she hadn't seen herself as having much value. She'd been a receptionist at a real estate company when she met Tony. Most recently she'd waitressed in a bar.

Of course Lily had a college degree. Jocelyn had dropped out after eighteen months when she couldn't pay tuition. The Associates degree she was working on left behind when she went to work to support herself. Maybe if she did marry Mark, she could return to school?

Startled at the thought, Jocelyn straightened in the chair. Somewhere in the last weeks she'd turned a corner and now saw marriage to Mark as having positives beyond a way for Emma and her to disappear. Perhaps it was because several times a week, Mark and Ethan joined them for dinner at Lily and Jackson's and spent the night.

The front door opened and Mark entered behind two boisterous children. Emma came across the room at her fastest pace, her arms opened wide. Jocelyn met her half-way and picked her up. Emma threw her arms around Jocelyn's neck and gave her a smacking kiss on the cheek and announced, "We got dinner for everyone."

Jocelyn's second look confirmed Emma's statement. Mark had a bag with the distinctive markings of a favorite local Chinese restaurant in each hand. He held them up, a broad smile on his face. "Pay back."

Just then the distant but distinct sound of the garage door opening registered. A few minutes later she heard Lily and Jackson's voices as they came into the house.

"Brought dinner." Mark held the bags up as he strode across the great room and placed them on the kitchen counter. "You two," he pointed to Emma and Ethan, "need to go wash up."

A glance at Jackson and Lily at the end of a long day and Jocelyn knew it was time for Emma and her to move on. They looked tired and yet still had a houseful of people.

She stood and approached the kitchen. "You two go on. I know the kitchen well enough that I can get dishes out, add water to the tea kettle and whatever else needs to be done." Turning toward Mark she said, "Dinner ready in ten?"

He turned and started toward her. "Definitely if not a bit sooner."

They worked well together as if they were members of a well-oiled team. Jocelyn's awareness of where Mark was in proximity to her was acute. Not unpleasant but not yet pleasant.

As they were cleaning up the kitchen, having banished Jackson and Lily to the couch and the children downstairs to watch a movie, Jocelyn bumped arms with Mark as they both reached for the same bowl to put in the dishwasher.

She heard his indrawn breath and bits and pieces of thoughts, of ideas about her future with Emma shifted into a new pattern.

Her throat tightened, her palms sweated, her knees weakened and her cheeks heated. "About your offer?"

Mark stilled.

A nanosecond later he replied. "I'm listening."

"Before I answer, can we talk?"

He swiveled to face her, his hands rose to rest on her shoulders, his gaze met hers. The heat from his hands warmed her skin through her sweater, his clean scent infiltrated her body. His face marked with concern and hope, he said, "Of course. When?"

"I-I-I'm not sure. Your schedule is," she laughed, a desperate sound with a hiccup at the end, "busier than mine."

"Why don't we both take the kids to Audrey's in the morning? We can talk in the car on the way to my office and if we haven't finished, we can continue in my office."

"I'll have to check...." Her hands twisted and then she clutched her elbows.

"Jocelyn, we'll work it out. If we can't finish before I have to see patients, you can take my car, pick up the kids, go to the park, whatever. I'll call you or have Anne call you when I'm seeing my last patient and you can come pick me up.

CHAPTER 29

Nausea threatened. There wasn't anything left in Jocelyn's stomach. She'd been sick during the night and had the dry heaves this morning. At best she was running on empty in terms of both energy and focus. But she could and would do this. She got Emma unbuckled from her car seat, kissed and hugged her as she set her on the pavement. "Have a good day, Pumpernickel."

Mark took the children inside. This morning they were a little more reluctant than usual. Instead of the usual dash for Audrey's front door, they walked, looking back at her still in the car. She smiled and waved but knew Emma was not fooled.

When Mark backed out of the drive and started down the street, Jocelyn knew the clock was ticking. She swallowed the bile rising in her throat and took a sip from the water bottle she'd brought along.

"About your offer." The words strangled out in chunks.

"Just so we're on the same topic. Are we talking about you living and working for my parents or marriage?" Mark kept his eyes on the road and his hands on the steering wheel.

Jocelyn's nerves jumped and she leaned toward the passenger door. "I-I'd forgotten about the job offer. I'm sorry, of course Emma and I would be grateful to accept that."

Mark's knuckles turned white as he gripped the steering wheel.

Jocelyn kept her eyes trained ahead but heard his sharp intake of breath.

Tension lashed through her and her eyes darted, looking for safety. "I-I'm sorry, Mark. I-I-I shouldn't have forgotten the job offer. I've just been so-so-so distracted lately with—."

"Don't, Jocelyn. Don't make excuses or apologize. I'd hoped when you said you wanted to talk it was about my offer of marriage," he said in a tired and defeated voice.

On a deep breath, she leapt into the void. "It was."

"What?" Mark swerved to the curb and put the car in park before he turned to face her.

Hands clenched tightly in her lap, Jocelyn plunged on. "Last night when I asked to talk to you, it was about the marriage offer. I had totally forgotten the offer of a job."

"Then why?"

"Because I'm out of my depths. I'm terrified to marry again." At the look of horror on his face, she hastily added. "I'm not terrified of you. I'm not even afraid of you. These past couple of weeks, being around you in general every day kinds of activities, I know I can trust you to not hurt either Emma or me. I wanted to talk to you because, while I'm honored you'd even think to marry me, I'm not sure I can be a-a-a wife to you. That is…," she twisted her hands, clutching her elbows and shaking her head to dismiss the fears and tears welling inside.

Mark started to reach for her, to comfort but pulled his hand back. He wanted to lean close, to reassure her, but didn't. "I don't know the details of your marriage, but I do know that Tony was a mean bastard, abused you and Emma physically, mentally and emotionally. It takes time to heal from that much abuse.

"Not going to lie here and say I'm not attracted to you because I am but if you are hesitating in saying "yes" because of physical intimacies, of sex, that's something we can work on.

"No one needs to know when we consummate our marriage. That's between us. My condo has three bedrooms," he paused. "But I think we would need to buy a house. Ethan and I have talked about a house with a real yard. We can look at four or five bedroom homes and that will be enough space—. What?"

Mark was so earnest, so—. Jocelyn didn't have the words to describe how he looked, his face animated, his hands gesturing within the confines of the car. He wanted her as his wife. It might be a marriage of convenience for her, and it may have started out that way for him, but now? Now he wanted a real marriage with her.

She flushed with pleasure. He really did want to marry her. But the cold seeped from her belly to her heart when she thought of those physical intimacies.

She froze. Mark needed to know she was damaged, was frigid, so he could find someone else. To bind him to her when she was broken? She couldn't, wouldn't do that to him.

She watched as if from a distance as her hands moved to hold his closest one. She took a deep breath and reached inside for the courage to tell him the truth about herself.

"I'm frigid. The very idea of being with anyone that way? I go cold inside and, from what I've learned about it, I do something called 'dissociating.' I don't know that I'd ever be able to be a real wife to you."

His fingers closed around hers, his voice husky, he said, "Give us a chance?"

Confusion shook her head. "I don't know what you mean."

"Let's get married, buy that house and see what happens. I promise I will never force you but I do not promise I won't try to kiss and cuddle.

"We even kissed once and for me it was very pleasurable. I've held your hand, put my arm around your shoulders and recently held you in my arms while you cried. It isn't like we've had no physical contact, Jocelyn."

A bud of hope like an early crocus poked through the winter of despair that claimed her body when she thought of sexual contact. What he'd said was true. She hadn't run away screaming much less had nightmares about him.

"I-I-I'm not sure locking you into a marriage—."

"I know I'm interrupting and I want to add this. Let's give it a try and see where we are in time. At least a couple of years? See how Ethan and Emma are doing? I know we can come to an amicable agreement if we both decide it isn't working.

"Maybe you can go to school, finish that degree? If you think it would help, my insurance will cover therapy."

She'd already floated out into uncharted territory by asking to talk about marriage.

"We'd have a pre-nup?" The bud of hope opened further.

"We'd have a pre-nup."

Jocelyn's heart still pounded but her anxiety eased. "Okay, if we can agree on the contents of a pre-nup, I'll marry you."

"For clarification. The pre-nup will be about the non-financial aspects of our marriage. It's important to me that if things don't work out, you and Emma are taken care of. Like you keeping your car, the two of you being on my insurance, maybe even child support, a home of your own—."

"You don't owe me any... ." Jocelyn's words trailed off at the look on Mark's face.

"That's the deal. You get final say on the non-financial parts of the pre-nup but I get final say on the financial pieces."

"People will say I'm taking advantage of you," she said, exasperation infusing her tone.

"People," Mark quirked his fingers in quote marks, "don't have to know we even have a pre-nup. You, me and an attorney. What about using Ms. Lawford if she doesn't see it as a conflict of interest?"

Mark's phone rang. He pushed the hands-free answer button. "I'm on my way. Be there in ten, fifteen if traffic is bad." He was already pulling out from the curb and heading to his office.

Jocelyn sat in numb amazement. She was getting married. A sense of well-being, different than happiness, filled her body, mind and spirit.

In front of his office building, Mark popped out of the car. Rounding the hood, he handed Jocelyn the keys, gave her a brief hug and kiss on the cheek. Jogging to the entrance, he disappeared inside.

Getting in on the driver's side, Jocelyn adjusted the seat and mirrors. In a daze she managed to put the car in gear. Pinching herself, she fought down the anxiety that chirped in her belly and drove off.

Before she turned onto the street, the one question she hadn't thought about, the one question they hadn't talked about popped into her mind. When and what to tell the kids. Hoping to catch him before he was inundated with patients, she called Mark from her cell.

He answered on the first ring. "You can't—," he started when she interrupted.

"What and when are we telling the kids? And what about Lily, Jackson, Eleanor, your parents?" Her words were rushed, her voice tinted with adrenaline.

"Good question. Glad you called. Let me think about it. I'll get back to you when I've gathered my thoughts. Right now what might work is to bring the kids with you when you pick me up. But that's just off the top of my head. I'll get back to you. Gotta go."

Jocelyn sat for a few more minutes letting the rush of energy fade, letting her mind clear of the litany of ways to defuse anger, upset or rage she would have faced if it had been Tony on the other end of this call.

But it wasn't Tony. It was Mark. Mark who was behind, had people waiting for him, people who depended on him. His voice was rushed not abrupt. His tone was focused, not angry. He would think about it and they'd talk about how to handle this.

When she played the conversation over again in her mind the first words registered. "Good question." he'd said. "Glad you called." Tears came unbidden as relief swept through her. *Maybe...* .

JOCELYN PULLED INTO THE "DOCTOR ONLY" parking slot just as Mark came out the door. "Perfect timing," he said, grinning as he opened the passenger door. "Hey guy and gal want to get out and run around the courtyard?"

He and Jocelyn easily got two eager children out of their car seats. Knowing where the courtyard was, they dashed off.

"How are you doing?" Mark held Jocelyn's hand as they walked toward the enclosed area. Noticing it was cold, he rubbed her fingers with his own.

"I'm okay. Well, I'm a bit scared that one or both of them might not like us getting married." She released a shaky breath. "Other than that? I'm good."

The invitation had been to run around the courtyard and Ethan was making good on it. Emma was making an effort to follow but her limping gait meant she couldn't keep up.

"Hey you two, come on over here," Mark said, sitting down on one of the benches. "We've got something to tell you."

Ethan paused and then slowly, dragging his feet, came toward them.

Emma froze, her head swiveled their way. Her gaze locked with Jocelyn's.

Getting up, Jocelyn crossed over to where Emma stood unmoving. "You might even think it is really good news, Pumpernickel," she said picking her up.

Back by Mark, she sat with Emma on her lap. Ethan leaned against Mark, clutching his arm.

They'd decided that Mark would talk first and that Jocelyn would add to what he said. He should have known better than to set it up this way, should have realized neither Ethan much less Emma could deal with this kind of surprise.

"Okay, here's the deal. Emma's mom and I want to get married. That would mean we'd be a family, and you two," he gestured to Ethan and Emma, "would be like brother and sister. We'd all live together in the same house. What that would mean for us, Ethan, is that we'd move."

"But," Jocelyn said when Mark paused, "we wouldn't get married unless both of you agreed it was a good thing to do."

"Would you be my mama?" Ethan speared her with a piercing look, his chin pointed.

"If you want to call me, Mama, I'd like that but you don't have to. You can call me Jocelyn like you do now."

"Same for you, Emma. You can call me Papa or not," Mark assured Emma, who was burrowed against her mom.

Mark focused on breathing and waiting. He'd thought both children would be ecstatic, jumping up and down, wanting to celebrate. This quiet tense response didn't fit his imaginings.

"We've had time," Jocelyn gestured toward Mark, "to think about what it will mean, the changes that we will all make." Jocelyn's arm was around Emma but she leaned toward Ethan, clearly including him as she spoke. "This is a really big decision. If you need some time, we'll understand."

"Where would we move to?" Ethan asked, looking up at Mark.

"I don't know. We'd have to look for a place that we all liked. It wouldn't just be something that you and I like, Ethan. It would have to be a house that not only we liked but Jocelyn and Emma liked also. That's part of being married, being a family, everyone has a say."

"So Emma would stay with us?" Ethan's brows scrunched.

"Emma and Jocelyn and you and I would be a family." Mark said, rubbing Ethan's shoulders. "It would be different than just us two. There'd be four of us, all living together, figuring things out."

"But Em would be with us?"

"Are you worried that Emma would be left alone? That something bad could happen to her?" Mark asked the questions he figured Ethan struggled with.

Ethan nodded. "And you could fix her." He looked up at Mark, determination written on his face.

Mark turned toward Jocelyn and Emma. "It would be easier to do if we were a family but I'd fix Em whether we were or not." His arm around Ethan, he leaned in Emma's direction. "What do you have to say about this, Miss Em. Do you want to be a family with Ethan and me?"

Jocelyn dared not move. She wanted, no needed, the answer to be totally 100 percent Emma's. Tears welled but she blinked them back when Emma nodded. "And I want to call you Papa."

"Ethan?" Mark tipped his son's head up and held his gaze. "What's your answer?"

"Em is my bestest friend, Papa. I can share. I'm a good sharer. And you'll fix Em and she'll be able to run if the bad man comes." Ethan looked at Emma. "Are you gonna share your mama with me?"

No pause, no hesitation, a definite nod and a quiet "Uh-huh."

"Shall we stop by Grandpapa and Grandmama's and tell them our news?" Mark asked as they stood and started back to the car.

"Yes!" was the eager chorus.

"And we'll let Lily and Jackson know we're bringing take-out?" Mark held Jocelyn's hand as they returned to the car.

"When we left to pick you up, Jackson had a big pot of spaghetti on the stove," Jocelyn told Mark. "We could do take-out but I think he planned on all of us for dinner. Maybe tomorrow we can do hamburgers or something?"

"Excellent idea." Mark held the passenger door open for Jocelyn. He wrapped an arm around her waist and whispered in her ear, "That went well." She nodded and as she got in, looked up at him and smiled.

The children were in their car seats. Mark slipped behind the wheel. As he started to pull out of his parking slot, he paused, took Jocelyn's hand in his and said "It's official."

CHAPTER 30

That weekend, Mark was on call. He'd lined up some houses to check out—at least driving by. One had an 'open house' sign so they all clamored out of the car and went inside. Large, spacious great room, good-sized bedrooms, everything updated with new appliances. The trend was granite countertops and Jocelyn was not a fan. Nor did she like the marble in the bathrooms.

"Too big," she pronounced as they piled back in the car and drove away.

"Did you like the configuration? The open concept? What about the yard?" Mark asked.

"It didn't feel right," Jocelyn replied. She shook her head to dispel the clear vision of the lawn with the old oak, a swing from a gnarled branch.

Looking out the passenger-side window she saw an old craftsman-style home. Her guess was it was built in the 1920's. The front lawn had a For Sale sign.

"Let's look at this one." Jocelyn said. Something about the house called to her.

Mark pulled up to the curb and everyone got out. As they started up the walkway, a car drove into the driveway and an older man got out.

"Can I help you?"

Jocelyn smiled. "We saw the sign and wanted to take a look."

Mark stepped forward, his hand outstretched. "Hi, I'm Mark Parker. My fiancé, Jocelyn and our kids, Ethan and Emma. We're getting married soon and are looking for a home that will fit all of us."

"I'm Collin Perth." He shifted the sack of groceries to shake Mark's hand. "Open House is tomorrow but since you're here, I'll let you take a look around."

"We really appreciate it Mr. Perth," Jocelyn smiled and reached out to take the sack of groceries from him. "Have you lived here long?"

"My wife and I bought it and raised our boys here. Too much for me to keep up any more." He unlocked the front door and gestured them inside. "Sadie, I'm back," he called out at the bottom of the stairs. "Brought a family who wants to take a look around." He turned to Mark. "My wife is bedbound so I'd appreciate it if you'd give her her privacy."

Mark ushered Ethan and Emma further inside, his hands holding theirs. "That's not a problem, Mr. Perth. We're grateful you're accommodating us as it is."

Mr. Perth nodded. "The only change we've made is we took down the wall between the formal dining room and kitchen and added decking out back. Everything is original, even the hardwood floors."

"I can see you love this place." Jocelyn waved a hand to include the large living room with a fireplace, built in bookcases with glass doors on either side. Mark had already guided the children across the room and all were looking out the windows into the backyard.

"Swing, Papa, can we swing?" Ethan bounced in place.

Mr. Perth smiled. "Go on ahead. French doors from the kitchen to the deck and stairs down to the yard."

Jocelyn, who still had the groceries, followed Mr. Perth into the kitchen. Her breath caught in her chest. It was perfect. Limestone counters, beautiful cabinetry but new appliances. The patina on the old oak floors glowed a dark gold. The walls were painted a sky blue and white curtains framed the windows over the sink and along the back wall.

And out those back windows? Mark strode across a large lawn, Emma on his shoulders while Ethan ran ahead toward a large, gnarled, old oak tree with a swing hanging from one branch.

Her vision. Jocelyn's hand fluttered to her lips, tears welled in her eyes. This place was what she'd dreamed of, what kept her sane in the insanity of her life with Tony. It wasn't that far from Mark's parents—maybe fifteen minutes or so. She could still go over and help out when they needed it. And unlike the other place they'd seen, this one didn't feel too big. It felt just right.

"How many bedrooms and bathrooms?" Her voice shook and her hands trembled as she took items from the grocery sack.

"We had a large pantry turned into a half-bath for this floor. Upstairs are four bedrooms and two bathrooms. The downstairs is finished. A large open space and two smaller rooms. When our boys were here, that was where the kids all gathered. Don't use it much at all these days. Stairs are hard for these old knees." Mr. Perth answered.

"Where do you want these items," Jocelyn pointed to the non-perishables.

"Just leave them on the counter. You go on out with your fella and see the yard. It's not much to look at right now but in the spring... ." His voice trailed off.

"I imagine those rhododendron and azaleas are spectacular." She saw how it would be, the riot of colors in her mind's eye.

He nodded and Jocelyn saw a touch of wetness in his eyes.

"Do you have any offers?" she asked, her heart in her throat.

"First Open House is tomorrow." Did she imagine his voice shook a bit?

Jocelyn turned and looked directly at Mr. Perth. "I don't know anything about real estate so I may be overstepping when I ask you this."

"Just say it."

Heart beating so loud Mr. Perth should have been able to hear it. "I don't know what Mark will say but I love this place and if he does also, can we make you an offer? Is that legal?"

"You see what your fella says and then we'll talk."

Jocelyn walked out onto the deck and when she stood at the top of the stairs leading down to the yard, the scene before her was almost an exact match to her vision. The differences? She clearly saw that the man was Mark and Ethan was also there. No blond or dark-haired child by her side. But maybe…maybe if they lived here she would heal enough that there would be.

Nerves skittered through her and she wavered as if a strong wind hit her. Taking her courage in hand, she waved from the deck. Mark and the children started toward her as she descended the steps.

"You are radiant," he said and slipped an arm around her shoulders.

She tipped up her head to see his face. "Tomorrow is the first open house. There are no offers." Without thinking, her arm reached around his waist as they strolled to the house.

"You like it?" He was watching the kids already at the bottom of the stairs as he waited for her answer.

"I love it. It feels like home. I've seen this yard in dreams and visions for so long. Just exactly this yard with the tree and swing." She stopped and he did also. Shifting to stand in front of him, her heart thumped wildly and her hands were damp. Jocelyn swallowed the lump of fear but her voice still shook. "In my dream there was a man and Emma was on the swing. A dark haired child was standing next to me."

Mark's chocolate brown gaze never wavered. "Let's talk to Mr. Perth and see what we can work out."

Relief was so intense she faltered. "Just like that?"

He smiled down into her upturned face and kissed her nose. "Just like that."

They'd started up the stairs and had reached the top when Mark's pager went off. He looked at the call and muttered something about timing.

"Mr. Perth, I just got paged. I've fifteen minutes to get to the hospital."

"Doctor then?"

Mark nodded. "We're very interested in this house but I can't stop and talk more right now."

"I can't stop the Open House tomorrow, but I can decline any offers until I hear back from you."

"I'll call this afternoon if I may." Mark held himself still for the few seconds it took Mr. Perth to nod.

"Here's my number." Mr. Perth handed Mark a scrap of paper just as a bell rang in the distance. "That's my Sadie. Just close the door when you go out."

Jocelyn was already herding the kids to the door and knowing the drill, in record time children were secured in car seats and they were headed to the hospital. "I'll call you when I'm ready and you can come get me. Here are the keys to the condo. It's closer. Food in refridge—."

Jocelyn stopped him with a finger pressed to his lips. "We'll be fine. Call when you're ready and we'll come and get you. Right?" She glanced in the back seat.

A chorus of "yes" erupted.

Mark kissed her cheek before dashing off.

She waited for outrage or fear or something to overwhelm her. Instead a warm sensation slid over her. A small smile tipped her lips as she got in the driver's seat.

Her prayers seemed to be coming true.

The Universe was watching over, guiding and protecting her. And maybe it always had been. In her heart she knew Emma would be dead if she hadn't come into her life. All the pain she suffered at Tony's hands was the price she'd gladly paid in order for this precious little girl to live and find joy and happiness.

Maybe she could heal and have a full marriage with Mark. She did like him, also trusted him, which was no mean feat. He was kind, gentle, honorable. A bit stubborn but then she had her moments too. In her innermost core, her soul, she knew if they could purchase the old craftsman, she could make it a real home.

Her mind on the future, she drove right past the street to Mark's condo. Ethan's "You missed it" along with Emma's "Mama" brought her back to the present. She drove around a few blocks and made a game of it, asking at every intersection "Do I turn here?"

Of course moving again would mean teaching Emma and maybe even Ethan about their new surroundings. If Emma ever got lost or, heaven forbid, kidnapped, she had drilled her daughter as to where to go and what to say when she got away or was found.

Those thoughts put a damper on the happy thoughts so she pushed them all aside as they went through the condo's front door. Thankfully Ethan knew the security code and also reminded her that the fob on the key ring turned it off.

So much to learn. So many changes. So much hope.

CHAPTER 31

Once he'd taken care of the emergency, Mark called and talked to Collin Perth and arranged to return with only Jocelyn so they could see the rest of the house. As they started up the walk, he took Jocelyn's hand.

Collin met them at the door, welcomed them both with handshakes and led them into the formal living room.

"Now my Sadie is in her room so that's off limits but you can look around upstairs. I'll tell you there is a bathroom off that room. Used to be five bedrooms up there but we took the smaller nursery room next to our room and turned it into a bathroom once the boys were older."

"I don't mean to be nosy but I do wonder why you and Mrs. Perth are selling?" Jocelyn's grip on Mark's hand tightened.

"My Sadie needs more care than I can really give her. My old knees just can't keep up with the number of trips up and down the stairs."

"So if there was a way for Mrs. Perth to have the care she needs here, you'd want to stay?" Mark asked.

Mr. Perth's eyes shimmered with tears. "Our sons think it's best to move."

Jocelyn let go of Mark and took the two steps to stand closer to the older man. Her hand on his arm, her voice gentle she continued. "Mr. Perth, if there was a way to take care of your Sadie and stay in this house, would that be your preference?"

He nodded. A heartfelt sigh escaped. "That's not possible. I can't do the stairs."

"But I can. Or, Mrs. Perth can be moved to this floor. The living room is large and has a magnificent view of the back yard and the mountains in the distance. Instead of moving out of this house that you both love, she could be here." Jocelyn gestured to the open pocket doors leading to the room.

"I know I'm most likely out-of-bounds here but as much as I love this house and hope we can purchase it, it breaks my heart to think of you and your Sadie living elsewhere."

Mr. Perth turned away. "Take another look around," he said, his voice quivered and he brushed a hand across his face.

Jocelyn started up the stairs. A few steps up she turned, an expectant look on her face. Mark motioned her to go on and mouthed "I'll be along."

"Has Mrs. Perth's doctor told you her prognosis?" Mark stood to the side and a half-step behind. His hand rested on Mr. Perth's shoulder.

"She's going on Hospice when we move, so not long."

"You do know she can be on Hospice right here."

"Son, I want what's best for my Sadie. We've been married for seventy years. Have had our ups and downs but never anything serious. I can't wrap my brain around the reality she won't be with me for much longer."

"Jocelyn and I, well, as much as we already love this place and can see ourselves living here, we both think you and Sadie need to stay here.

"The living room could easily be transformed into a bedroom or the downstairs could become your private quarters. The main room set up with a hospital bed. There's a bedroom down there also but the view to the yard and beyond is best from the main room."

"My Sadie can't walk, how…?"

"How were you going to move her to a new place?"

"Medical transport."

"They can just as easily move her to the downstairs as move her to another place. Especially if all is in readiness, it will be a much easier move for her. I can help you order a hospital bed and whatever other supplies you may need."

"I thought you wanted to buy this place," Mr. Perth argued.

"We do want to buy this place but we also want what's best for you and your wife. If her final days are happier, more peaceful because she's in her own home, that's more important to us," Mark said in his professional tone. "Talk to her and see what she says. Jocelyn and I'll look around a bit more and will check in with you before we leave."

Jocelyn descended the stairs, a smile on her face. "Did your sons enjoy this?" she asked Mr. Perth, her hand sliding down the banister.

"That they did." He grinned.

Jocelyn stood on the bottom step, a soft smile on her face. "You've kept this house immaculate."

"Cleaning service the last few years."

She took the final step to the floor. "A good one by the looks of it."

Mark took Jocelyn's hand. "We're going to look around a bit more while Collin talks to Sadie about your idea."

Jocelyn nodded but her brow wrinkled in question.

They strolled through the house to the breakfast nook attached to the kitchen and the door leading to the back deck. Outside they stood next to each other and leaned on the railing. "What idea?"

"The one about moving Sadie to the living room. I also embellished that plan with them moving downstairs." His gripped tightened a fraction as he leaned toward her. "They've been married seventy years."

"I didn't know that." Jocelyn's mind whirred. Seventy years and still devoted. And Peter and Peggy Parker who, while not anywhere close to seventy years, were at least near forty years. Maybe?

Mark was still talking. "Excuse me," she said, "my mind wandered."

"And she's to be admitted to Hospice."

Jocelyn looked up at Mark, looked up into his chocolate brown eyes and saw what? Saw him waiting for her to say something. "Can't she be on Hospice here?"

"Of course she can." Mark shifted closer, draped his arm around her shoulders and kissed her temple. "I've got a crazy idea."

She leaned into him. "I'm listening."

"What if we offer to purchase the house with the stipulation that the Perth's can continue to live here. I think the best plan is for them to take over the downstairs. While it is a wonderful space and will be a natural hangout when the kids are older, we can live without it now.

"It would mean you'd have cooking for them added. Well, maybe not. I'm... ."

"Are you assuming I'd become a housewife and cook and clean and do laundry all day?" She laughed and patted his cheek.

"What I mean is we'll make sure they have their meals. There is already a small refrigerator down there that can easily keep medications, juice, etc. Easy to add a microwave, maybe even a larger fridge, electric tea kettle. You know, whatever they might need.

"We'd talk to the Hospice people, her doctor, etc. and get everything set up for them downstairs and then have her moved. Maybe on her moving day, we'd move some things in also."

"What about the children?" Jocelyn asked, thinking ahead to how to make it all work.

"Something to talk about with them. We'd have these two floors. Maybe one of the bedrooms upstairs could be the play area. There is access to the backyard from this level so we wouldn't need to go downstairs." He turned to her, brought her hand to his lips and kissed her knuckles. "Your face glows with love for this place. I can hear it in the tone of your voice and saw it in the way you touch the banister. I've never seen you as relaxed as you are right now and I've got an arm around your shoulders, I'm standing close to you and have even kissed you."

Jocelyn tipped her head up and kissed his jaw. "Yes, you did and now I've kissed you." She leaned and rested her head on his shoulder. "I don't know what it is about this place that calls to me. It looks just like this recurring vision I've had for several years."

He rubbed a hand up and down her arm. "When did it start?"

She was quiet for several minutes. Mark let the time pass, enjoyed the feel of her so close, breathed in her clean scent. Smiled at the knowledge that neither of them used fragrance-infused products. The more he was around her, the more perfect she fit and the more he wanted her in his life and in his bed.

"The earliest I can remember is after I met Tony. I'm not sure if it was the first time he hit me or later, but I used to curl up with Emma and I'd see the green lawn, the tree and swing. When I was in that vision, I felt safe."

A throat cleared behind them. As one they turned to see Mr. Perth, a smile on his face. "My Sadie would like to meet you."

MARK HELD the passenger door open and Jocelyn slid onto the leather seats. She watched as he paced round the hood of the car and noted the serious look on his face when he got in. Her stomach tightened but then she saw his eyes dancing with merriment.

"You look very happy with yourself."

"I am and I know you are also. They'll still have the open house, we'll still go through the realtor because she's a longtime friend of the family, but we've got the house."

Inside Jocelyn wanted to fist pump like Emma and Ethan. Outside she wanted reassurance this was happening. "And you're sure the contract or whatever it is that allows them to stay in the house as long as they want is a good idea?"

"Don't you? It was your idea to begin with."

Jocelyn's heart beat so fast, she put a hand on her chest. Looking out the passenger window, her head slowly shook. "Reality is setting in. A part of me, a very large part, cannot believe I will be living in this home," she said in a whispery voice.

"In two weeks we'll be living there. Monday I'll help Collin get things set up to move Sadie downstairs. We'll order the bed and whatever else is needed, make arrangements for moving her, etc. Give them a few days in the new space before we invade."

"You mean before we move in. We... ." Her breath caught in her throat when he reached out and squeezed her hand, leaned over and kissed her cheek.

"We'll be just fine. This is a 'win-win' for everyone."

Her gaze sought his dark brown eyes, connected and held. "You forget they have three sons who might object to their parents being relegated to the 'basement.'" She quoted the last word with her fingers.

Mark started the car and pulled away from the curb. "They might object but I don't think too strenuously. They are, of course, welcome to check us out. You do remember Collin saying that each of their sons had offered to move them closer to them but they'd refused. This is their home and this is where they want to live. That part of the conversation has already been conducted."

"And they'll know they have a doctor in the house." Jocelyn smiled and added "an orthopod but an MD nonetheless."

"And they'll know there is a loving, kind, caring woman also available to support their parents through this time."

Jocelyn held Mark's hand, her fingers tightening as she talked. "I expect they'll want to be here when Sadie is closer to dying." She paused. "I really like her. She's so sweet and yet strong. Kind and caring but tough. The way they look at each other as if no one else in the world matters." She sighed.

"Maybe we'll look at each other like that when we've been married seventy years," Mark quipped.

"You are dreaming. I've no plans or inclinations to live so far over 100. Really, Mark, do you?" Puzzled by her response to this conversation, Jocelyn looked out the window. She was joking with Mark, she was relaxed and, a sharp intake of breath cemented the feeling. She was happy.

Before she could find words to express her feelings other than the mundane word 'happy', they pulled into the senior Parker's driveway. They'd been gone ninety minutes and she imagined Peggy and Peter Parker were counting the seconds until they returned.

Mark escorted her, hand on elbow, to the door and with a single knock, opened it and guided her in. He was proprietary at times but not in a way that frightened. *He listens to you.*

"We're here," Mark called out.

Jocelyn listened for the pounding of little feet charging towards them but heard nothing. She glanced at Mark, her brow quirked in question.

He strode across the living room and looked out on to the deck and into the yard. No one was there.

"Where is everyone?" Jocelyn's worry meter notched up.

"Come with me. I think I know." He flashed his devilish grin and grabbed her hand.

Jocelyn followed him through the kitchen to the stairs leading to the lower level. Flickering lights came from a smaller room off the main one. No sound?

When they stopped at the door and looked in, there everyone was —head phones on, watching a movie on the big screen t.v. Emma was sitting with Peter and Ethan with his grandmama.

They backed out of the room recognizing, because this movie was a favorite, that there were only a few minutes left. Sitting together on the couch in the main room, they waited until they heard voices.

"We're here." Mark called out.

Mere moments later two small bodies hurtled through the air and landed on them. Jocelyn wrapped her arms around Ethan who'd ended up in her lap. A quick check confirmed that Emma was happily snuggled with Mark.

"So what's the news?" Peter asked, his arm around Peggy who obviously leaned on him.

"We got the place." Mark announced.

Both Emma and Ethan fist pumped then jumped down and did a happy dance.

After a minute or so, Jocelyn quietly said, "There's more. Do you want to talk about it here or," she looked over at Peggy, "is it better to go upstairs."

Peter guided Peggy over to the loveseat across from the couch.

"Our offer has been accepted. There are still some tasks that need to be done because—," She paused, wiped her hands on her skirt and looked at Mark who nodded.

"Well, we've offered to have the Perth's remain in the house," she rushed on. "Mrs. Perth will be on Hospice in a day or so and they've lived in this house most of their seventy-year marriage."

Mark picked up and added, "They'll have the lower floor. We'll help them get that set up for Mrs. Perth and also help Mr. Perth move his belongings down there. The plan is we'll have the top two floors until such time as we don't."

"Can she be my grandmama," Emma asked. "Ethan has a Grandmama and a Grandpapa. I want one too."

"I can't promise that, Emma. That's something that can take time and I don't know how much time Mrs. Perth, Sadie, has until she dies. She's very sick now and will not get better."

"She'll need lots of love then." Emma nodded at the rightness of her statement. "I can make her pretty cards and I could even tell her stories."

Joy bubbled up and Jocelyn smiled at her daughter. "You make the very best pretty cards. I still have every one you ever made for me."

Peter's frown had not diminished. "Are you sure this is wise?"

"I'm not sure how wise it is but we know," he reached over and held Jocelyn's hand, "it is the right thing to do. I'd be surprised if Sadie lasts six months and I don't think Collin will remain with us much longer after she's gone.

"We get a fantastic house at a great price. We can keep as many of the furnishings as we want. Emma may end up with her own grandmama and grandpapa. We can move in in two weeks, which leaves us enough time to pack."

Jocelyn picked up the thread. "Mark had been approached by a neighbor who said if he ever wanted to sell, to let him know because he had a friend who would love to live in that complex. So that's taken care of—pretty much anyway."

"They've even said Jocelyn and I can get married there. If the day is warm enough we'll be outside under the oak tree. If it isn't? The fireplace in the living room is magnificent and a perfect setting."

"Well, you've lots to do then," Peggy said, sounding perkier than Jocelyn had ever seen her. "Do you need help planning the wedding?" Peggy's look was hopeful.

Nerves singing, Jocelyn hold on Mark's hand tightened. "I'd certainly appreciate your help. It won't be a big wedding. Mark would invite his partners and their wives. I'd invite the Montgomery's and maybe the Kenner's. At the top of the list are the two of you."

"If we marry before we move Sadie downstairs, the children could all be down there and watching a movie or something. Once she moves down there, we'll turn one of the upstairs bedrooms into a play area." Mark turned to her, his brow raised, inviting her to participate.

"The wall between the formal dining room and kitchen was removed so there is plenty of open space to create a play area there is we want to. We've options and will have time to figure out what works best." She smiled at the thought of being a stay-at-home mom, taking care of two children, supporting the Perths.

Jocelyn waited for nerves, for the sense of being "less." She waited in vain. She'd make sure the Perth's had whatever they needed, keep the house up, do all the housewife tasks she never thought she'd want to do. She would scrub bathrooms, keep floors up, dust, laundry, vacuum, cook—straightening her shoulders, she gritted her teeth. Whatever it took, she'd willingly pay the price to live in her dream house, to be safe and most important, to keep Emma safe.

In the relative scheme of things, it wasn't really such a high price —was it?

CHAPTER 32

Exhausted, Mark made his way to his car in the office parking lot. Too many bone-crushing accidents where his expertise was needed. He shook his head, clearing the images. In his car, he settled into the seat with his briefcase on the passenger side floor. He rubbed the back of his neck to stave off the first signs of a headache. It didn't seem to help.

The demands of his work wasn't the problem. Getting married tomorrow and no ring was. His original plan had been to take Jocelyn to pick out one but every time they'd set something up, he was called in. The life of a doctor had perks but also a downside.

No ring but everything else was in order. Jocelyn had made all the arrangements, with the help of his mom and Lily, for a simple wedding. Lily had gone dress shopping with her. He smiled as the image of Emma, so happy she was walking on air, flitted through his mind. His smile widened to a grin remembering how very tight-lipped she was about the dresses she and her mama would be wearing. Had he properly thanked his dad for making sure Ethan still fit in the suit he'd worn for Lily's wedding?

Instead of planning two weddings dependent on the weather, it was Oregon in the fall after all, they decided to have the ceremony in the living room in front of the fireplace. His mom was in her element taking charge of the flowers and cake. His worry that it would be too much for her was quickly set aside. His mom liked Jocelyn and was already in love with Emma, as was his dad.

He started the car. Tonight Ethan and Emma were spending the night at his parents' house. The idea was that he and Jocelyn could have a little more time to themselves. He wasn't sure what would happen. They were getting along well. She no longer tensed if he kissed her temple or cheek, put his arm around her shoulder or just held her.

If he had to, he could remain celibate. Ethan was worth more than sexual pleasure or just physical release. Shoulders tensed, fists clenched every time he thought of what Jocelyn had endured, had survived during the time she was with that rat-bastard. He'd never really considered hitting someone, he had surgeon hands, but Tony? The satisfaction of hearing bones crunch, seeing blood coming out the bastard's nose, lips split? He could almost make a case for taking a swing or two.

It was dark early this time of the year. Where could he go to get a ring? What was her size?

His car still in park, Mark pulled his cell phone out and called. She answered on the second ring and the background noise signaled bedlam did not reign.

"What are you doing?" He heard the tension, the impatience in his voice.

"I'm about to fix dinner." Jocelyn's tone was cool.

"Have you started?" He rubbed his neck, pressing the points that could alleviate the headache.

"Almost. Why?" He heard the hesitancy in her voice.

"Do me a favor and stop. I'll pick you up in ten. I've something important to talk to you about. We'll stop and pick something up to feed everyone."

"What do we need to talk about?"

Not hesitation, confusion. Was that good or bad? He didn't take the time to figure it out. "Trust me on this, Jocelyn. I'm on my way."

He backed out of his slot and headed towards his parents' house. "You'll need a coat, it's chilly out," he said into his Bluetooth headset.

"I'm wearing a sweatshirt."

"I don't know if it will be enough." He paused. "Scratch that. You'll be fine. I'll be there in less than five."

"Okay, I'll look for you. Just honk and we'll come out."

He held back the sigh that threatened to erupt from his throat. "Okay, I'm about four blocks away."

Mark pulled into the driveway and beeped his horn—toot, toot, toot—toot. By the time he tapped the final sound, the front door was opening and Ethan, Emma and Jocelyn stepped out.

He put the car in park and set the emergency brake but left it running because it was chilly out.

Getting the children settled in their car seats took less than two minutes. They had it down to a routine.

Fifteen minutes later, he pulled into the closest mall and everyone piled out. He took Jocelyn's hand and Emma's while Ethan grabbed Jocelyn's free one. Inside the Mall, he gravitated to the map. Scanning he located the closest jewelry store and headed that way.

As they approached, he saw the employee begin to pull the guard down. They were closing. "Just a minute," Mark called out and quickened his pace. Emma couldn't keep up so he reached down, swung her up and perched her on his hip as he strode to the shop.

"We're closed," the clerk said pulling the guard down a few inches.

"I know we're cutting it really close." Mark said, plastering a smile on his face.

The clerk nodded and pulled the guard down another few inches.

"You see, we're getting married tomorrow and things have been a bit hectic and we need a ring."

Mark turned to Jocelyn. "This isn't how I wanted this to go—."

"A simple ring. A plain gold band is perfect. We won't really take up much of your time. We'd be ever so grateful for whatever you can do for us." Jocelyn smiled and Mark relaxed when he saw the clerk's hesitation.

"Mama," Emma and Ethan chorused. "Look here!"

The clerk glanced around to see both children had slipped through and were now peering into a case of rings.

"Step in so I can close the guard," the clerk grumbled.

Strolling over to the case as the clerk secured the space, Mark saw the children were gazing in awe at diamond rings.

Jocelyn pulled away from him. "Not those rings," she said and moved one case over where the plain gold bands were. "One of these."

"Nuh-uh," Ethan shook his head. "One of these. This one." He pointed at the diamond rings but Mark couldn't discern which one had caught his eye.

"Ethan, a fancy ring like that isn't a good choice when I'll be cleaning house and keeping up the yard."

Ethan's chin set in its stubborn line.

The clerk was behind the case now. "Which ring did you like?" He was talking to Ethan.

"Since it's my ring, I think you need to be asking me." Jocelyn pointed to her chest.

"Of course," the clerk opened the case and took out the tray of gold bands. He also took out the tray that Ethan had pointed to.

Emma now stood beside Ethan. "I like this one." She held her finger over a simple solitaire diamond.

"This one is prettier." Ethan pointed to another ring that had an emerald solitaire surrounded by diamonds. "This one is like Mama's eyes when she's happy."

Jocelyn's lungs seized and tears welled hearing Ethan claim her as his mama. She held on to the counter, letting the plain gold band she had tried on fall back on the tray.

Mark picked up the ring Ethan had picked out and took her hand. "Let's just see how this fits."

She started to argue. He nodded toward Ethan and Emma who looked on with rapt interest. He noted when she capitulated and heard her sigh as he slipped the ring on. A perfect fit.

"It's too... ."

"It looks like it belongs on her hand." Mark held her hand in his, her fingers curving to show the ring at its best advantage.

"Ooooh, Mama, it's soo beautiful," Emma sighed, her hands clasped as in prayer.

"Yep, it looks just right," Ethan declared with a fist pump.

"It's too expensive." Jocelyn's voice was soft and dreamy, her eyes focused on the ring.

"I think it's just the right price." Mark pulled out his wallet and extracted a credit card. He might have to transfer some funds from savings to cover the cost but he wasn't going to worry about that right now. Seeing the look on Jocelyn's face as well as Ethan and Emma's made the price of the ring immaterial. "We'll take it."

"It also comes in a set, including a ring for the groom," the clerk said now in full-sales-clerk-mode. He showed them how it looked as an engagement ring and then as an engagement ring with wedding band. The addition of the ring of emeralds and diamonds made precisely to fit on either side of the diamond encircled emerald solitaire was stunning.

"I-I-I can't accept... ." Jocelyn pulled her hand from his and started to take the rings off.

He captured her hands, held them in a loose grip and leaning close whispered "Yes, you can. You deserve something beautiful and we can afford it."

"But they'll get damaged." Her soft voice trembled, the struggle evident in her gaze that sought his.

"No they won't." Mark slipped his arm around her shoulders. "What do you have to protect them?"

"We have ring holders, ring boxes and one of our most popular choices is a simple chain that can be worn around the neck." The clerk gestured to the holders and boxes on a shelf behind him but held up a simple gold chain with a large lobster-style clasp on the end. "It's very simple." He demonstrated with another ring how easily it could be secured.

"What do you think?" He tipped Jocelyn's face up and saw the indecision etched in the worried look in her eyes, the wrinkled forehead and pursed lips.

Jocelyn worried her bottom lip with her teeth. The rings were weightless as if made of gossamer instead of gold, emeralds and diamonds. How could she justify the expense? She couldn't. She shook her head, opened her mouth to refuse when the faces of Ethan and Emma registered. Mouths slightly open in anticipation, they were holding themselves so still they vibrated.

Mark still held her hand but had also slipped his other arm around her shoulders. Cocooning her in his embrace. Her body warmed from his touch. His clean scent comforted.

"I don't deserve…," she whispered.

His breath tickled her ear. "Not good enough."

"The-the-they're so expensive," she stammered looking up at him.

He kissed her temple. "We can afford it."

"But…."

He turned her toward him, his chocolate gaze intense. A gentle shake. "These rings were made for you. And the set comes with a ring for me that also is a perfect fit. And, having Ethan and Emma pick them out? What more of an omen do you need. These are the right rings."

She nodded. Surprised at how bereft she felt when she took the rings off and handed them to the clerk.

He rang things up and handed Mark the small bag with the ring box along with another one for the safety chain.

Back in the car, Mark called in an order of Hawaiian pizza—a large family size.

Dinner over, Jocelyn loaded the dishwasher and cleaned up the kitchen, while Peggy and Peter supervised bath time and bedtime stories.

A final swipe of the kitchen counter, she hung the dishcloth on the faucet and turned. Mark leaned against the kitchen island, his hand held out to her. Jitters. She had jitters. Not flutters like in butterflies but jitters like in Mexican Jumping Beans. This time tomorrow, they'd be married and spending the night alone at his condo.

"Come," he wrapped his hand around hers and guided her into the living room. Illumination from the hall and a street light gave the room enough ambient light with which to see.

Resting his forehead against hers, he held both of her hands in his. "Thank you for saying "yes" to both my proposal of marriage and this." He lifted his head to gaze in her hazel eyes and as he slipped the emerald and diamond solitaire ring on her finger said, "I promise to—."

She brushed her free hand across his lips to silence the rest of his words. How could she accept promises from him when she wouldn't truly be his wife? Her stomach rebelled and she fought down the surge of bile at the thought of being intimate.

A ray of light caught the diamonds, rainbows sparkled. Her attention drawn to her hand still in his. She no longer flinched at his touch, no longer froze when he was near. Maybe…she shut off that line of thinking. That way lay madness and a whole ream of "what ifs."

CHAPTER 33

Jocelyn and Emma were met by Mr. Perth at the bottom of the stairs of the old Craftsman house. He gave her a hug before escorting her to where Mark and Ethan waited. Lily and Jackson, Peggy and Peter and Mark's partners and their wives settled on chairs set in a semi-circle. Anne, Mark's receptionist, video camera in hand, documented the ceremony. Even though this was a hobby of hers, Anne made sure she had formal and candid shots of the wedding party, the cake and decorations including the bouquets of white and green carnations.

The wedding cake was three tiers. The top layer was a carrot cake, Mark's favorite. Next was Jocelyn's layer. A spice cake with a light cinnamon flavored filling and icing. The bottom layer was a chocolate/vanilla marbled cake with vanilla pudding filling and chocolate icing, Emma and Ethan's favorites.

Champagne punch for the adults, the same punch without the alcohol for the children. Ethan and Emma were on their best behavior, usually holding hands, and never very far from one another.

Jocelyn noticed when the children went off with Anne. Just when she was getting nervous, they reappeared. Anne put her finger to her lips and made the zipping motion. Emma and Ethan beamed and copied her.

Mark had filled her in on the wives of his partners who were educated, professional women; one a nurse and one an attorney. How could she compete with these women? She'd finished high school and had started that Certificate program but—. Her stomach clenched and nerves fizzed under her skin. She was so out of her element.

The few things she and Emma had were already moved into a bedroom upstairs. It would be Emma's room. Ethan's was just across the hall. She wouldn't be surprised if they snuck into each other's rooms at night. Worries about Emma's adjustments roiled through her and she stopped eating before she got sick.

"What's wrong?" Mark leaned over and whispered in her ear.

"Nothing."

He laughed and his breath feathered across her cheek. "Of course there is. But if this isn't the right place to talk, I can appreciate that. After all, it is our wedding day."

Jocelyn's chest tightened, her breathing shallow and her hands clammy. She focused on the positives of this day. Ethan safe. And Emma? Marriage to Mark was another layer of protection.

She gripped the stem of her champagne glass as feelings of being unworthy overwhelmed. She gripped Mark's hand trying to find her equilibrium. The feelings—they all circled back to fear of not being good enough. She fought against the litany playing through her mind.

Cool air tickled her senses. She was standing by the front door, Mark still holding her hand. She nodded and shook hands, smiled and hoped the few words she spoke to Mark's partners and their wives were good enough that she didn't embarrass him.

Peter and Peggy and Lily and Jackson were the last to leave. Emma and Ethan were bundled up in warm jackets, small backpacks dragging beside them. "We'll take good care of these two," Peter said, shaking Mark's hand and giving him a quick hug. "An official welcome to the family," Peter said as he hugged her. "We're delighted."

Tears welled as Peggy followed Peter. "Life as a doctor's wife can be a challenge. Always know you can come talk to me. I promise I'll understand and only give advice if you ask for it."

Mark laughed. "Mom means it now when she says it but be prepared that she might slip a time or two."

"I'm ignoring you." Peggy blew Mark a kiss and took Emma and Ethan by the hand. "Let's go you two. We've places to go and things to do."

"And people to see?" Ethan asked as they headed out the door.

"I think we've already done the people to see part," Peter answered, transferring Ethan's hand to his and taking Peggy's arm as they went down the steps.

Jocelyn blew Emma a kiss when the little girl turned to look back at her. Peggy leaned down and said something. Emma nodded. Ethan switched from holding Peter's hand and came around to Emma's side. He said something and she latched on to him. In another few steps they were out of sight.

"You do know she'll be okay." Lily's voice brought her back to the foyer.

"I-I-I. It's hard for me to stay in trust." Jocelyn breathed deep to stop the tears.

"But you are moving forward," Lily said, her hand on Jocelyn's arm.

"I'm a work-in-progress," Jocelyn said, her voice soft.

Lily laughed and wrapped her in a fierce hug. "We all are. Even when we don't look like it, it's still true." She stepped back but kept hold of Jocelyn's hands. "There are still times I pinch myself, expecting to wake up from this dream. A year ago I'd just met Jackson and was—."

"She was smitten." Jackson said slinging an arm around Lily's shoulders.

She arched a brow and shook her head.

"Intrigued?"

And Jocelyn knew this was a game they played. Her part? "And what about you, Jackson. Were you smitten when you first met Lily?"

Lily chortled. "He thought I was scamming his mother."

A bashful look on his face, Jackson nodded. "I did at that."

Mark slipped his arm around Jocelyn's waist. "He was even jealous of me for—."

Jackson snorted. "As if—."

"On that happy note," Lily grinned. "We'll be going. We're off to Ireland in the morning to see Elizabeth."

"That's right, you're spending Samhain with her," Jocelyn said and smiled.

They stood in the doorway, Mark's arm around her waist, her head resting on his shoulder as the Montgomerys left.

Closing the door, they turned to see Mr. Perth waiting.

"Everything is set up for the day after tomorrow. We'll be out of—," he said, gesturing toward the living room.

"You'll be settled downstairs and we'll be settling in upstairs." Jocelyn reached out and laid her hand on his arm. "We'll be back tomorrow."

"Most likely early afternoon." Mark added. "Is there anything you need before we go?"

Mr. Perth shook his head. "My Sadie and I are just fine."

He started to say more but Mark reached out and shook his hand. "We'll see you tomorrow then."

Grabbing her coat from the rack by the door, Mark slipped it around her shoulders. His hand at her elbow, they walked out into the night.

CHAPTER 34

Her skin buzzed as nerves danced through her body. Jocelyn fought the surge of bile that threatened. She was married and her wedding night awaited. Could she do it? Could she consummate her marriage to Mark? She glanced at him out of the corner of her eye. He looked relaxed, one hand draped over the steering wheel as he maneuvered the car into the driveway of his condo.

Business like, almost brusque, he escorted her to the door and inside. Switching on the lights, he took her coat and hung it on the hall tree, doing the same with his jacket.

The concern in his eyes when he turned back and faced her punched her in the stomach. How could she turn him away? He was her husband and even in the 21st century, he had the right to assume they'd consummate this marriage.

"How are you doing?" His fingertips brushed her cheek and she leaned into the soft touch.

"I-I-I'm okay." Her thready voice sounded far away.

Mark reached for her, drawing her a step toward him as he closed the distance. "Talk to me Jocelyn." His warm breath ruffled the air by her ear. His body heat edged away the cold that claimed her.

"I-I-I don't know what you want me to say." Her forehead on his chest, her words spoken into his shirt.

"Can I get you anything? Wine? Water? I think there's some cranberry juice. I can fix you tea. Come, let's see what's in the kitchen before we decide." He wrapped his arm around her shoulder and together they walked down the entry hall to the kitchen. He settled her on a stool at the breakfast bar and began rummaging through cupboards setting out three boxes of tea.

When he stuck his head inside the refrigerator, his voice dimmed. "We've cranberry and a pear and pineapple juice." He took out a carton of milk, took a whiff and put it on the counter. "That's gone bad. Thankfully there's another half-gallon here that hasn't been opened nor has the date expired so we're good. What can I get you?"

"You go ahead. I'm good." She managed five whole words without her voice shaking.

Mark closed the refrigerator door and took the few steps until he stood across from her, the breakfast bar between them.

"We can make this work." He leaned across the island and reached for her hand. He didn't pick it up, just rested his on top of hers. "We can find our way forward in this relationship and have a good marriage."

"And, what is a good marriage to you?" Jocelyn kept her gaze locked on Mark's brown eyes.

He smiled and patted her hand. "See, I knew we could do it."

Flustered, her face burning with embarrassment, Jocelyn pulled her hand out from under his and folded it in her lap.

Mark rounded the breakfast bar and straddled a stool, leaving an empty one between them. "I'm not trying to embarrass you." He leaned forward, "The one thing all successful marriages have is good communication. You're willing to talk about what I think a good marriage is all about and I want to hear your ideas also. That's a start and as desperate as I am to keep Ethan, I never would have asked you to marry me if I didn't like you, care about you and adore Emma, if I didn't think we could talk or that we wouldn't even try."

He got up and paced to the other side of the counter. "Look, I'm attracted to you. Would I like to go upstairs and make love to you or with you? Of course I would, Jocelyn but—and it's a big but, I won't. Not tonight or tomorrow night or the next night. I'm an adult and I can control myself. Maybe not keep my body from being aroused but I don't have to act on it.

"We'll wait to consummate our marriage until you're ready to do so. I don't expect a pity or gratitude fuck so put that thought out of your mind if it was even there. No one needs to know what we do, when we do it much less how."

Jocelyn's battled nausea, feeling both hope and despair. "But won't Mrs. Fester want to know?"

"Mrs. Fester will want to know. We'll show her our bedroom, the king sized bed that we'll share. Why will we share it? Because she'll also talk to Ethan and Emma and if we are not sharing a bed, that won't look so good.

"If it makes you feel more secure, we'll put a bolster pillow down the middle at night and use it as decoration with a bunch of smaller pillows during the day."

Jocelyn's nerves calmed. "So if she asks, we'll lie?"

He arched a brow and stared at her. "Now it's your turn."

Jocelyn knew her cheeks were red but her lips tipped up in the first smile she'd shared with her husband since they came in the door. "I'm not sure I can match that look."

"You don't have to. You just have to have your own look."

She leaned on the counter. "What do you think she'll ask?"

"My guess is she'll ask you how often we have sex and whether you like it or not."

Jocelyn's face burned, her mouth popped open and just as quickly closed but no words emerged until she sputtered. "What an abominable question."

"And your answer would be?"

"A thousand times better than with anyone else I've known," indignation colored her tone.

A burst of laughter erupted from Mark. His face wrinkled, his eyes crinkled as the sound rolled out of him. When he quieted to a chuckle, he wiped a trace of a tear off his cheeks. "Perfect."

He came around the breakfast bar again and slipped his arms around her. He snuggled against her back and held her. "We'll make it Jocelyn. I know in my heart we'll make it through whatever lies ahead."

His heat against her back, his arms wrapped around her waist, Jocelyn relaxed against him, let him support her weight and began to believe or maybe it was hope he was right.

CHAPTER 35

Jocelyn woke during the night. Sleeping with Mark was not the same as sleeping with Emma. He was a restless sleeper, at least he was on this night. He didn't snore, at least he didn't on this night. He was a considerate person, man, but husband? She blew a puff of disgusted air, inwardly chastising herself for not being able to call him her husband.

He hadn't made a big deal of anything. Not fluffing pillows from Ethan's bed and stuffing them down the middle of this bed, or showing her the en-suite bathroom, or asking if she needed anything. When she'd shaken her head, he'd excused himself saying he was going to check messages and emails and call his dad to see how the kids were doing. No, he wasn't going to talk to them, just check in with his dad.

She'd taken a hot shower and finished her nightly routine: rubbed lotion into her skin, brushed her teeth, dried her hair and donned her best nightgown which meant it had no holes and still retained a modicum of color. She allowed her thoughts to wonder why she cared enough to wear it when she took a final look at herself in the mirror.

Finished, she'd padded out to the third bedroom that Mark had transformed into his office. She'd knocked on the door jamb and he'd looked up from a game of computer solitaire.

"Are you winning?" she'd asked from the doorway.

"About 50-50." His gaze had swept over her. "Jocelyn, would you be upset if I gave you some funds and asked you to purchase a few things?"

She'd gripped the door jamb waiting, wishing she'd put something else on, berating herself for trying to look her best for him.

"If you give me a list, of course I'll go shopping for you," she'd managed.

He'd smiled and turned back to the computer. A few clicks later, it was off and he'd strolled across the room toward her.

Jocelyn's feet had been like blocks of ice frozen to the floor. As he passed her in the doorway, he'd brushed against her, a light almost nothing touch of fabric to fabric. A touch that had had her heart racing, her breathing fractured, her cheeks flaming, her eyes fluttering. And then he was gone. She'd staggered two steps before connecting with the solid wall across the hall. Steeling herself, she'd walked to the bedroom they now shared.

Mark had been nowhere in sight.

Water had been running.

A smile blossomed when she'd identified the other sound —humming.

The king-sized bed had loomed in the center of the room. She'd slipped under the covers on the side opposite from the night stand with an alarm clock and his cell phone. With her back to the bathroom, she'd scrunched her eyes closed and waited. It seemed a lifetime before she heard the door open.

The bed had barely registered Mark's weight when he climbed in. "I left a nightlight on in the bathroom in case you need to get up during the night."

"Thank you," she'd whispered.

Light slid into the room from the gaps between the curtains, making streaks of white and pale yellow against the dark carpet. Morning had arrived. Jocelyn had slept in fits and starts, got up once to roam through the condo until she'd settled enough to get back in bed. Had she awakened Mark? She didn't think so but she wasn't sure.

She grabbed clean underwear, a pair of jeans, a V-necked print top and headed to the bathroom where she took care of her morning needs and got dressed. This was the first day of her real marriage.

Leaning on the counter, she stared into her eyes and let the memories of that first night with Tony surface. He'd told her when they were dating that he wanted their first time to be when they were married. It was so romantic at the time and he'd kiss her and touch her until she was to the point of begging for completion. Tony liked it rough and that first time had been terrifying. She might have left then if she hadn't already fallen in love with Emma.

Over time she'd been able to divorce her feelings from the memories but her body always reacted. A rapid heartbeat, stuttered breathing along with the stark haunted look in her eyes and pale cheeks were her normal reactions to these daytime memories. Will they ever go away? Don't go down that road, she chastised the woman in the mirror.

Pinching a bit of color in her cheeks, she left the bathroom, slipped on shoes and headed down to the kitchen.

Mark had set two places at the small table in the breakfast nook surrounded by a bay window with a view of the backyard. A backyard that looked a bit worse for wear with dying asters and chrysanthemums.

"How would—"

"I can—"

They both spoke at once.

"What do you want to say?" Mark watched her from his place in front of the stove.

"I was going to say I can freshen up the backyard. You know deadhead the flowers. That sort of thing." She hoped her voice sounded casual because inside she was a mass of nerves.

"That might be a good project for Ethan and Emma to help with," Mark said, putting a skillet on a burner.

"I think it would be." She smiled and added. "What were you going to say?"

"How would you like your eggs? And do you want toast, bagel or English muffins?"

"Oh, Mark, you don't have to fix breakfast for me." Jocelyn was on her feet hurrying across the kitchen. "I can... ." She stopped a foot away, her hand within inches of his as she reached for the frying pan.

"Mrs. Parker." Mark leaned close. "This is your first day as Mrs. Parker actually, Mrs. Mark Parker and as such you get your breakfast made to order." He grinned, brushed his lips over her temple and added, "I've no idea when this urge to fix you breakfast will strike again so you'd better take advantage of it."

"You mean I'm not Jocelyn Parker?" She pouted but laughter lit her eyes.

He shook his head.

"What about Dr. Parker's wife? Or she who has no name of her own?"

He laughed. "Won't happen. You will always have a name of your own. I'll become known as Jocelyn's husband." He bumped his hip against hers. "So, Mrs. Mark Parker or Mrs. Jocelyn Parker, how would you like your husband, he who has no other name, to fix your eggs?"

"What are my options?" Jocelyn batted her eyelashes and bumped hips back.

"Well, Mrs. Jocelyn Parker, my specialty is scrambled with a hint of sea salt and a bit of cheese. I can also do a bit of cheese and sea salt with eggs that are scrambled."

A giggle escaped. "Your cooking prowess is amazing, husband. However, I think you are leaving a couple of options out. I've heard Ethan talk about having your version of a McDonald's favorite with eggs and muffins and stuff. I'm not sure what the 'stuff' is but... ."

He was watching her mouth.

"What?"

"You giggled."

A flush traveled from her neck up to her forehead. "I did. I-I-I—."

"I liked it."

"Oh." Her cheeks were hot from the flush but it was a pleasant rather than crushing feeling.

"And I've decided to do the whole nine-yards for my new bride this morning. Two special Eggs Benedict's coming up."

"Really? With Hollandaise Sauce?" She heard her own astonishment.

"What's an Eggs Benedict without Hollandaise Sauce?" he said in a mock serious tone.

Jocelyn laughed. "It wouldn't be an Eggs Benedict. You make your own Sauce?

"I do. And it is a work of art. Just watch and be amazed!" He plucked the muffins from the box with a flourish and dropped them into the toaster but didn't push the lever down. "Timing is everything if you want quality Eggs Benedict."

Jocelyn watched Mark slip the eggs into simmering water once the Hollandaise Sauce was in the blender. When the muffins were toasting, he got plates down and set them on the counter near the stove.

He didn't seem self-conscious as he puttered around the kitchen creating a masterpiece breakfast. He also cleaned up as he went along.

"I could help," she'd offered at one point.

"Consider this your bride's gift."

"My bride's gift?" Her brow puckered.

"Surely you know that once upon a time, it was the tradition for a bride and groom to exchange gifts the morning after their wedding."

"I do remember reading about that in historical novels. Are you a fan of them?"

"Nope. Not sure I've ever read one but I've heard about the tradition. Maybe this is something we can do on our anniversaries?"

She heard the question in his tone. "You make breakfast for me or …?"

"We can take turns. Next year you can make breakfast for me. The year after that I'll make it for you, etc. etc. etc."

He wasn't even looking at her as he casually rattled off establishing a tradition for years to come.

"You really see us staying married?" She was shocked to hear her voice saying the words.

Mark turned from the counter, the plates with their breakfast in hand. He set them down on the table and turned to where she sat on the stool at the kitchen island.

"I not only see us staying married. I see us happily married. I see us with at least one more child. I see us growing old together." He was standing so close the heat and scent of him enveloped her. His hand gently gripped her elbow and he half-lifted her off the stool. "Let's eat our breakfast before it gets cold."

His arm steadied her the three steps to the table. He held her chair out for her when she sat and when he leaned over to hand her her napkin, he brushed a soft kiss on her forehead.

"My words are not meant to discombobulate you, Jocelyn." He spoke in a calm, gentle voice and he rested a hand on her shoulder for a few seconds.

Instead of a response, she picked up her knife and fork and cut into her food. "This is delicious." Her eyes closed, a small moan escaped as the rich Hollandaise Sauce coated egg and muffin played with her taste buds. "Where did you ever learn to fix this?"

"Mom and Dad love food so, as their son, I had no choice but to enjoy eating it."

Curiosity got the better of her and she wanted to know more. "But you said you aren't a great cook."

"I'm not. I've a couple of meals I've learned to fix, this being my breakfast meal." He quirked his fingers as he said the last two words.

"And lunch?"

"I make a decadent Reuben because I load it with all the ingredients and make my own dressing that's a combination of Thousand Island and Russian."

"Reubens are one of my favorite sandwiches." She sipped her juice, waiting for him to go on. When he didn't she kept the conversation in this safe place. "What about dinner?"

"Ethan would say it's my spaghetti but after having Jackson's? Nope. Mine is good but not as good as his. I can grill a good steak. I can poach salmon—similar to poaching eggs so it isn't that I've gained a new kitchen skill."

"What about your hamburgers?"

"What do you mean? Can I grill them? Yes."

"Your grilled hamburgers with your Reuben dressing? With Swiss cheese even? And if you have a deep fryer, I make excellent homemade fries both regular and sweet potato or even potato chips."

"We'll make sure we have a deep fryer in our new home. Maybe try out the grilled hamburgers tonight? The kids will love it because we'll let them help."

She raised an eyebrow.

"I do the slicing but Ethan puts everything on the plate and carries it to the table."

"Ahh, I do something similar with Emma. She reminds me of the time so nothing burns and she sets the table."

Mark's face shifted from light and amused to dark and serious. "Can you see from this conversation how we are a good fit?"

She looked out the window hoping words would come. Words didn't come but emotions welled from her belly bringing with them her breakfast. Her hand to her mouth, she mumbled "excuse me" and dashed from the table.

Once her stomach was empty, she curled on the bathroom floor, her tears dampening the tiles.

Something warm covered her. She struggled to open her eyes, on the one hand amazed she hadn't startled and on the other thankful she felt safe. Mark hunkered down by her feet, his brow furrowed, his eyes filled with concern.

"I'm not exactly sure what it was I said but I never meant to upset you so," he said concern laced his words.

She tried to move and then realized she was stiff from being on the cold tiles.

"May I help you up?" Mark asked, standing and offering his hand.

She nodded and reached up. "Sit first."

When she was sitting, Mark moved the blanket, wrapping it around her shoulders. "I'm fairly sure now isn't the time to talk, but I do want to, at some point, so I don't create this situation again."

Jocelyn gathered the blanket around her and stood. "Let's find another place to talk." It wasn't that she really wanted to talk but while she was heaving her guts out and sobbing on the bathroom floor, her brain whirred with thoughts. Thoughts this man who was her husband deserved to hear.

CHAPTER 36

Mark stood aside so Jocelyn could precede him from the bathroom. She was pale and he stuck close in case she fainted. A soft smile flitted across his face as he recognized the steel beneath the pale. His wife would not faint, at least not when she was so determined.

In the bedroom she climbed on the bed and pulled the blanket around her. She sat with her back against a pile of pillows, one of them in her lap and her legs akimbo. She snuggled back against the cushions and his sense of loss was profound. Would she ever be able to snuggle like that with him?

He debated whether to pull up a chair, perch on the bed beside her or stretch out. An internal shake and he decided he'd mirror her. So he sat in the same position she did but a little to the side at the foot of the bed using the bed post for stability.

Jocelyn fidgeted with the blanket, smoothed and then fluffed the pillow, clasped and unclasped her hands all the while never once glancing at him. He waited.

At least a minute if not two passed before she sighed, glanced up at him and then down at her hands that were now holding the opposite elbows.

"I'm—."

Mark interrupted when he saw the misery etched on her face, heard the defeat in her voice and knew, just knew the next word out of her mouth would be 'sorry'.

"If you are going to apologize, don't. You've nothing to apologize for," he said in his calm, professional tone.

Her eyes glistened and tears streamed down her face. "I-I-I've spoiled your bride's gift." With the edge of the blanket she swiped at the tears but the misery that radiated from every cell of her body remained.

"Jocelyn." Mark used his gentlest tone and her name in an effort to soothe. "You've ruined nothing." He held up his hand to stave off her rebuttal. "Hear me out."

When she nodded, he continued.

"I've been considering marriage ever since Mrs. Fester came into my life so it's been several months not a week or maybe two like you. I don't come from a depraved abusive relationship and you do. That means I've had more time to prepare for this change and it's easier for me.

"I'm not going to tell you I love you with all my heart but I will tell you I believe it highly likely someday I will. You're a brave woman, a fantastic mother, a compassionate and caring lady. I like you. I admire you. And as much as you love Emma, you would not have agreed to this hare-brained scheme if you didn't have a modicum of trust in me. That is your greatest gift to me. You trusted me enough to marry me and see what happens. We'll have some rough spots. Even the best marriages do. But we have similar core values that will see us through."

Jocelyn glanced at him. "Why have you never married?"

He smiled. "Yeah, the whole doctor/husband thing. I think my mom said something to you in passing that it isn't all a bed of roses. My partners are covering for me right now and they will the rest of this week but my turn in the rotation will be back before you know it. Then there will be those phone calls in the night. My coming home haggard and silent. And I stay silent because when I've had a really hard night or day I can be harsh, rude and abrupt. Ethan knows the signs and I'm sure he'll be more than happy to share what to do and what not to do when "Papa's like that."

Jocelyn shifted, the pillow rested on her lap. "To be honest, I haven't thought beyond the immediate future about being married… that is until this morning when you were talking about future anniversaries."

"You mean went on and on and on about them," he said his tone rueful.

"No, you weren't just talking." Jocelyn looked him in the eyes. "Future anniversaries were in your thoughts. You could see us together one, two, three years from now. I only see us together today. I'm not even able to look at tomorrow yet."

"Yet." Mark stretched out his foot and tapped her closest knee. "Already the seed is planted that there can be more. That's enough. We'll live today and in the morning we'll live tomorrow. This time of year creates opportunities to live a little bit into the future. Costumes for Halloween. Deciding what to do, where to eat on Thanksgiving. And then there's Christmas. Do we want… ?" his voice trailed off at the stricken look on her face.

"But today is today. We'll pick up the kids and head back to our home. What else?" Mark asked, a thread of relief sliding through him.

"We can make sure the pantry is stocked and that we have the fixings for you to grill hamburgers and make your famous sauce?"

"Sounds like a perfect day to me."

"Since you cooked breakfast, I'll clean up the kitchen."

"We'll clean up the kitchen together and maybe you can get a bit of food down you before we head out to get Ethan and Emma," he said noting her color was still off.

"Maybe we'd better check in with your parents to see how things are. We can always get them and then come back here to finish straightening things up."

He noted her hesitant tone and was glad she was talking. They'd make it if they could keep talking, even about simple things like what to have for dinner.

"Good idea." He shifted onto his knees and crawled up the bed, reaching past her for his cell phone. "Speed dial," he said as he punched one number before holding the phone to his ear. "Hey Dad, how are things going? Jocelyn and I can come get the munchkins now or in about an hour. What works best for you?

"You're sure they aren't wearing Mom out? Or you? No kidding. You engaged them in a reading marathon? Okay then, we'll see you in an hour or so. Bye now.

"You'll never guess what Mom has done?" He waited.

Jocelyn sat without moving, amusement having replaced misery. She waved a hand. "Go on, you said I'll never guess so I'm not going to. You did mention a reading marathon."

He slanted a mock frown in her direction. "She had them get ALL their books together and sort them by author and then the alphabet before they started reading. She'd written the ABC's in large letters and let them work it out. The reward was once the authors were sorted they read a story. Once half the authors were alphabetized they read another one. Once all of them were organized, they started with the "Z's" and are working their way back to "A".

"What about the bigger books with several stories in them?" Jocelyn smiled, glad her stomach was calm.

"They were separated out but still organized. Bedtime is when one story from one book is read. Since these also are alphabetized the arguments about what to read and who gets to pick have been virtually eliminated."

"Your mom deserves a special gift." Jocelyn smiled.

"I agree. We'll ask her what she'd like." Mark relished the small victory of a smile and color back on his new wife's face.

"So, we are going to finish up here and then go pick up the kids?"

"That's the plan. And, I think we might just stop at the store and get the fixings for dinner and breakfast tomorrow. That way we know we've got food for the munchkins and ourselves."

"What will we do with the rest of the day?"

"You can make a grocery list if you want. And there isn't anything that says we can't go to the store again. We'll want to check on Sadie.

The kids have things to put away in their rooms. I've an office to organize. And you," he turned and put his hands on her shoulders, "you can do whatever you want. You can watch, supervise, find a corner and read, go down and visit with Sadie. Your options are almost endless. The only deterrent to you doing anything you want is you have to be home for dinner."

Jocelyn arched a brow. "Have to?"

"Yep, a new Parker Family Rule. Whomever decides what we're having for dinner must be at that dinner. Now take the pledge." His face was solemn but his eyes shone with humor as he put his hand over his heart.

Jocelyn laughed, shrugged out of the blanket and stood. "Can't do this lying down. This is serious Parker Family business.

"I, Jocelyn Parker, do swear that I will always be at the dinner table if I choose the meal. Now you." She poked Mark in the ribs but he slung an arm around her shoulders.

"Now here is where one of the Doctor Parker Family rules comes in to play." His tone became serious. "When I'm On Call, I can be summoned in the middle of a meal, minutes before it is served, etc."

"Then we'll find a stand-in for you."

He raised his brow.

"If it is a Parker Family Rule then it is a "rule" and we, as parents need to set a good example. I understand there may be times when you have to leave and cannot be physically here. So, your task today is to decide who/what will be your 'stand-in.' What will be your place holder at the table when you aren't here?"

"You mean like a stuffed animal or something?"

"It's up to you and in reality it may be fun for each of us to figure out who or what our stand-in will be. I can see into the future enough to know that Emma and Ethan will be having activities, sleep overs, etc. where they will not be here for dinner."

Mark pulled her against his chest, nuzzled her hair and sighed. "You are amazing. Don't fight it. Just acknowledge it. You can even say "I am amazing."

Jocelyn stepped back, her face flushed with happy embarrassment. "Yes, you are amazing."

Mark cocked a brow at her and folded his arms across his chest and stared her down.

"And, and, and there are times when I might... . "

He shook his head.

"When I am..." she paused, took a deep breath and let the words rush out between her parted lips, "amazing too."

CHAPTER 37

*J*ocelyn smiled as both Emma and Ethan raced to the front window, noses pressed against the glass, hands waving wildly. "Papa, Papa, Papa," peppered the air.

Mark was home.

She'd already taken food down to the Perths and made sure they had everything they needed for the evening. She'd collect the dinner dishes when she took lunch down tomorrow. Sadie was doing better. Or it seemed that way to her. Her color was good, she was eating a little more and she had more energy. Jocelyn considered asking Mark what he thought. She sucked in a deep breath. She would talk to him. She could talk to him. He'd listen, maybe ask a clarifying question or two but his tone would be calm, moderate, inquisitive, interested.

In the week they'd been married, she'd grown comfortable with a kiss when he left for work and again when he came home. He hugged her as they readied for bed. Warmth flowed from within blooming in a bright smile. She was sleeping now, quite well in fact.

This afternoon when the children were playing a game and she was fixing dinner, she'd actually pinched herself, pinched hard enough that her skin was still a little red. This was her life now. It wasn't a dream. And when dinner was in the oven and she sat with a cup of tea looking out at the backyard, she thought of Mark, his warm hands on her shoulders, his gentle caress of her arms, his clean scent that had come to mean she was safe. When his arms came around her and he held her close, she relaxed now.

Trust was the first step.

Being safe was the second step in becoming his wife in all ways.

Being relaxed was the third step. Her breath hitched but easily released a sigh at their progress.

Fourth might be kissing? Well, they did that. A bit more than a peck but not anywhere near passionate. *If she was ready.* She paused. *When I'm ready.* She nodded and continued. *When I'm ready, I can—?* Her lungs squeezed and her heart rate quickened. The operative word is "when" and obviously that isn't now.

She followed Ethan and Emma to the door but stood back as it opened. One look at Mark and she knew he'd had a very bad day.

She moved forward, gently tugging the children aside. "Okay, let Papa in the door. Ethan, you take Papa's coat and put it on the chair. Emma, you take Papa's hand and help him into the living room so he can sit by the fire."

She ushered the trio to where a blaze burned brightly, very glad she'd followed her instinct that having a fire today would be a good thing.

Once Mark was settled in the big chair, she called the children to her side. "Now we're going to see what Papa wants us to do. You can see he's very tired tonight so we want to take care of him.

"So Papa, your choices are to have kisses and snuggles or to be left alone for a bit until dinner is served. You can also choose to have Mr. Dragon sit in your seat at the table and have your dinner in here so you have a bit more quiet time."

She watched Mark carefully, never having seen him in quite this state. He was doing something internally. His eyes were closed, his arms rested on the chair, his hands unclenched, his breathing slowed. "Or, you can sleep for a bit and then decide," she whispered.

Bending over, her voice soft, she said to Ethan and Emma, "Let's let Papa sleep a little. He looks very tired." She herded them into the kitchen and was trying to think of what to say to Emma whose eyes were large and worried when Ethan patted Emma's shoulder. "Papa sometimes has hard work and he needs a nap when he gets home. That's why he sometimes didn't pick me up at Grandmama and Grandpapa's right away."

"Thank you for telling us, Ethan. I feel better knowing Papa just needs a bit of a nap. What about you, Emma?"

Emma stood very still, her voice quavered. "Is it like when you're really scared and have to run away?"

Jocelyn laid a hand on her daughter's shoulder. "In some ways it is like that, Em. We were always so very tired when we got to our new place we slept right away, didn't we." Emma nodded, her blue eyes glued to Jocelyn's face. "But we were scared. I think Papa is sad more than scared."

"Sometimes people do really stupid things," Ethan said with authority. "I heard Papa and Grandpapa talking about stupid people doing stupid things and stuff like that."

"And that means they didn't think ahead as to what the consequences might be." She noted their confused look and added, "Consequences are what can happen because of what your choices are, like throwing a ball without paying attention to where it could land."

"Like breaking a window?" Emma asked, her brow scrunched.

Jocelyn nodded.

"Or going into the neighbor's yard. And then you have to go knock on their door and 'splain and ask for your ball back and promise you'll be careful." Ethan hung his head and heaved a big sigh.

Jocelyn turned to the stove to hide her smile while saying "That's a perfect example of a consequence Ethan."

Her body registered a difference in the air. When she looked up, Mark was standing in the kitchen. He still looked weary but not as wiped out as he had when he came through the door.

"Where's my welcome home hugs and kisses?" He squatted with his back to the wall. A good thing when the two small bodies attacked him.

Joyous chatter ensued as they wrapped around him, smothering him with kisses and hugs. He managed to stand, one kid in each arm but still braced against the wall. Jocelyn walked to him and stretched up on her toes to kiss him on the lips. "Welcome home, Papa."

∽

Mark would have staggered back if he wasn't already leaning against the wall. He would have slipped his arms around her to prolong that kiss if his arms weren't filled with Ethan and Emma. But since he was against the wall and his arms were full of children, he caught her gaze and held it hoping the need that radiated from his own didn't scare her.

"I smell something delicious," he said and with great exaggeration sniffed the air before bending over and nibbling on Ethan and Emma. Their giggles and clinging to him gave false to their "No, No, No."

He lowered them to the floor and held them until they were steady on their feet. "Do I smell pot roast?"

"You do," his wife said, a saucy smile on her face. "Can you guess what's for dessert?"

He sniffed the air again, picked up a hint of chocolate and something else—maybe mint? "I'm hoping its chocolate pudding pie."

Jocelyn put her finger to her lips and then made the zipping motion. Both Ethan and Emma did the same. "If you eat all your dinner, you can have some dessert. These two," she patted Ethan and Emma on the shoulders, "were creative dessert chefs today."

He looked down at the two excited, jiggling children. "I bet it's going to be very good, excellent in fact. Maybe as good as Jackson's ice cream." He licked his lips, smacked them together and rubbed his hands. "Let's wash up so we can eat. I'm hungry as a bear." For good measure he growled and reached for them with his hands curled into claws.

Of course they squealed and dashed for the bathroom. As the thunder of their feet quieted when they reached their destination, he approached his wife. "Sorry to—"

She reached up and laid her hand on his cheek. "Don't apologize for coming home at the end of the day tired and needing a nap. Ethan told us that some days you have stupid people to take care of and that makes you tired."

He groaned. "Little ears. I've never knowingly said anything like that in front of him."

She smiled and turned back to the stove. "He heard you and your dad talking. And it wasn't a bad thing. We had a good talk about consequences and people doing things without thinking what could happen. He gave an excellent example of throwing a ball that went into the neighbor's yard. Very dramatic rendering of the event."

Mark chuckled. "I've seldom seen him walk so slowly. One would have thought he was going to face a firing squad." He grimaced. "Not a good example. He, hopefully, doesn't know about firing squads yet."

"Now both he and Emma know what the word consequence means. And they know about being exhausted or really tired because Emma likened your nap to when we've had to run. As soon as everything was inside and the doors were locked, we'd fall asleep. We didn't even unpack."

His arm wrapped around her shoulders. "Those days are behind you. Over and done with." He kissed her temple when she leaned against him. Waited for her arm to slip around his waist. And waited.

"Papa, you have to wash your hands too!" Ethan and Emma chorused as they stood in front of them, hands on hips.

He saluted. "Yes I do. If you'll excuse me, I'll take care of that right away."

Mark staved off fatigue by being engrossed in dinner and dessert. Ethan and Emma had made a chocolate mint pudding pie. At least one can of whipped cream decorated the top and it resembled a massive snow-covered mountain.

As a family they cleared the table. Jocelyn put perishables in the refrigerator.

"I'd like a pot roast sandwich tomorrow." He spoke to her back side because she was halfway in the appliance.

When she backed out, a smile was on her face. "Good. I actually cooked two so we can have sandwiches. I also made extra gravy so we can have open-faced sandwiches or just pot roast with gravy. But tomorrow night is chicken night."

He stifled a yawn. "Are you fixing two chickens?"

"Most likely I'll fix three or four and make chicken soup, shred some so we can have chicken tacos, or maybe chicken salad for sandwiches. I know Sadie will enjoy chicken soup. Thought I'd make both chicken noodle and chicken vegetable. We've the big freezer so nothing will go to waste if—."

He put his hand up to stop her, saw her flinch and immediately dropped his hand to his side.

"Jocelyn, I totally trust you to handle things here. You're doing an amazing job. And, if we have leftovers that get freezer burned or spoil in the refrigerator, just think of it as compost and helping fertilize the soil."

"I'm—."

"Don't," he interrupted her. "Do not apologize for anything right now. Why? Because you have nothing to apologize for." He paused, thought to lean in and kiss her lips but stopped. "I'm going to start the kids on their bedtime routine, if you can finish up I'd appreciate it. I think I'd fall asleep if I read them a story."

"Just tell them good-night and let them tell you the best thing about their day and then go to bed. I can supervise baths and story time," she said while cleaning off a plate.

"Kitchen?"

"While you are doing this first part, I'll load the dishwasher. That's really all that's left to do." Jocelyn opened the dishwasher door.

He smiled. "Yeah right. When I get up in the morning the kitchen will be spotless. I don't know if you can even go to bed much less sleep if there is a speck on the counters or stove top."

She nudged him. "Go, they're waiting for you. I'll be along shortly."

With that she turned away from him and began putting plates, glasses and silverware in the dishwasher. She was humming when he left her. The tune sounded familiar but he couldn't place it.

Jocelyn hummed one of the songs she'd learned and loved when at the 14th Moon Gathering. It was a simple song with an upbeat tune and all about being blessed. Sometimes it was difficult to separate her past from her present like just now when Mark wanted to stop the apology that automatically came to her lips.

But was it automatic anymore? No, it wasn't. She was beginning to trust that she didn't have to apologize or explain. When she gave herself a moment to reflect on her life now, what stunned her was how close this life was to her dreams and visions. The backyard in this house was exactly like the one in her recurring vision. She loved the old craftsman style house. It was a full time job keeping it up but it was also a labor of love. Getting more organized was the answer to keeping the dust at bay.

Expanding her repertoire of foods she could prepare was next on her list. Pot roast, chicken, soups, chili had been mastered. Mark was a whiz at grilling steaks and hamburgers as well as hotdogs. Weekends when he wasn't on call seemed to be the better times to put grilling on the menu.

Truth be told she'd been alarmed at his state of exhaustion when he came in the door. She paused and looked around the kitchen. She really should mop the floors tonight. A glance at the clock had her moving toward the stairs. Bedtime routine first and then a quick mop before she went to bed.

Tonight would be the first time she'd climb into bed with Mark already there, already asleep. No time to mull that over she chided herself as she reached the top of the stairs.

Hearing water splashing she opened the bathroom door. Mark was sitting on the toilet asleep. Emma and Ethan? A water fight.

"Enough." Her voice was loud and forceful.

Mark startled awake.

"You," she said and pinned Mark with a look, "go to bed. Now." She emphasized her order with a pointed stab at the door.

"And you two." Two very worried little faces eyed her cautiously. "Your bathing is done. You will get out and after you dry off, you will wipe up the extra water on the floor and then put your towels in the tub."

She folded her arms over her chest and waited while Mark shuffled to his feet. He gingerly crossed to the tub and helped each child out, giving them their good night kiss as he did so. His head hung at a decidedly sheepish angle as he approached her. "Do I get my goodnight kiss?"

"Once these hooligans are in bed, I'll see that you're tucked in too. You'll get your goodnight kiss then."

"It'll be worth staying awake for," he said in a low voice for her ears only.

Heat flashed through her as his breath caressed her ear. She attempted a glare but knew she'd fallen short when he smiled.

Tugging her attention away from him, she focused on Emma and Ethan who had managed to wipe up the worst of the water. The floor was tile so it could wait until she got them into bed. Pajamas on, wet towels in the bathtub, Jocelyn got out the hair dryer and started in. By having them stand next to each other and using the blow dryer on first one and then the other, they were both done about the same time.

"No story tonight," she announced as she ushered them to their room. Tucking them in, she kissed their foreheads.

"Remember, tomorrow is a new day." She blew them each another kiss when she turned off the light and partially closed their door. "Night Mama" echoed in her heart as she headed back to the bathroom.

On her hands and knees, using the driest towels from the tub the mopping of the floor took only a few minutes. It took two trips to haul the wet towels to the upstairs laundry and start a load. That finished she started downstairs to take care of the kitchen floor and take another swipe at the countertops.

In the kitchen entry, she stopped dead in her tracks when she saw Mark putting the mop away. "What?"

"So the munchkins are in bed?"

She nodded.

"And now the kitchen is ready for morning. Let's go to bed, wife." He strolled toward her, his gaze never wavering. "It felt strange to go to bed without you."

His arm slipped around her waist as he guided her back to the stairs. Once in their room, he closed the door and kept the lights dimmed. "I did come in here and brushed my teeth, etc. so the bathroom is yours." He headed toward the walk-in closet, taking items of clothing off as he went. Shirt, undershirt, belt, shoes. She watched transfixed as he undressed, feeling the heat rise in her cheeks but unable to look away.

Off came his slacks and briefs and then socks. He was naked, his back to her but naked nonetheless. He half-turned to get the pair of sweat pants he slept in. She thought he was aroused and that was enough to get her feet unstuck from the floor.

In the bathroom she quickly brushed her teeth, washed her face and ran a comb through her hair in case there were tangles. Of course there were and in her haste she tugged too hard. "Ow," she hissed.

"Let me." His hand took the comb and gently, so very gently combed her hair easing any snarls out. "There."

Her body quivered under the onslaught of his touch, his light massage of her scalp, she wanted to lean into his strength, his heat, feel his arms around her. She fought the urge and, instead, turned, took the comb from his hand. "Thank you."

She started past him but he stepped in front of her. "My good night kiss?"

She nodded and rose on her toes to brush her mouth against his.

"I want to touch you but don't know where I can and not frighten you." Mark confessed.

Gentle quivers shivered through her at his words. His tender gaze roamed over her face. "Where do you want to touch me?" she whispered.

"Eventually everywhere but for now anywhere." His voice was rough with the emotions she saw in his eyes.

"Just tell me where you want to touch me so I'm not surprised."

The gentle quivers morphed into shudders, heating her from the inside out.

His hands rested on her shoulders. "May I hold your head in my hands and give you a goodnight kiss?"

Jocelyn stifled the internal quaking. Nodded. "You may."

It was a gentle kiss, he touched the seam of her mouth with his tongue and Jocelyn found herself opening and tentatively welcoming him in. He didn't stay long but lingered a bit by kissing her jaw, her cheeks, her temples, her forehead ending his leisurely perusal of her face with his lips with a quick kiss on the tip of her nose.

Somewhere along the way, she'd raised her hands and lightly gripped his forearms. When the kiss ended, her hands dropped away.

"Thank you, wife. That was just what the doctor ordered so he could go to sleep." His hand reached for hers as he headed toward the bed. Pulling the covers back he positioned the bolster pillows down the center before offering his hand to help her into bed. He tucked the covers around her, kissed her forehead and then padded around to the other side. The bed shifted as he climbed in. The covers rustled as he pulled them up over his shoulder.

Jocelyn waited until she heard his breathing slow in sleep before she turned into her pillow and wept.

CHAPTER 38

Mark grinned. His fingers tapped on the steering wheel in time to his humming, He was on his way home from a day at the office with its normal challenges and he was happy. Since Ethan had come into his life, he usually was happy to get home but this was a different happy.

He waited at the stop light, sorting through the concept of different kinds of happy. Different kinds or was it more like different places or…. Of course he was happy with his practice, partners, office staff and patients. He chuckled—most patients. The light changed and he started forward. The truth was, he thrived on many of the less cooperative patients. There was something about showing a person that they could heal, become whole and active again. And in those worst case scenarios, helping them make peace with their new normal. His chest tightened, his brow puckered and he grimaced. *New normal? I hate that phrase.*

A full stop at the next stop sign extended into an additional pause. Here he knew people tended to pause instead of actually stop. His humming continued as he drove on.

His newly-married life was developing a normal routine. His breathing eased as he shook off his negative connotation of the word, routine. However they seemed to be creating a family that worked for them. He looked forward to the charging bodies hurtling his way. Even Emma came at him as fast as she could. Tucking them into bed and reading bedtime stories always righted a difficult day.

Jocelyn took care of the house and kids during the week. Weekends he took the lead with the kids and helped with the meals. Hope banished any residual tension and he relaxed more fully into the car's leather seat. Jocelyn was an excellent mom to Ethan. And she was carrying and compassionate with the Perths. When the two of them were together they had an easy-going friendship—most of the time. Except for physical intimacy, he was very happy with this marriage. He shook his head and reminded himself they'd only been married two weeks.

The thought he'd been ignoring surfaced and with it came an acid stomach, iron bar tension in his shoulders, arms and hands. Tomorrow was the hearing for permanent custody of Ethan or hopefully for adoption. He knew if the judge talked privately to Ethan, his son would confirm that Jocelyn loved him and vice-versa.

For a moment he knew he was going to be sick and he looked for a place to pull over. Tears blurred his vision and he drew shuddering gulps of air into tight lungs. Fought the bile rising in his throat into submission. He didn't pull over but became more determined to get home and hold his son.

His chest swelled with pride and the darkness receded as he focused on Ethan. His son could have been a mean little boy having endured so much meanness in his young life, but he wasn't. He was a caring and compassionate child, wise beyond his years, who had a healing touch. Maybe or maybe not in terms of his physical touch. Time would tell on that. But Mark had no doubts in his mind, Ethan was a healer.

And then there was Emma. Emma had opened up and become much more carefree—much more like a little girl her age.

Then there was the counseling. His jury was out on how much it helped. Right now, both he and Jocelyn were up at night because of the nightmares after a counseling session. To be fair, the nightmares were also laced with fear due to the court hearing. He was ever so grateful Jocelyn and he had talked about the nightmares even before they were married.

When they were single, they'd welcomed their child into their beds. Comforting Ethan and Emma in their own beds was what they did now. Last night both children were so frightened they clung. He and Jocelyn had crawled into bed and held them through the remainder of the night.

The original plan that the children would have their own rooms had failed. When anxiety and nightmares ran rampant, they slept together. He was confident time would heal things and they'd be able to sleep in their own beds.

Both he and Jocelyn slept in nightclothes and since they were not yet intimate there wasn't anything for the kids to walk in on but.... He was ever-hopeful that would change. She wasn't immune to him. She wasn't rigid when he kissed her good-night or hello or good-bye. She wasn't stiff when he added a hug to his kiss or just put his arm around her. In fact she often leaned into him.

And then there was the night she'd watched him strip. That event had tried his patience on every level. Not necessarily his patience with her. He totally understood her hesitancy about sex. Tony had been despicable, terrorizing her and Emma. He'd bet he didn't know the half-of-it. And what he did know created a hot flashing anger that consumed him every time he considered, even for a moment, what she and Emma had endured. He couldn't help but wonder if he knew it all, it would ease her mind about being intimate with him.

He drew a calming breath as ideas popped up.

Lily'd be back from Ireland or maybe she already was. He could talk to her about Jocelyn. No, he could but he wouldn't.

Maybe suggest the women get together? Or maybe Jocelyn could join Lily's women's circle?

She'd been in the house for two solid weeks not even going out for groceries.

Well, that was something he could change. Ideas continued to flow.

This weekend they'd all go somewhere. Maybe to the park and the ice cream parlor? Maybe, if there was a kid's movie showing anywhere, they could do that? The least they could do was get out of the house, go for a drive, have dinner out.

His grip tightened on the steering wheel. Crap—he was On Call this weekend so maybe anything that required a chunk of time was out but—if not this weekend, then maybe the next?

Wait, Monday. He had Monday morning off. No patients until 1 p.m. Well, rounds at the hospital if anyone was admitted over the weekend. They'd go out for breakfast. Maybe make that a family tradition – breakfast out on the Monday after he'd been On Call for the weekend.

Now humming a tuneless sound, he noticed a car at the curb when he pulled into the driveway. Not one he recognized. Maybe visiting the neighbors across the street? He grabbed his briefcase and headed to the front door, clicking the fob to lock the car and set the alarm.

Something hit him on the head.

He rubbed the spot as looked up to see Ethan hanging out the window. What?

The look on his son's face was reminiscent of the early days when he was still in the hospital.

"Papa, a bad man is hurting Mama and Emma."

CHAPTER 39

Mark's heart burst into a rapid tattoo, his feet froze to the walkway. When his brain kicked in a mere moment later, he checked the windows to see if anyone inside could see him. Ducking down, he moved to the driveway while putting his finger to his lips and making the zipping sign for Ethan.

A chilling scream rent the air.

He motioned Ethan to duck down, pulled his cell phone out and keyed in 911. He secured his ear piece as he tucked the phone in his pocket and headed to the door. He paused when he heard the 911 operator's voice. Name, address and the word "intruder" were delivered in a rapid-fire, no-nonsense tone.

Adopting a feigned calm, he opened the door. "I'm home," he announced as he crossed the threshold. His grip on his briefcase tightened at the scene before him.

He didn't need an introduction to know it was Tony who held a knife to Jocelyn's neck, her left arm bent behind her in a hold that was just short of dislocating her shoulder or breaking her arm.

Emma clung to Jocelyn's right hand, the look of terror and determination on her little face gave him pause. What was she up to?

"Well, look who's home?" The guy sneered, tipped Jocelyn's head back as he ratcheted the pressure on her arm. "What no screams? You know I like to hear you scream, Bitch. Come on, just a little one."

Jocelyn's face was stained with tears, blood trickled down her neck from a nick near her jugular vein. She was on her tiptoes. Muscles trembled from the strain. He couldn't begin to imagine the terror she and Emma felt in that moment.

"Bitch," Tony crooned. "Scream for me. Just a little one." The knife nicked another spot, more blood trickled down to stain the neckline of her blouse.

From the moment he'd come in the door, her eyes had focused on his. Her gaze never wavered. He read the plea in them. But it was a plea he ignored.

He was not leaving her.

Sometimes there is that moment in time when you know what you need to do. He'd had that moment when he first met Ethan. He knew he'd met his son. Everything he'd done since that time had been to have that realization be his reality. This was another one of those moments in time. He may have suggested he and Jocelyn marry to secure the children, but now? Now the reality of how much he loved her flowed through him like a hot lava flow.

He left the front door ajar, set his briefcase on the bench, resisted the urge to take off his coat and ignored the 911 operator's voice in his ear.

Instinct had him tense for the charge across the space but he stifled the urge to move closer. "I don't believe we've been introduced. I'm Mark Parker. I see you've met my wife. Is the knife against her neck necessary?"

Tony flicked the knife point creating another stream of blood. "Think she's your wife? Used goods. And not even very good at the only thing bitches are good for."

He needed to keep Tony's focus on him. The 911 despatcher said police were on the way. He discarded words and phrases that flew through his mind. The truth: "She's perfect in every way for me."

"Must be she's showed you some of the tricks I taught her. Right, Bitch? You suck him dry?"

Jocelyn's demeanor underwent a slight change when Tony's words were followed by him grinding himself against her back. She no longer held Mark's gaze with her own. Her eyes blanked and she looked at some point beyond his left shoulder.

"You taught me how to please—." Her thin voice was rough with a brittle edge to it.

"Watch it, Bitch. What have you done with him?" He used the knife to point at Mark but quickly returned it to Jocelyn's neck. "Remember what happens to the kid if you say the wrong thing."

Jocelyn leaned back against Tony, her words barely a whisper. "I've not forgotten anything."

Mark hoped the 911 operator heard Tony. He knew she couldn't hear Jocelyn. He was across the room and barely caught what she'd said. He blocked out everything except his wife, daughter and the monster before him.

What the hell? Was he hallucinating? Was Jocelyn rubbing her butt against Tony? Mark double-checked Tony's face to see if his shock had registered. Obviously not.

A grin split Tony's face. "Miss me?" He cooed in Jocelyn's ear.

Jocelyn's hips never stopped moving. "I've thought of you constantly."

Tony shifted and began to pump against her.

Mark stood transfixed watching the scene before him.

Jocelyn let go of Emma's hand and pushed her away. With slow stealthy steps, Emma moved back a few steps. She slipped behind Tony and crept to the stairs. She hunched down and crawled up the stairs checking between each step to see what was going on or maybe to see if she was out of sight?

Mark didn't know for sure why she stopped between each step but he did know for sure this wasn't the first time Jocelyn and Emma had done this.

Tony's breathing was a little faster and as he rocked into Jocelyn's body, she pushed back. He lowered Jocelyn's arm to where Mark thought his crotch to be.

At the movement, Jocelyn whimpered in pain.

Instinctively at the animalistic sound, Mark took a step forward. Tony grinned. "Want to come play with us?"

∼

SHE WAS FLOATING ALMOST TOUCHING the ceiling, looking down on the scene below.

Dear God, what was happening? She'd lost herself in her vision of happiness. This house, this backyard with the green grass, oak tree and swing where she and Emma were safe and happy.

She was supremely grateful that the Perths were out at Sadie's doctor appointment when Tony broke in. She'd known when she heard the glass breaking he'd found them. Of course he knew Emma was here. He cursed and threatened to hurt her even more if Emma didn't show up. Jocelyn had tried not to cry out but it had been long enough since she'd been hurt that the noise came without her intending it.

Emma knew what Tony was capable of so she'd come out of hiding. Stood next to her while Tony made threats, cut her and made more threats. Her prayers had been that Mark and Ethan would be safe. Her plan was to go with Tony and leave Emma behind. It was a plan she and Emma had talked over in the past. The only way Emma had agreed to it was because she could then call the police and give them a description, tell them what happened, and Jocelyn would know help was on its way.

And then Mark walked in the door. Did he know what was happening? He seemed so calm. She imagined that was the persona he presented when dealing with people who were in horrible accidents and maybe would never walk again or lose a leg or arm or... .

The image of him undressing while she watched replayed in her mind. He was nothing like Tony. He'd never threaten her, hurt her, demean her. He'd never try to force her to prostitute for him. Why had she ever denied herself the gift of intimacy with him?

"Want to come play with us?" Tony's cock ground into her hand. A hand that automatically made the movements it had been taught to make.

The pain in her shoulder radiated down her arm, a new cut from the knife digging into her flesh brought on a new blood flow. A part of her wanted to be floating on the ceiling, away from the pain, the terror. But for the plan to work, she had to be present.

Had Mark moved closer? She locked gazes with him, willing him to go away, to stay safe.

Emma's hand clung to hers. The knife dug into her flesh and blood began to flow again. His exertions made Tony's sour, whiskey-laden breath and unwashed body odor suffocating.

Tony was close to release and while he was not so lost that she could escape, from past experience she knew he wasn't as aware of what was going on peripherally.

A slight squeeze and she let go of Emma's hand and brushed her back and away.

She inwardly sighed with relief when Emma didn't hesitate. At least Emma would be safe. Emma and Ethan would be able to stay together and that was what mattered.

She stared at Mark. Did he understand her message? Stop. Stay safe.

Tony grunted in her ear with his release. Through his pants his semen dampened her hand. "Change of plans, Bitch. Decided to take you on a trip, show you a good time." His snarled laugh chilled her.

"Move Bitch!" Tony wrenched her left arm behind her as he bumped against her, shoving her into the knife.

"Fucking Bitch!" he yelled. "I said Move!"

Jocelyn shuffled forward, as best she could with her leg muscles screaming from being stretched, her arm twisted behind her and a knife at her throat. She kept her gaze on Mark, taking comfort and gaining strength from that connection. Emma would be safe and that's what really mattered.

"Tony, I already told you I'd come with you. We could get out of here faster if you eased your grip on my arm." Her voice rasped, her throat hurt and she knew besides the cuts, bruises were forming from when he'd first arrived and choked her. A shudder ratcheted through her as her body remembered her world turning black when he'd squeezed her neck.

He lifted her feet a few inches from the floor. Pain shot through her shoulder, the scream erupted of its own accord. How could she have forgotten how important it was to measure every word?

They were even with Mark now.

In another moment she would pass him and lose the lifeline looking at him gave her.

"You first," Tony waved the knife at Mark.

Mark sidled toward the front door not turning his back on her although his gaze shifted from her to Tony's.

At the doorway, Tony motioned him again to precede them.

On the broad porch, Jocelyn shivered in the cold November air. Eight steps from the porch to the ground. She and the kids counted them backwards. Eight, seven six, five, four, three, two one—they were on the ground.

She could feel Tony turning his head from side-to-side.

"Is that your car?" Mark asked, taking a few steps to one side while pointing toward the car parked at the curb.

"None of your fucking business." Tony stabbed the knife at Mark. "Get going, Shithead," he snarled.

A sound from her left—a pop.

The knife fell away.

The tension on her arm released.

The press of Tony against her back gone.

And the world went crazy.

Mark charged across the lawn.

Her peripheral vision filled with police officers, guns drawn.

Mark reached her first, his hands skillfully tracing her head, face, neck, arms, shoulders, inspecting and assessing.

Gulping sobs threatened to choke her.

Darkness crept in and claimed her.

Gentle pressure on her cheek, the kiss on her forehead after sweaty strands of hair were brushed back. Emma's small hand held hers.

Mark held her other hand as he talked to the officers and identified Tony adding he had a long history of physical, mental and emotional abuse. Ms. Lawford's name was mentioned.

Too much, too many details to take in. Start at the beginning. Her back was wet and cold from the grass. Emma and Mark held her hands. Ethan? Where was Ethan?

"Just a minute," Mark's voice interrupted the other one. "I'm a doctor and this is my wife. She needs medical treatment. Now. Most likely she'll need stitches."

She gripped his hand.

He squeezed it in response, his lips brushed her forehead. "You'll be okay, Jocelyn. We're taking you to the hospital. You don't need to talk, to say anything until you're checked out."

"Mama, I love you." Emma kissed her knuckles.

"Me too." Ethan patted her shoulder.

Mark's larger hand was replaced by a smaller one. Ethan was with her.

Her panicked brain, still fogged with pain, spewed questions that ran rampant. She tried to talk, but nothing happened.

Where was Tony? What happened?

The vision of Mark charging across the lawn was the only image she could dredge up.

Panic consumed her. She had to get up, take Emma and get away.

Little hands held her shoulders. "I'm still here, Mama. Papa is talking to the police officer and ambulance people have something for you to lie down on." Emma patted her cheek. "Tony's on the ground and he has a hole in his head. A police lady took his knife."

Jocelyn tried to speak, the words squirreling through her mind, but no sound emerged.

Was it over? Would she and Emma be safe? Ms. Lawford said there was enough evidence to keep Tony away from them. Was that true?

"One, two, three." Hands lifted her and shifted her onto the gurney. Blankets were wrapped around her. Mark took her hand.

"My folks have just arrived. They'll bring the kids to the hospital. I'm coming with you."

The cold slipped through her and she shivered. Everything seemed so far away.

"Shock," Mark's voice cut the air.

The outside air was cool, the ambulance heated. She hovered somewhere in the ether while an IV was started and warm blankets wrapped around her. Mark never left her side. Sirens blaring, the ambulance raced off.

CHAPTER 40

A large warm hand enveloped hers, the sound of breathing other than her own registered. Eyes closed Jocelyn identified the sounds and sensations around her. The hand holding hers was Mark's. She knew that for a certainty. A smile twitched the corners of her mouth.

She cracked her eyes open. Mark was right beside her, his hand through the hospital bed railing, holding hers. His eyes were closed, his breathing deep and even. He needed his sleep after what he'd been through.

A stab of guilt wrenched her gut.

He startled awake. "You're back," his sleepy voice rasped. He stretched with one arm, not letting her go.

She tugged, but he held tight. "Not letting you go," he said, standing and leaning over her.

"Mama?" Emma popped up on the other side of the bed with Ethan right beside her.

Tears pooled in her eyes as Emma and Ethan's happy, smiling faces greeted her.

The bandages around her neck constricted but she worked her throat, swallowing a couple of times before she tried to speak.

"Are you okay?" she whispered.

Emma's enthusiastic nod was accompanied by Ethan's fist pump and Mark's gentle squeeze of her hand.

"We're all okay. We took a vote and decided we'd be better than okay if we spent the night with you. Right?"

"Best of nights, right Papa?"

"As soon as the doctors fixed your Mama up, it was a very good night."

He turned to Jocelyn, kissed her temple and looked her in the eyes. "You had a close call, dear heart. Most of the cuts were shallow but a few were deeper. You lost a bit of blood."

She swallowed and focused on making herself heard. "Home?"

"Today."

Her grip on Mark's hand tightened. "Tony?"

"Dead. The police sharpshooter had a clean shot. When you are up to it, the police will come by and take your statement. Ms. Lawford has already filed papers with the court for us to adopt both children. She's amazingly fearsome."

Her forehead wrinkled. "How?"

"My parents. They had Ms. Lawford's name or knew her name and called. Left a message with her service about what happened. She called them back. Filed papers first thing this morning. Guess she had a rough draft and just added the latest incident to it."

She shuddered as spikes of fear stabbed. "Tony?"

"Jocelyn, he's dead." Mark leaned close, his chocolate brown gaze focused on her hazel one. "And the police did talk to Emma and Ethan so they know what they heard before Emma came downstairs. And they know what he did to you and Emma before I got there."

Tears threatened. "I...."

"I know you'd do anything to protect Emma, and now Ethan and me. I know, Jocelyn. You are the bravest of women and I am a very lucky man. I love you."

His words were filtered through her disbelief. "I...."

"You need say nothing. Just know you are fantastic and you have three lifelong fans right here in the room with you."

Emma patted her hand. "Mama, the doctor said you can have all the ice cream you want."

Jocelyn saw two eager faces in her line of vision. She managed a thumbs up while tears streamed down her face.

Wrapped in the protection of her disbelief, Jocelyn looked at Mark. How could he love her after what he witnessed? What he'd heard?

But when she looked at his face, looked in his eyes, she saw his truth. Under the onslaught of his love, the last layers of her disbelief slithered away.

JOCELYN SAT in the front seat of the car, her gaze rapt on the house of her dreams. Her brain scanned her body for signs of distress. Her fear upon leaving the hospital was that Tony had taken away her dream house. She was uneasy about going inside, uneasy about what she'd find, what she'd feel when she visited the scene of her living nightmare.

She remembered what the police officer and hospital social worker had said about how to deal with returning to the scene of trauma, of the crime. Mark had sat in on the meeting and actually offered that they stay in a hotel for a while or even move back into his condo.

His condo had been rented and was being moved into next weekend. And a hotel? "I'll feel better surrounded by my own things," she'd said, refusing both options. But here she was, still in the car, seat belt on, her brain still grappling with what she faced when she got out.

The front door opened and Mr. Perth stood there, a smile on his face, his hand raised in a welcoming wave. Ethan and Emma ran to him, each with a sack of ice cream held tight. They clamored up the stairs and he enveloped them in a hug. He saluted the car and that's when she noticed Mark was standing next to her door and it was open.

"Shall we?" His voice was warm with a hint of anxiety and he held his hand out as if inviting her to dance.

She wasn't sure what caught his attention but he added "Remember, this house is full of people who love and adore you. Remember, we have options. Remember you are not alone in this. I'm right here and I'm not going anywhere."

A flare of guilt assaulted her gut. "Your practice—."

"Is being covered by my partners until I come back."

She was terrified and yet hopeful. Maybe? "Mark?"

"Jocelyn, let's go in. I'll be right there. I shouldn't tell you this but a surprise is waiting for you. Emma, Ethan, my parents, Lily and Jackson and the Perth's have worked on it. I think you'll like it—and even if you don't, we can make changes until you do—or—we'll find another house in which to be happy."

Mark leaned in and unbuckled her seat belt. His nearness warmed her. The patience, kindness in his eyes soothed but the apology was there nonetheless. "I'm sorry...."

"Shh. Remember, no apologies. You'll be okay. I'm here to help you maneuver. You need to protect your left arm or wear the immobilizer."

She shifted and placed her hand in his. With his help she stood. He slipped his arm around her waist. She leaned into him, leaned on him, took solace in his strength.

What she wanted to do was tip her head back and look up at him but the bandages on her neck constricted her movements. She wrapped her right arm around his waist and let him guide her to the house.

It did not escape her notice that he went out of his way to block her view of the police tape in the form of a body still up on the front lawn. It did not escape her notice that there was police tape on the front lawn. It did not escape her notice that every time she looked out the windows onto the front lawn, she'd see the spot where Tony died. Would she ever be able to move past the horror of those few hours?

Walking in the front door was transformational. While she was gone, the place had been made over. It was the same house and yet not. Furniture was rearranged. Books had been changed out in their shelves. The focus in the living room was still the massive fireplace but the large couch and overstuffed chairs had been moved into a different configuration.

Because long ago the Perth's had removed the wall between the formal dining room and the kitchen she could see through the archway from the front door to the kitchen. The open concept wasn't as grand as a great room but only because it was smaller.

"I know you love the view of the backyard, so we came up with this arrangement," Mark said and gestured at the loveseat and chairs placed to show off the yard. The breath from Mark's words stirred the hair by her ear. She leaned her head against his shoulder, his arm tightened around her waist.

"You did all this for me?" Amazement and awe filled her tone as she struggled to speak.

He didn't answer. Instead he guided her a few more steps into the house and gestured for her to look around.

Emma and Ethan stood stock still, their intense gaze watching her every move, anticipation shimmering off them in waves.

"What a surprise!" she managed, still stunned with all they'd accomplished in twenty-four hours. "You must have worked very hard to do all this."

"We had lots of help," Ethan said, his head nodding.

"Who?"

"Lily and Jackson, Sophia who filled up the freezer with morsels of decadent goodness. My partners came by last night and helped move the furniture around. We had the cleaning service come in earlier in the day and clean, change beds, etc. Laundry is done thanks to the Perth's. It was a team effort. Team Jocelyn."

Jocelyn's head reeled. "But you were at the hospital with me."

"My parents supervised everything. Remember they came by the hospital this morning. And yes, they watched the kids, but they also kept them involved, asked their advice. This is what Team Jocelyn came up with as starters. Any or all of it can be changed around."

Tears threatened as tangled emotions flooded through her. "I don't know what to say." The whispered words were muffled in Mark's shirt as she turned into his arms and wept.

"It's okay kids. These are Mama's happy tears."

Jocelyn heard Mark's voice, felt one hand rubbing her back as the other held her tight.

"Mama doesn't cry happy tears." Emma's worry infused her words.

Mark's arm stopped traversing her back. "I'm sure you're right, Emma. But it's different now. I guarantee these are happy tears. Your mama is happy to be home, happy to see all the work we've done, happy to see everyone is safe."

A small hand patted her arm.

"Is Papa right, Mama? Are you crying happy tears?"

She nodded. Without stepping away, she let go of Mark and reached for Emma, holding her close to her side. When Mark let her go with one arm, she knew he now had Ethan by him.

"We are a family," Mark's voice reverberated in his chest. "And families stick together, they share their happy tears and their sad tears."

The doorbell rang.

"Let's see who's there, okay?" Mark kept ahold of Jocelyn's hand as they turned to the door. Ethan and Emma looked out the front window. "It's Lily and Jackson!"

"We can't stay long," Lily announced as they came in the door. "We brought you food. It's still warm so if you want it can be your dinner or you can save it for another day."

Jocelyn found herself wrapped in a warm, loving hug. "You are in everyone's prayers. And, if you need to talk or just want to be with someone, let me know. Ash will take the kids for an afternoon if that will help or she and Amanda will come over for a visit. I'm a phone call away. Call anytime, Jocelyn. Any time at all."

She grinned and patted Jocelyn's left arm. "I see you are without an immobilizer. Do be sure and let me know if he bullies you into wearing one. I've lots of practice on how to do things wearing one."

"I have a list of restrictions and if I fail to stick with them that's the next step," she managed to say before her throat seized.

Lily laughed. "That sounds so much like the Dr. Mark Parker I know." Her tone serious she added, "See what I can do?" She raised her arms over her head, stretched behind her and rotated her shoulders. "I know why he was so stern with me. I would have gone my own way and not healed as well as I did if he hadn't been."

"And I knew she would have been non-compliant and gone her own way." Mark chuckled. "I'm hoping my wife is more compliant because I will strap an immobilizer on her myself if she isn't."

His arm slid from her waist and he walked away.

"I don't know whether to be affronted or pleased," Jocelyn said to Lily in her whispery voice as she turned to see that he was joining Jackson and the kids in the kitchen.

"You can be both," Lily said and grinned. "He loves you and his protective streak is at the forefront of all he is doing now. Try to remember he wants what's best for you.

"Changing the subject, Jackson brought his spaghetti sauce, some homemade noodles, a loaf of bread. He was told the plan was to stop at the ice cream store and stock up since you can have all the ice cream you want." Lily's eyes twinkled and a smile tipped her lips. "Your kids are thrilled that was one of the doctor's orders."

Jocelyn smiled. "I think he gave that order for them."

"He might have. Something to divert them from their worry about you. You do know they think they are responsible for the cuts."

Jocelyn staggered under the weight of those words. A harsh and guttural "No!" filled the air.

All eyes turned to her. Mark started toward her. Emma and Ethan froze, their eyes large with fear.

"That bastard can't do that to us." Tears coursed down her face, leaving damp drops on her blouse.

Lily held her hand. "Jocelyn, let's sit down and talk this out, okay?" Lily guided Jocelyn to the sitting area overlooking the yard. "Come join us," she beckoned to Ethan, Emma and Mark.

"Now, let's be clear about this." Lily's tone brooked no argument. "Tony is responsible for everything bad that happened. No one else."

"But Mama got cut bad and I—." Ethan's face scrunched up and tears pooled in his eyes.

"Tony had the knife, Ethan," Lily said looking him in the eyes, "that's why he is responsible for the cuts on your mama and all the fear and worry everyone felt. You and Emma were very brave."

"I don't know what would have happened if you two had not done what you did." Jocelyn wished she had more power in her words, more confidence in her tone. In time she would as she'd been assured of a full recovery but for now she had this raspy, whispery hoarse voice.

"I don't want Tony to be my dad," Emma's tear-stained voice quavered.

"Sweetheart, Tony's dead and that means he can't ever hurt us again." It hurt to say even these words as Jocelyn's throat tightened even more.

"Did he go to heaven?" Ethan's face scrunch in concentration.

Jocelyn's heart skipped a beat and her lungs seized. Leave it to a little boy to ask such a question. She reached out and took Ethan's hand. Looking him straight in the eyes, she cleared her throat before she answered but her words still came out in a whisper. "As bad as Tony was, I don't believe he was born that way. Lots of times people have bad things happen to them."

Ethan never broke eye contact but he nodded.

"So when bad things happen to us, we have a choice. We can decide we'll do bad things too. Or, we can decide we'll be different. Tony made the decision to do bad things. But deep inside him, he was that little boy who had bad things happen to him. I believe that little boy will go to heaven.

"I believe we are all connected to each other through Spirit or The Divine. That Spirit or The Divine is a part of all that is. So, when I look outside at the old oak tree, I see a part of myself, a part of each of us. Does that make sense?"

Ethan's brow furrowed. "Is that like when I saw him," he gestured to Mark, "I knew he was my papa?"

Jocelyn's throat constricted with emotions, tears filled her eyes as she nodded. "Yes, it's just like that. And you and your papa made a choice, even though bad things had happened, not to let that keep you from being happy together."

"If the court hearing goes as we hope," Mark sat beside her, but on the arm of the chair, still holding her hand, "you both will have Jocelyn and me as your mama and papa."

"I can't imagine the court not granting you both custody and permission to adopt," Lily added.

Jocelyn sat a little straighter and looked directly at both children. "You saved my life. Emma, you came downstairs and stood by me. You remembered everything we talked about and did exactly as we'd planned. Ethan, you alerted your papa that something bad was happening so when he came in the door, he was prepared. And, he talked to Tony and distracted him enough that Tony didn't know the police were there. All three of you gave me the strength to do what I had to do to survive.

"While I love the idea of Team Jocelyn, I think it's more accurate to say "Team Parker."

CHAPTER 41

Team Parker was joined by the Perths and the senior Parkers for a big spaghetti dinner with ice cream for dessert. After Peter and Peggy left and the Perths returned to their living quarters, Mark and Jocelyn sat on the floor in front of the fireplace with Ethan and Emma snuggled in their laps. As the fire burned down and the room cooled, they gathered throws from the couch and chairs and wrapped themselves up in the soft fabric.

"What about a campout?" Jocelyn wondered aloud as Emma burrowed deeper when Mark mentioned bedtime.

Mark looked over at her. "Here?"

"Yes, here." She might regret it in the morning but tonight she wanted more than anything to ensure the children slept well. Peter and Peggy would be back tomorrow to take the kids out to the park and maybe shopping or a movie. They'd be gone for several hours. She could nap then.

"Perfect idea," Mark kissed her temple and shifted Ethan over toward her. "I'll get supplies."

He levered himself up and stretched, twisted and worked the kinks out.

"You need a massage," she commented.

"We could all do with one." He lean down and kissed the top of her head. "I shall return."

"Mama?" Emma's sleepy voice recalled her to the present.

"What Pumpernickel?" Jocelyn relished the weight of her daughter nestled against her right side.

"Where'd Papa go?"

"Just upstairs for a few things. He'll be back in a few minutes."

"I miss him." Emma snuggled closer, a soft sigh and her breathing resumed its sleeping rhythm.

I miss him too. Jocelyn missed his heat, his strength, his unwavering support, his scent, the sound of his voice, his kiss, his … . The promise she'd made herself when Tony's knife was cutting her, when he threatened all she loved, rose in her mind. She was certain she and Mark would not be intimate tonight but soon. She would no longer deny herself intimacy with a loving, kind man because a monster had treated her brutally. She deserved better than that.

Jocelyn did not delude herself that it would be easy, that she'd undergo no fear or hesitation or—. But the reward when she was on the other side of it, when she'd experienced intimate tenderness with a man who loved her, took care of her and looked out for her; a good man, a good father. And, as she heard his footsteps signal his approach, added, a good husband. That reward would be more than worth it.

She started to chuckle but stopped when the bandage around her neck constricted her movements. A pair of legs were partially hidden behind a swath of blankets. Before she shifted to get a better view, the entire pile landed in a heap at her feet.

Mark leaned over and picked up Emma, holding her close to his chest, he took the few steps to the overstuffed chair. Ethan was the next to be moved. Mark helped her to stand and ushered her to the side. "How are you doing?" His brow furrowed and concern shone in his eyes as he gazed down at her, running his hands up and down her arms.

Warmth traced his movements and joy filled her heart. "I'm doing okay." She gestured to the pile. "And this?"

"And this is our camping out bed." He plucked cushions off the couch and tossed them on the floor. Blankets came next, then pillows. Another pile of blankets would be their covers.

While she was up, she walked around the living room a bit, testing her legs that, while not injured, were sore from the stress of standing on her tiptoes to keep the knife at bay.

Back at the scene of living room campout disarray, she said, "I can help."

"Let me do this, Jocelyn. Let me take care of you tonight."

His intensity, his need to do this registered in his unwavering gaze and the soft plea in the tone of his voice.

She nodded. "I'm going to go brush my teeth."

"Do you need any he—."

She put a hand up to stave off his words. "I'll be okay. Nothing bad happened to me upstairs and you and everyone else are making wonderful memories for me here. I'll be okay."

Upstairs she used the toilet and took a good look at herself in the mirror as she washed her hands and brushed her teeth. There was something about knowing Tony was dead and unable to come after her that soothed. She saw a lessening of the tension she'd carried for so long she'd stopped noticing it. Now, she was safe. She and Emma were safe. She and Emma had Mark and Ethan. She and Emma were part of a family, regardless of what the court ruling would be.

Tonight at dinner, she had easily seen the Perths were Emma's grandparents just as Peter and Peggy were Ethan's. She wasn't their blood relation. As a matter of fact, Emma wasn't even her blood relation. *In this instance the old adage blood is thicker than water, is not true.*

Sadie seemed to have a new lease on life now that they were living downstairs and she had the view of the yard. She needed help to come up the stairs to the main floor but with her walker was managing to move around downstairs on her own.

Before this all happened, they enjoyed tea time virtually every afternoon. Jocelyn fixed tea and plated cookies or fruit or maybe a few bites of pastry on a tray she took downstairs and shared with Sadie.

Before this all happened, she'd asked Mark about installing one of those chair lifts so Sadie could more easily come up to the main floor.

Before this all happened…she was still inspecting the face of the woman in the mirror as her mind rambled with random thoughts.

Before this all happened she'd denied herself joy and happiness; she'd denied her worth to herself or others; she'd been so fearful, so guarded, so intent on seeing the negative.

She believed each life experience held a gift. The gift in Tony's abuse? Besides having Emma? Now on the other side of it, she had clarity. She knew exactly what she wanted in a life-partner, in a marriage, in a family. Her own parents' marriage had had an undertone of negativity. Certainly not abusive like the one she'd had with Tony, but laughter was not a daily occurrence in her family home.

She sensed him before she saw him by her side through the mirror.

"You okay?"

She shifted to look at him. "I'm getting there."

"Good." He held out his hand.

She looked back in the mirror. "She was reminding me of the gift Tony gave me by coming here."

Mark stepped closer so he stood behind her. His hands rested gently on her shoulders, his gaze locked on the eyes of the woman in the mirror. "Do you think she'd share that with me?"

Jocelyn didn't hesitate, speaking in a clear yet raspy voice. "She wants you to know that Jocelyn did her best but became too overwhelmed by fear and doubt. She became too negative. Tony coming here now reminded her that she is worth much more than he could ever see, could ever recognize. And because he came here and was defeated, she is now free to live a full life. To invite love and happiness into her home and her heart."

"She's very wise." He kissed the crown of her head. "Need anything more in here?"

Lightness filled her body and she relaxed against him. "No." A simple word, no. And yet a complex and complicated one. This *no* locked a door to her past, sealed it shut. She was not so naïve to think nothing would ever leak out but she was confident she had the key to locking it away again.

Mark took her hand and escorted her down the stairs where the floor was covered with cushions, pillows and blankets. Emma and Ethan were tucked in the middle of the mess.

"Let me help you," Mark said as he assisted her down onto the pillows. "Will this be okay?"

Jocelyn, on her right side, tucked a pillow so it supported her head. Mark pulled blankets up and over her shoulder before he turned the lights off and took his place on the opposite side of the kids.

"Let me touch you," Mark's request whispered across the pillows.

He stretched out his hand until he found her.

She ran her hand up his arm, not quite to his elbow before she traced the corded muscles in his arm back to his hand. The burnished embers in the fireplace gave off minimal light but she could see his face.

He reached out and brushed his fingertips over her cheeks, her nose, traced her chin.

Finding his hand again, she wrapped it in her own. Her thumb stroked the back of his hand. His breathing slowed. She knew when he'd fallen asleep because the tension in his hand eased.

Her fingers traced his knuckles, his wrist and circled around as she explored the palm of his hand. The last thing she remembered as sleep overcame her was *I'm safe.*

CHAPTER 42

Mark woke before the sun rose. He remembered this great idea of camping out on the living room floor had been his. The part that wasn't so great? His hips were on the hardwood floor, his feet were cold. Not chilled but freezing. He wiggled them and tried to bend his knees to get them under blankets. What also registered was the warm body curled into his chest and someone holding his hand. Cracking one eye open to better get his bearings, his lips tipped in a smile.

Jocelyn still held his hand.

Careful not to wake Ethan, he shifted his son so he could roll off the cushions and get to his feet. He stretched and bent to touch his toes, rubbing the tops of his feet to get some blood moving. Balancing on one foot and then the other, he pulled wool socks on before heading to the bathroom and then the kitchen. He started coffee for himself and water for Jocelyn's tea. After checking the refrigerator, he figured he and the kids would make French toast for breakfast.

Movement captured his attention and his hand automatically fisted.

"Awful early. Heard someone moving around," Mr. Perth said, a rolling pin in his thin, frail hand.

"Thanks for checking. I've got coffee if you'd like a cup."

Mr. Perth smiled and held out his hand. "Best way to start the day is with a cuppa."

They sat in the eating nook off the kitchen and watched the sun light up the backyard while turning the sky a soft rose with touches of lavender.

"Have you thought of upgrading the security system?" Mr. Perth said into the silence.

"I have now." Mark smiled his thanks. "Haven't gotten past one minute to the next until right now."

"Understandable. My Sadie and I will split the cost with you."

"Thanks for the offer but that won't be necessary." Mark noticed the older man's shoulders slump at his words. "What is necessary is that you be here with Jocelyn when the security company comes so you can weigh in on what is needed and what is superfluous. You and Sadie know this house better than anyone."

Mr. Perth sat tall. "You can count on me."

"You have no idea how much Jocelyn and I do count on you and Sadie already. We're very...." His next words died in his throat.

"We're very blessed to have you and Sadie and this house in our lives," Jocelyn said coming to stand next to Mark, her hand resting lightly on his shoulder. "I'm the one who should apologize—."

Two male voices interrupted. Mark snaked his arm around her waist and pulled her down on his lap. "You should be asleep, resting, taking care of yourself," he chided as he kissed her temple.

"Did we wake you?" Mr. Perth asked.

"No, Mother Nature did that and then I heard voices and came to investigate." She snuggled closer to Mark, rested her head on his shoulder.

"How are you feeling this morning?" Concern registered in Mark's voice, his hands lightly checking her left shoulder, arm and hand.

"Physically I'm stiff, sore. Emotionally I'm drained. Mentally I'm managing."

"You have some pain pills you could take." Mark suggested in a neutral tone.

"I think a couple of aspirin will be enough. I'm surprised my neck doesn't hurt more than it does." She started to stand.

"Let me wait on you." Mark stood, setting Jocelyn in the chair before he crossed to the stove where the tea kettle simmered. He knew she liked her tea on the weak side so he filled the mug and brought it, an assortment of teas and a spoon to her before sitting in a vacant chair.

Adopting a casual posture and keeping his voice calm, Mark said "Mr. Perth suggested we update the security system. He's prepared to be here and act as a consultant because he knows the house inside and out. What do you think?"

Jocelyn sipped her tea before answering. "I think that's an excellent idea." She smiled at Mr. Perth. "I'm fairly certain it wouldn't have stopped Tony from breaking in because he was so intent on harming Emma and me but—" she turned to Mark, "I'm sure it will deter the general run-of-the-mill kind of thief."

"I'll call today and set up an appointment. It may be someone can come today or tomorrow and I'll also be here." Mark said in his take-charge way.

"You don't have to stay home because of me. I'm fine."

"Well, you may be fine, he crooked his fingers around the last word, "but I'm not."

Jocelyn heard the hard edge in his tone and paused before answering. What had this whole ordeal done to him? To Ethan? She'd put them both in danger because she'd agreed to marry Mark.

"I'm so sorry—."

Mark abruptly stood, sending the chair back a foot. Hands fisted at his side he stared at her.

"Jocelyn," Mr. Perth's gentle voice broke her gaze from Mark's intense stare. "I think your husband needs time to be with his family. To have the reality that everyone is safe settle in his bones.

"It's hard for a man to watch someone he loves in trouble, in pain or in jeopardy and be unable to rush in and save her. I know that's true with my Sadie. She suffers from a disease and there's nothing I can do except be there with her, hold her hand when she needs that or just hold her in my arms when I need to be close to her."

She reached across the table and placed her hand on his. "Thank you. I've been wrapped up in myself and lost sight of the impact on others."

Mr. Perth patted her hand. "And you should be wrapped up in yourself. Not saying anything about that. Just saying everyone else is wrapped up in themselves too. Need to make space for everyone to sort things out."

Jocelyn rose and stepped in front of Mark. She started to tip her head back to look in his eyes but the bandage constricted and the stitches pulled. She stopped. "Come sit with me." She held his hand and tugged him back to the table. When they were both seated, she held his hand in both of hers. "I can't imagine what it was like to come home and know the danger that Ethan and Emma were in."

He cocked his head, raised an eyebrow and stared her down.

She flushed and looked away. "Well, and me. I know you like me."

He leaned forward, turned her face toward him with a firm touch. "Let's get one thing clarified. I love you."

Out of the corner of her eye, she saw Mr. Perth quietly get up and leave.

She took a deep breath. Unshed tears pooled and she blinked several times to clear her vision. "That's good because I love you too." Her voice shook and tears slipped down her cheeks. "I'll make a deal with you."

"I'm listening."

"We talk to each other at the end of the day, before going to sleep. A check-in so we each know how the other is doing. I've been through this before." At the look on his face she hurried on. "Not exactly like this. He held a gun on Emma once so I'd agree to do something he wanted—."

Her heart beat so hard she felt the pulse in every fiber of her being. She slowed her breathing until her voice was steady. "Emma and I saw a counselor once. She told us that everything would get better in time but there was always the possibility of something triggering the memory and our bodies would respond as if we were back in that situation.

"She said it was important to remember these were passing thoughts that seemed real and to create a process to keep us grounded in the present. One way to do that was to return to our normal routines as best we could.

"That advice has helped Emma and me through tough times. It's why I said you could go back to work. It isn't that we don't want you here, that I don't want you here. It's that I want you moving beyond yesterday."

Mark's thumb stroked the back of her hand, he leaned forward and kissed her cheek. "You are amazing. I'm not sure when my feelings for you changed from liking you to loving you but that's where I am now. If you ever want to talk in more detail about your life with Tony, I promise I'll listen. If you never want to talk about it, I'm okay with that."

"Not even curious?" She smiled but it was a faint imitation of her happy one.

"I'm always curious but I can control my curiosity. I want you and Emma to feel safe here with Ethan and me. I want you to know the joy that comes with unfettered freedom to be yourselves.

"And, as sick as this may sound, I'm glad Tony found us. I'm glad I got to see with my own eyes what a sick, tormented bastard he was. I totally understand your hesitance to be intimate with me, why you flinch or shy away at times, why Emma is so hypervigilant."

"Papa, Mama?" A hint of panic sounded in the two voices calling out.

"We're in the kitchen," Mark called out.

As Emma and Ethan charged into the room, he opened his arms and scooped them up. "Who wants French toast?"

A chorus of "Me" and "I do" was followed by small bodies jumping up and down.

"Okay then. We'll make French toast for Mama. Ethan you get the eggs out of the fridge. Emma you get the bread. And you," he pointed to Jocelyn, "supervise." As Ethan got out the eggs, Mark reached over his head and grabbed the milk.

They created an assembly line once the egg and milk mixture was ready. Emma dipped the bread in the mixture and dropped it into the pan. Ethan got out butter and syrup along with jam and a shaker full of cinnamon and sugar.

As the toast cooked, Mark put it on a plate in the oven until the pile was high. "Ready?" At eager nods, he shooed them to the table, took out the platter and began putting the French toast on plates.

He also saw that Jocelyn's tea was replenished, his coffee mug refilled and Ethan and Emma had glasses of milk.

"You make an excellent cook," Jocelyn commented just before she brought a bite of cinnamon-sugar covered French toast to her mouth. "Perfect," she mumbled around a mouthful.

Mark leaned over and kissed her cheek. "We aim to please."

CHAPTER 43

Ms. Lawford had been hard at work. The hearing that was to have taken place the day after Tony's attack was rescheduled ten days out. Enough time for them to start to recover but not so much time as to create more anxiety.

Mark returned to work part-time the following Monday. He checked on any patients in the hospital, took his On-Call nights and kept office hours from noon to three.

The morning of the hearing finally arrived. No one had slept well. Mark had been up and down all night with Ethan and Emma who were having "bad dreams." She was going to get up but remembered Mr. Perth's advice—this was something Mark had to do for her. And, she thought, for himself.

Although grateful the large swath of gauze around her neck was off, it meant all the bandages covering the multitude of cuts were visible. Ms. Lawford advised she wear a scarf if she was self-conscious. She debated whether to cover up the evidence of their nightmare or make a statement. In the end, she wore a rainbow colored scarf she'd been gifted at the 14th Moon Gathering draped around her neck.

Mrs. Fester was sitting with the state's attorney when they entered the courtroom. Ms. Lawford was at an adjoining table. They'd talked about what to do and decided Jocelyn would sit with the children and Mark would sit with Ms. Lawford.

Lily and Ashley sat directly behind her. She startled then relaxed when Lily patted her shoulder and said, "Remember, you're not alone."

A strange sensation filled her stomach—not the familiar nausea, cramping or clenching she was used to. Warmer and comforting it expanded and filled her body.

Another layer of support: Peggy and Peter Parker sat next to Lily. Her surgery to remove the tumor was scheduled for day after tomorrow. Despite the arguments her husband and son plied, she was adamant that she be here for the hearing.

Mr. Perth sat beside Ashley. He and Sadie had been staunch supporters, especially since Tony's break-in and death. He had been with her when the security company installed updated equipment. And, he'd suggested a way to transform the front yard.

Yesterday Jackson, his friend, Daniel and Mark planted an oak tree. Her grandchildren and great grandchildren would have a tree to climb and swing from in the front yard. Four smaller circles representing the four directions were planted with flowers that would attract butterflies and hummingbirds. The ugliness that was Tony was gone.

"All rise." The Bailiff called out.

Judge Peterson strode into the courtroom and took her seat in the chair behind the bench.

"You may be seated" The Judge picked up the paperwork before her, glanced over it and said to the state's attorney, "You may proceed."

Jocelyn held both Emma and Ethan's hands and willed her grip to be firm but not tight as the attorney read the petition stating why Ethan should not be adopted by Mark.

Thankfully, Ms. Lawford had told them that was the recommendation so they could talk to both children and prepare them as best as they could.

"Ms. Lawford, I see that you have filed a counter-petition asking the court to approve the adoption of Ethan and that you have also included a request that this court approve the adoption of the daughter of the now deceased Anthony Barger's daughter, Emma, to both Mark Parker and his wife, Jocelyn."

Ms. Lawford rose and gestured to Jocelyn and the children before focusing back on the judge. "Your Honor, you see before you two children who have had a challenging start in life. Ethan, as you know from the file, was severely injured which is why he's been in care. The birth parents have agreed to their rights being terminated upon his adoption.

"You will note that Emma has also come from an abusive background. Her biological father broke bones and did not seek medical treatment. He staged a fake marriage to Ms. Jocelyn Edwards who then became Emma's stepmother. It is because of Jocelyn Edwards Parker that Emma is alive today.

"I'm sure Mrs. Fester's report has been amended to include the disturbing incident that caused the original hearing to be rescheduled. What may be missing is that Mr. Barger is dead. Had he lived, he would have faced criminal charges here and in Illinois.

"However, what's pertinent in this case is that both of these children feel safe with Dr. and Mrs. Parker. Both of these children have clearly indicated in therapy sessions that they want to remain together and that they want to remain with Dr. and Mrs. Parker.

"It is in the best interests of the children for the court to grant Dr. Mark Parker's petition that he and his wife adopt both children."

"Mrs. Fester, do you have something to say before I rule?" Judge Peterson's gaze focused on the social worker.

Mrs. Fester stood. "Your Honor, these children are young and could easily make a good adjustment in a loving home. Dr. Parker and Ms. Edwards married to thwart my recommendation. Theirs is not a marriage based on love. It is a marriage based on a mutual goal of keeping these children with them. Studies show that children do better in a home where the parents love and respect each other."

"May I?" Mark raised his hand as he spoke.

"What would you like to add Dr. Parker?" Judge Peterson asked.

"Mrs. Fester is right that the idea to marry was so I could keep Ethan. I love him as if he were my own flesh and blood and we'd created a good life. Mrs. Fester insisted that I must marry and stated that she couldn't with a good conscience recommend adoption of a small child to a single man.

"However, I stand before you as a married man. I am married to the bravest, most courageous, loving and compassionate woman I've ever known. She is kind and caring. She has a core of steely resolve so that when she's determined to do something, she follows through until she's successful. When Mr. Barger threatened to hurt Emma, held a gun to that little girl's head until Jocelyn agreed to prostitute for him—" his voice broke and he ran a hand down his face.

"I can't imagine... . Well, what I mean to say is that was the impetus for her to find a way to take Emma and run. The decision to take Emma with her made it more difficult for her to escape and disappear.

"To keep this little girl safe, my wife and Emma made plans for what to do if Mr. Barger ever caught up to them. I won't bore you with the details except for one. If he ever caught up to them, and Emma could escape, she must do that. She must get away and get help. Jocelyn assured her that she'd be okay if Emma got away. No matter what he did or said, Emma was to stay hidden unless Jocelyn called to her.

"Having seen what he did to my wife in an effort to ensnare Emma, to have another hold on my wife was terrifying. But this little girl knew her mama had a plan. So when Jocelyn told her to come, she did. She stayed right beside her mama, held her hand and when the signal came, she slipped away.

"Ethan missed all of this because he was upstairs hiding. But when Emma came back up, they hatched a plan. Getting baseball bats, they were going to sneak down the stairs and, with all their might, hit Mr. Barger. Bats aimed at his knees and when he fell, hitting him on the head.

"I'm grateful they didn't actually act on this plan but I'm grateful they had a plan. Ask yourself this, how would a four and five year old know where vulnerable body parts are? They certainly don't get that from watching any television at our house because neither my wife nor I watch that kind of program. They knew this because Jocelyn had taught Emma the best places to hit someone and be able to get away.

"I can't remember a time in my life when I begged for something, but, Your Honor, I'm begging now. Ethan and Emma are already the children of our hearts, please make them our legal children. They are well loved. They are safe and in some ways safer than they would be in a family who'd never experienced violence.

"And, just to set the record straight. I may have married Jocelyn because I liked and respected her and for the selfish reason of keeping Ethan but I can solemnly state now that I love her unconditionally. I thank God that I asked her to marry me because I can't imagine sharing my heart with anyone else."

The room was quiet when Mark sat down. Jocelyn no longer held Ethan and Emma by the hand, they were cuddled on either side.

"Papa did a good job, didn't he?" Ethan's whisper carried in the stillness.

"Papa did an amazing job," Jocelyn replied and kissed the top of his head.

"You must be Ethan," Judge Peterson said. "I'd like you to come up here and talk to me."

"Can I bring Emma?"

"Why do you want to bring Emma?" Judge Peterson leaned forward, a smile on her face.

"'Cause we do everything together when we get scared," Ethan announced, his voice trembling.

"Then bring Emma with you."

Jocelyn shifted and helped the children into the aisle. The Bailiff opened the gate and ushered them to the witness chair.

Judge Peterson leaned forward and asked "Do you both want Dr. Parker to be your father?"

The look of horror that raced across both Ethan and Emma's faces chilled the air.

The judge leaned closer. "I was told you both want Mark and Jocelyn to be your father and mother."

Wide open fear-filled eyes and shaking heads followed that statement.

"In my chambers, now!" Judge Peterson rose from her chair and strode out of the room.

Ethan was crying, Emma's arms were around him. Mr. Perth approached them. "Now, come and sit with me and your Grandmama and Grandpapa. Everything will work out."

"What's going on?" Judge Peterson's tone ripped through the air.

"I told you this wasn't a good home." Mrs. Fester's righteous voice hit Jocelyn in the gut.

"Your Honor?" Jocelyn spoke up.

"You can shed some light on this debacle?" Judge Peterson gestured to go on.

"I can tell you why the children reacted in such a strange way to your question. One of the things that drew them together is the horrendous abuse they'd both received at the hands of men who were called their 'dad', 'daddy' or 'father'. They would never refer to Mark as anything but 'Papa' because 'Papas' are safe. I know if you ask them if they want Mark to be their papa, you'll get a very different answer."

"Your Honor," Mrs. Fester spoke up.

"Wait here." Judge Peterson exited the room.

It seemed forever before the door opened and the Bailiff asked them to return to the courtroom.

Judge Peterson sat in her chair and on her lap were Ethan and Emma who were telling her a grand tale. A tale that had the judge smiling.

Mark's hand tightened and she squeezed back. The fear of losing the children lessened.

When everyone was back in their appointed places, except for

Emma and Ethan who were still with the judge, she gave her gavel to Emma who rapped it twice on a wooden block.

Ethan, his most serious look on his face, said "The Judge has made her decision."

"Very good." Judge Peterson beamed a smile at both of them. "You'll make wonderful judges yourselves someday." Her focus returned to the courtroom.

"Mrs. Fester, other than your opinion that Dr. and Mrs. Parker do not love each other and theirs is a marriage of convenience, I've heard nothing to convince me they are unfit to parent these children.

"Therefore the Court is granting the adoption of Ethan to Mark and Jocelyn Parker.

"In the matter of Emma. The Court is giving legal custody of this child to Mark and Jocelyn Parker until such time as the required home study is completed. At that time the court will approve the legal adoption of said child by the Parkers."

Judge Peterson leaned down and whispered something to the children.

Emma and Ethan gave her hugs before tearing down from the bench throwing themselves into Mark and Jocelyn's arms.

"Mama, Papa, The Judge said you are going to always be my mama and papa." Ethan's small arms hugged Jocelyn tight.

"And she said that we can always live with you forever and ever." Emma kissed Mark's cheek.

"And she said, Papa can fix Emma just like he fixed me."

Mark looped his free arm over Jocelyn's shoulder. "Shall we take this brood home?"

"With pleasure."

CHAPTER 44

The house was ablaze with lights when they pulled in the driveway. Mr. Perth stood in the doorway, Lily and Jackson just behind. Ethan held Emma's hand as they went up the steps.

Jocelyn's knees wobbled and she leaned on the hood of the car.

"It's real," Mark said, his breath feathering her neck. "Our home, our family is real."

Tears teetered before tracing damp paths down her cheeks. Her head rested on Mark's shoulder and she held his hand. "I can hardly believe this is real. I feel like I'm living in a dream right now."

Mark shifted and caged her against the car, leaned down and kissed her forehead and cheeks. With his thumbs he erased the evidence of her tears. "You are my dream come true." He smiled and drew her into a hug. "Rather miraculous isn't it that we both are living our dreams right now." He bent down and looked in her eyes. "Shall we go in and see what else our dreams have in store for us?"

"Yes." As she said the simple word, took her husband's hand and started toward the house, Jocelyn floated on the air of happiness.

"Come see, come see," Emma and Ethan met them at the door, tugging them into the house and the living room.

"It's a surprise," Emma bounced on the couch and patted the spot beside her.

"Uh huh." Ethan sat on the other end.

"You two are to be in the middle," Lily said. Once Jocelyn and Mark were settled, she turned the television on.

Anne's face came on the screen. "This is my gift for you and your family, Dr. Parker. Jocelyn, just so you know, everyone at Fremont Ortho is delighted you and Emma have joined our family. Now on with the show." She waved her hand in a dramatic manner and disappeared.

Jocelyn relived her wedding day. The house, the flowers, the ceremony flowed on the screen before her eyes. Each guest looked directly into the camera and made personal remarks. She had a hint as to what was coming next because both Emma and Ethan's excitement was palpable.

She grasped Mark's hand as the camera focused on the two children. They were upstairs in the room they now shared. Emma's serious face filled the camera.

"I love you, Mama." Tears dribbled down her face and she swiped them away with one hand while reaching out of camera range with the other.

Jocelyn wasn't surprised when Ethan appeared. His lowered voice carried to the camera microphone. "We were going to do this alone."

Emma held tight and Ethan heaved a sigh and sat next to her. Another swipe at the tears. A tissue appeared and Emma leaned forward to grab it. "I love you, Mama. And I love Papa. I'm going to be really good and pick my toys up." She smiled, "I love my new dolly and I have my own books too. Ethan's Grandmama let me pick out books for me to keep all by myself."

Jocelyn's cheeks were damp.

Mark handed her a tissue.

"I promise I'll be really good. I won't forget. I still know how to pack my suitcase and backpack and I teached Ethan how to do it real quick."

"Anything else, Emma," Anne said.

Emma shook her head. Then looked directly in the camera. "Don't forget to call me "Pumpernickel."

"Ethan?" Anne coached.

"Papa, I love you this much!" Ethan flung his arms wide.

Emma ducked and rolled her eyes.

"You got me the best Mama in the world and," he paused, earnestness infusing his features as he stared into the camera, "the bestest everything." He lowered his voice, "I let Em teach me the packing stuff but I know you'll never let anything bad happen to us."

Mark's arm was around her, his head rested on hers. They both dabbed their eyes with wadded tissues.

Anne's face was back on the screen. "We're wishing you the best of everything. Emma and Ethan's heads popped into the picture from each side. "Love you a bushel and a peck" Emma said. "Doodle, oodle, oodle do" she and Ethan chorused.

CHAPTER 45

Jocelyn walked into the bedroom, closing the door behind her as anticipation thrummed through her. She looked forward to making love with her husband. It would be their first time. They'd talked a few days after Tony's assault. She'd assured Mark she wanted to be his wife physically, to be intimate and finally be his wife in all ways.

But Mark wanted to wait until her wounds were better healed.

"I can't nibble on your neck, barely get to your ear with all the bandages," he'd said while kissing her temple and holding her close.

Even though the large gauze bandage around her neck was removed, there were numerous smaller and three medium sized ones covering the cuts. They talked each night as they had agreed to that morning after she was released from the hospital. And with the court hearing looming, they decided waiting until they knew for sure about the kids would be best. When they became lovers, they wanted to totally focus on each other, on the joining of their bodies.

Jocelyn's body warmed at the thought of making love with Mark. She smiled as she relived the passionate kisses of last night. If they hadn't made a pact, she thought they'd have finished what they'd obviously started.

But she was grateful they'd pulled back because tonight would be so much better. She was Ethan's legal Mama and would soon be that to Emma. The home study process had already started. It was just a matter of time.

Sitting in bed with covers pulled up to his waist was her husband. The fact that the sheet was the only thing between him and the night air was obvious because the bottoms of his sweats were on the floor next to his side.

"Been waiting for you," he said and patted the bed.

Her heart beat a bit faster. Her body softened with desire. "I read an extra story to the end, even after I was fairly sure they'd fallen asleep. Just to be on the safe side."

"So, no interruptions?"

She smiled and untied the belt of her robe. "No interruptions would be nice."

"No interruptions would be crucial. I've never made love to a wife with children in the house."

She laughed. "You never had a wife before."

"Nope, I waited for the perfect woman and lo and behold, here she is." His hands swept in a wide gesture.

Jocelyn slipped the robe off her shoulders and laid it on the bench at the foot of the bed. The nightgown she wore was a shimmery swath of fabric that covered her from head to toe. "I bought this just for you because you said green was your favorite color."

Mark held his hand out when she approached his side of the bed. "I love this on you but will adore it off." He reached for the hem.

She brushed his hands aside and slipped and slide the fabric up her body.

EPILOGUE

September 2004
Labor Day Weekend

Bare feet planted on the ground, Jocelyn stood in the center of the circle of forty women with her circle sisters, Carol, Meagan and Molly. She wore a four inch wide pendant of intricately woven brass, her Intercessor talisman. "Please join me in opening this sacred circle." Arms wide, she slowly turned until she faced the arch marking the East Entrance. She stopped, raised her head to see the night sky and continued lifting her arms palms out until her hands were even with her head.

"Spirits of the East, rising sun, new beginnings, new life, Robin and Flicker, I invite you into this circle of women to be our guides and protectors as we celebrate together."

She lowered her arms before turning to the South. Once again she lifted her arms in prayer before speaking.

"Spirits of the South, noon sun, of ripening, of manifestation, Hummingbird and Blue Jay, I invite you into this circle of women to be our guides and protectors as we celebrate together."

The earth hummed energy through the soles of her feet and up her body as she shifted to the left.

"Spirits of the West, setting sun, reflection, recharging, Raven and Heron, I invite you into this circle of women to be our guides and protectors as we celebrate together."

Heat and light infused her body, her voice strong, she reached for the sky when she faced the North Gate.

"Spirits of the North, moon, ancestor wisdom, instinctive knowing, night hunter Owl in her many forms, I invite you into this circle of women to be our guides and protectors as we celebrate together."

She stepped to the side and motioned for Carol to step forward. Unshed tears glistened as one-by-one, her circle sisters called in the energies from Above, Below and Center. Months ago when they had balked about participating in the Opening and Closing Ceremonies, she'd responded. "I am the Intercessor and we are to follow my Spirituality. My Spirituality includes the sharing of Opening and Closing Ceremonies. When you are Intercessor, you may do as you wish."

Jocelyn remained in the center of the natural circle of eighty to one hundred foot Douglas firs. She breathed in the scent of the night and the trees as each woman introduced herself and shared why she was here, what she brought to this circle and what she hoped to take away. Some stood when they spoke, others remained seated on the ground or in an outdoor chair. Jocelyn listened carefully. There were parts of the ceremonial prayers where she was in trust the right words, some of them prompted by this sharing, would come through her in right time.

They lit the sacred fire that would burn until after tomorrow night's Crone ceremony, ending this year's 14th Moon. Jocelyn made sure everyone understood they would be called back to this sacred place with drumming and song. And after everyone's questions were answered, she raised her arms once again to the sky as the stars twinkled and winked and the light of the moon graced her upturned face.

In reverse order, Carol, Megan and Molly released the spirits of the Center, Below and Above. Turning to the North Gate, her arms still raised, Jocelyn's voice rang strong in the dark.

"We thank you Spirits of the North, moon, ancestor wisdom, instinctive knowing, night hunter Owl in her many forms, for being with us at this time. We release you with our gratitude." A cool breeze danced along her skin as she shifted to the next direction.

"Spirits of the West, setting sun, reflection, recharging, Raven and Heron, we thank you for being with us at this time. With our gratitude, you are released to go." A sigh whispered from someone and her own body echoed the release as she made a quarter turn.

"We thank you Spirits of the South, noon sun, of ripening, of manifestation, Hummingbird and Blue Jay, for being with us at this time. We release you with our gratitude." Jocelyn paused. The sounds of the night filled the air, an owl hooted, frogs croaked and in the distance a coyote howled. Her feet moved toward the East gate as if she had no control over them.

"Spirits of the East, rising sun, new beginnings, new life, Robin and Flicker, we thank you for being with us at this time. With our gratitude, you are released to go. Calm energy flowed through her and she lowered her arms.

"Thank you all," she said to the group.

A quick huddle with Carol, Megan and Molly and then a shared hug. When she turned, Lily stood waiting. "You are the perfect Intercessor for this 14th Moon," Lily whispered as she hugged her.

Jocelyn didn't go to the food tent and hang out. Instead she went straight to her own tent, collapsing on the sleeping bag already rolled out. Hands linked behind her head, she gazed at the stars through the open flap. A yawn escaped as she willed herself to relax.

Yesterday she and her circle sisters had come to the land to complete the finishing touches for the Friday afternoon to Saturday night Ceremonies. They'd set up their tents, decorated the gates, replenished the firewood for the sacred fire, set up the food tent and made sure they had everything needed for registration. After sharing a communal meal, they'd sought their tents and solitude.

Jocelyn's sleep that first night was deep and dreamless. Most likely because of the hard physical work required for finishing up all the details. On this second night, after being in the sacred circle, her dreams were vivid. She floated on the night air, looking down on Ethan and Emma asleep in their own rooms and Mark curled around her pillow. She saw beauty in flowers, rivers, felt the ocean's breeze on her cheeks. She awakened rested and at peace with her choices, grateful her life was filled with love and joy.

After the communal breakfast, Carol led the women in a morning prayer to The Goddess. She was getting her feet wet, so to speak, in preparation of being next year's Intercessor. Jocelyn had passed on Lily's wisdom that no matter how prepared you were, the reality was you'd have some doubts.

Was that still true for her? Jocelyn was aware that Carol was determined to banish any and all doubts before she took over as Intercessor Sunday morning, but for her? Where was she on the doubt continuum? Jocelyn's body had fully healed from the horror of Tony. She was now the legal mother of two wonderful, healthy, loving children. She was loved by an amazing man. She offered prayers of gratitude multiple times a day.

When was it she'd left doubt and fear about being Intercessor behind? After all she'd been through, a stumble over a word or a pause in a prayer were barely blips on the screen of life. Mistakes happen. That was part of living an active life, engaging with other, seeking new experiences. If she was living her life to the fullest, there would be mistakes. And since she believed every mistake had a gift, it really wasn't a mistake. She recognized another truth Lily had imparted. "You'll find times when you just drift off. It happens. Refocus when it does and all will be well." She did that now. Refocused because the Maiden's part of the 14th Moon was starting.

Megan had wanted to work with the Maidens. Being in her late 20's, she was closer in age and had formed close ties with the ten young women who comprised this year's group. Sitting as part of the circle, Jocelyn listened in particular to the messages imparted by the young women who'd been coming to Ceremony for several years. Their sharing about the importance of this gathering in their lives created a future vision in Jocelyn's mind's eye of being here with Emma.

Having had their first menses but being neither married nor a mother, these young women who were twenty-four or younger talked about finding strength and support here. They could ask anyone for ideas, information or feedback. Being particularly responsible to aid the Crones was an honor and one they carried back to their other lives. Jocelyn resolved to check out Emma's interest in creating a daily spiritual practice with her or even on her own.

Carol led the Matron Ceremony. She, Megan, Molly and Jocelyn had talked for hours about the importance of self-care for these women, some of whom were mothers, all of them twenty-five but not yet Crones.

Matrons themselves, Jocelyn's group of four had taken on the role and responsibility to create this weekend, this time-out-of- time. As they worked together, they had shared fears and frustrations. It was during one of the more intense conversations they had their epiphany: *At the core of everything they did was their spiritual practice.*

With this in mind, Carol came up with the idea of creating a sacred space in which each Matron could clarify and consider the what, when and how of her personal spiritual practice and then focus or commit to her creation. So now in The Circle within The Circle, fifteen Matrons sat on a large yellow cloth with a pad of paper and colored pencils.

The questions? What is your spiritual practice now? What do you want it to be? How can you make that happen given the realities of your life? Time was given for each woman to write out and then stand and share her plan. What was amazing was each woman made a vow that she would keep to a daily spiritual practice until next year.

And the Crone Ceremony? To be a Crone the women were at least fifty-one years wise and been through menopause for at least one year. Fifteen amazing women were honored this year. In other times and places, the Crones were the wise women, healers and teachers. Lily's circle had asked if they could lead the Crone's Ceremony. Of course most of their work had been preparation of Crone staffs and Crone gifts and coaching the Maidens in the practices that were a part of the 14th Moon's purpose which was to honor these women.

VISIONS OF HAPPINESS

At the end of the day, as darkness descended and the lights strung in the bushes and shrubs began to glow, Jocelyn sat on the ground at the feet of the Crones. She listened with an awareness that these trail blazers, these survivors were passing on the gifts, the wisdom they had gleaned from living their lives as best they could. And really that was all any of them could do—their best to manage, to handle, to survive life's challenges and then to find the gift in each of those events.

One day she too would sit with the Crones and experience what it was to be honored, respected and looked up to. She was grateful to be part of a Ceremony that made that happen in the now for these women.

It was Saturday night of Labor Day Weekend, 2004. Hard to believe her first 14th Moon had been last year. Jocelyn internally shook herself in amazement as the time approached to close the sacred circle. Throughout this time-out-of-time she'd floated in and out of the present as visions appeared before her or took her to another place and time. She'd approached Lily at one point. Her friend had smiled before saying, "It is as it is and always will be." Then Lily hugged her, a long, nurturing hug full of love and compassion.

And now it was over.

Jocelyn stood before the East Gate having just released the last of the guides and protectors. Flashes of memories and moments of being with this group of women streaked in front of her eyes. She'd bore witness to tears, laughter and healing as women talked and did the work needed to leave here whole. Various women had approached to talk with her and she'd listened intently and trusted Spirit to tell her how to respond. Lightheaded with exhilaration, the reality that she had done it was sinking in. She had been this year's Intercessor.

A year ago she hadn't yet met Mark and Ethan. She had sincerely doubted her ability to be Intercessor. All the questioning, second-guessing, negative talk about how she couldn't do it and even more damaging, wasn't worthy, roiled up and faded away.

She lowered her arms and patted cheeks moist with tears. These were happy tears. Happy tears that now flowed more rapidly as the memory of Mark assuring Emma and Ethan that first time she cried happy tears. Happy tears that she had had a spiritual practice that sustained her through the dark times in her life and that sustained her now in the light.

Happy tears because standing in this circle one of her visions flared, brighter and clearer than ever before. She was on the back deck of their home, Emma was on the swing on the old oak with Mark behind her. Ethan? Ethan was beside her. It was Ethan's light-brown hair she ruffled, Ethan whose small body leaned into hers.

The dark haired child? He was still there, calling out to her. "I'm coming," he said. "I'm coming to be with you." A flutter in her core followed that message. She rested her hand on her abdomen.

In a few hours she'd be home. She'd stand on the deck with Ethan by her side watching Mark push Emma on the swing. She'd see the joy on her daughter's face, hear it in her laughter and feel it when Emma ran across the lawn and jumped into her arms for a hug. It would all be there just like in the vision that had kept her sane through the dark times. But one piece would be different in what she now referred to as "the updated" version. In this version her womb pulsed with new life.

A REQUEST

If you enjoyed reading **Visions of Happiness**, I'd be grateful if you would spread the word by telling friends and family, posting on social media and writing a review. Any and all of the above will be greatly appreciated and are a perfect way to support me.

LEARN MORE ABOUT THESE BOOKS

Get the Latest News about New Releases, Special Events, Special pricing/sales

You have just finished reading *Visions of Happiness* the eighth book in the Sacred Women's Circle series.

Be the first to learn about future releases, any pre-release pricing or sales and special events by signing up for my mailing list here. I do not spam and you are free to unsubscribe at any time.

For More Information on The Sacred Women's Circle series check out:

My website: www.JudithAshleyRomance.com
My blog: www.JudithAshley.blogspot.com

READ MORE BOOKS IN THIS SERIES

Lily: The Dragon and the Great Horned Owl
Elizabeth: The Lady and the Sacred Grove
Diana: The Queen of Swords and the Knight of Pentacles
Ashley: Dragonflies and Dreams
Hunter: The Drum and The Dance
Gabriella: Chaos to Symmetry
Sophia: Every Ending Is A Beginning

ABOUT JUDITH

What do you do if you see visions and hear voices? If you're Judith Ashley, you write these stories down.

It helped that her visions and the voices were of seven women creating a sacred women's circle, a haven from whence they deal with the issues and struggles many of us face in everyday life.

It also helped that Judith experiences firsthand the healing power of supportive relationships and spiritual practices.

Judith's Prayer for you: *May your dreams manifest in "right time" and may you know the peace of unconditional acceptance, support and unconditional love.*

http://www.judithashleyromance.com/

facebook.com/JudithAshley.Romance
twitter.com/JudithAshley19
bookbub.com/authors/judith-ashley

WINDTREE PRESS

For more books from the heart in fiction and non-fiction please visit Windtree Press

http://windtreepress.com

www.ingramcontent.com/pod-product-compliance
Lightning Source LLC
Chambersburg PA
CBHW071304110526
44591CB00010B/765